DATE DUE			

REASONS FOR ACTIONS

Library of Philosophy and Logic

General Editors:

P. T. Geach, P. F. Strawson, David Wiggins, Peter Winch

IDENTITY AND SPATIO-TEMPORAL CONTINUITY

DAVID WIGGINS

THE LOGIC OF POWER

INGMAR PÖRN

CATEGORIAL FRAMEWORKS

STEPHAN KÖRNER

REASONS FOR ACTIONS

A Critique of Utilitarian Rationality

RICHARD NORMAN

BARNES & NOBLE, Inc.

NEW YORK

PUBLISHERS & BOOK SELLERS SINCE 1873

Printed in Great Britain

. . . it seemed to K. as if at last those people had broken off all relations with him, and as if now in reality he were freer than he had ever been, and at liberty to wait here in this place usually forbidden to him as long as he desired, and had won a freedom such as hardly anybody else had ever succeeded in winning, and as if nobody could dare to touch him or drive him away, or even speak to him; but—this conviction was at least equally strong—as if at the same time there was nothing more senseless, nothing more hopeless, than this freedom, this waiting, this inviolability.

Franz Kafka: *The Castle*
(Penguin edition, p. 105)

Contents

Preface

This book is mainly a revised version of a Ph.D. thesis written at the University of London during the period 1966–9. My greatest individual debt, both intellectually and for personal help and encouragement, is to my supervisor during that time, Professor Peter Winch. Anyone familiar with his work will be able to detect his influence throughout this book. If I add that the book should not be taken as a reliable guide to his views, this is not simply out of a regard for the etiquette of prefaces. In the first place, I know that he would disagree with some of the things that I have written. (Most fundamentally, I doubt if he would agree with me about how important the very notion of 'reasons' is to ethics). Secondly, even at those points where I would say that I had been directly influenced by him, I am not at all sure that I have properly understood or appreciated the nature of his views.

I am also extremely grateful to Miss Ruby Meager, who has, in a sense, helped me from the opposite direction: she has defended the position which I have attacked, and her willingness to argue the matter with me has been invaluable. If I have succeeded at all in doing justice to the strength of conflicting views in ethics, it is to her that I owe it.

Parts of the book originated as papers for seminars on ethical philosophy at Birkbeck College, where I benefited from the comments of other members of the seminars, especially Lloyd Reinhardt and Stephen Burns, who sometimes appeared to agree with me. I am also grateful for advice and criticisms from David Benjamin, Larry Blum, Nancy Calahan, David Lloyd Thomas, Anthony Quinton, and David Wiggins.

I dedicate this book to my wife, who not only gave me practical help but also, and even more importantly, encouraged me to think that the whole thing was worthwhile.

University of Sussex
1970

PART I

Wants and Reasons

1. The Search for Foundations

We are frequently faced with questions of the form 'Why should I do this rather than that?' These in turn give rise to the philosophical question 'What can legitimately count as a reason for performing an action?' One answer to this question has appeared and re-appeared again and again in the history of ethics. This is the theory that all reasons for performing actions must ultimately be derivable from statements of human wants or desires or satisfactions. I shall refer to it as the 'utilitarian' view of practical rationality, thereby using the term 'utilitarian' in a somewhat wider sense than is usual. Utilitarianism is not confined to the works of Bentham and Mill. Vestiges of it, in various half-articulated forms, pervade the moral and political thinking of our own society. As a philosophical tradition it has proved equally persistent. Many recent ethical philosophers have declared their allegiance to some kind of utilitarian account. Others again, while not explicitly accepting the label, have employed certain fundamental assumptions of a broadly utilitarian character. These assumptions do, indeed, possess considerable plausibility, which I shall try to account for. Utilitarianism is an important theory because it goes to the heart of the problem of reasons. The issues it raises are so deep-rooted that one cannot properly criticize it without being led to indicate some alternative general view of ethical rationality. This, at any rate, is what I have supposed in writing this book. The two views of 'reasons for acting' which are developed here—the one which I reject and the one which I propose—seem to me to be the only two possibilities. One of them, or something like it, *must* be right.

I do not intend to attack utilitarianism as a possible way of life, as one morality among others. What I do intend to dispute strongly is the claim that *all* reasons for acting *must* ultimately rest on utilitarian foundations. I shall look first at some modern versions of this claim. One of my further concerns will be to clarify the relation between the concept of 'rationality', the notion of practical or ethical 'reasons', and the role of 'reason' in ethics. Recent ethical philosophers have concentrated on the last two notions rather more than on the first (this will, indeed, be the substance of one of my criticisms of them). In the present chapter I shall look at three main accounts which have been offered of 'reasons for acting' and of the place of reason in ethics. In the form in which I shall present them, none of these is intended to correspond precisely to the position of any one particular philosopher. They will all be, to some extent, 'ideal types'. Nevertheless, I shall at the same time try to indicate which recent philosophers have seemed most inclined towards each of the three accounts. In the second chapter I shall argue that these three accounts can be situated within the utilitarian tradition, and I shall discuss some general features of the tradition. In the remainder of the book I shall undertake a fundamental criticism of the tradition and outline an alternative account of ethical and practical rationality.

1. FIRST ACCOUNT OF REASONS FOR ACTING

According to the First Account which we shall examine, there are two main functions that reason can serve in connection with practical or moral problems. In the first place one can, by the use of reason, determine relevant facts about the performed or prospective action. One can determine what kind of an action it is, and what its consequences are. And secondly, one can, by the use of reason, derive a judgement that an action, characterized as of such-and-such a kind and having such-and-such consequences, is right (or wrong), from a more general principle that actions of a certain kind are right (or wrong). This principle may in turn be similarly derived from an even more general principle, and so on. But eventually this chain of reasoning must come to an end, when one reaches an ultimate principle, i.e. a principle which is so general that it cannot be derived from any more general principle. At this point, therefore, one cannot give any further reasons in support of the principle that actions of this kind are right (or wrong); all that one can say is that one just does approve (or disapprove) of actions of this kind. Thus the following would be a typical sample of moral reasoning:

A: Why are you going to give some money to that beggar?
B: Because if I don't, he may starve.
A: But why should you part with your money just to stop a beggar from starving?
B: Well, if I can prevent a beggar from starving, then I am preventing a great deal of unnecessary suffering.
A: And why should you prevent unnecessary suffering?
B: I can't give you any reason why one ought to do so. It's just what I feel.

Reasoning of this kind can be formalized as the deduction of a practical conclusion from a minor premiss stating that the action or kind of action in question is one of a class C, together with a major premiss stating that actions belonging to class C are right (or that they are wrong; or that one ought to perform them, etc.). Thus the above example can be set out formally as the following two syllogisms:

First syllogism:
> Major premiss: I ought to prevent people from starving.
> Minor premiss: If I give money to this beggar, I shall prevent him from starving.
> Conclusion: I ought to give money to this beggar.

Second syllogism:
> Major premiss: I ought to prevent unnecessary suffering.
> Minor premiss: To prevent someone from starving is to prevent unnecessary suffering.
> Conclusion: I ought to prevent people from starving.

In this case, then, the premisses of the syllogisms constitute *reasons* for B to give money to the beggar. And the major premiss of the second syllogism constitutes, for B, an *ultimate reason*, i.e. a reason for which no further reason can be given.

This account of practical reason is very close to the one offered by R. M. Hare in *The Language of Morals*. Hare exhibits a certain reluctance to say that, when we get to ultimate principles, our adherence to them is a matter of 'attitudes' or 'approval'. He prefers to say that we just choose, or just decide, without having any further reasons (p. 69).[1] But this 'just choosing' does seem to be indistinguishable from the having of a psychological feeling or attitude; and I think that Hare would in fact probably agree that one's adherence to an ultimate principle is a matter of psychology. Elsewhere, he does make use of Nowell-Smith's term 'pro-attitudes' (e.g. *Descriptivism*, p. 131); and he frequently seems to imply that the only difference between desiring or wanting something and thinking it good is that in calling something 'good' I am logically committed to regarding as 'good' anything else which is like it in the relevant respects. I suspect that Hare's preference for the notion of 'choice' or 'decision', rather than that of 'attitudes', stems from a wish to differentiate his position from that of the emotivists. Perhaps the intention is to emphasize that this 'decision' is something which a man comes to reflectively and after due consideration of all the facts, and is in this respect to be distinguished from a mere state of feeling. Still, the point is that for Hare these 'facts' are only contingently related to the decision; it is the 'decision' itself which gives these facts the status of 'reasons', and therefore this 'decision' is not

[1] Details of all works which I refer to are given in the Bibliography.

importantly different from a felt psychological impulse or attitude. Again, Hare perhaps wishes to emphasize that the 'decision' is not a feeling aroused by a concrete thing or situation, but a judgement about a certain *kind* of action or thing (hence the importance attached to 'general principles'). But I do not think that this is a point which emotivists like Ayer and Stevenson would have denied, even though they did not positively emphasize it either.[1] And with this difference—which is, when all is said and done, a difference in detail—the role assigned to reason by Hare is fundamentally the same as the role assigned by the emotivists. The function of reason is, for them, simply to ascertain the characteristics and consequences of the action in question.

The notorious weakness in the emotivist account of reasons is the suggestion that any fact can count as a reason for a practical or moral judgement if it is capable of influencing someone to accept that judgement. This, of course, leaves no room for any distinction between genuine reasons and mere propaganda. It was partly in order to bring out this distinction that Hare emphasized the possibility of *logical* reasoning about moral questions. But if, at this point, the emotivists had emphasized the first-person element rather than the imperative element in their analysis of moral judgements, and had suggested that what a person properly gives as reasons for a moral judgement are the facts about the thing or action that make *him* have the attitude that he does have towards it, then their account of moral reasons would not have been essentially different from Hare's.

The historical ancestors of such an account are certain of the 18th-century British philosophers, and perhaps the classic statement of it is in the ethical writings of Hume. The following well-known passages from the *Enquiry Concerning the Principles of Morals* present it most succinctly:

One principal foundation of moral praise being supposed to lie in the usefulness of any quality or action, it is evident that *reason* must enter for a considerable share in all decisions of this kind, since nothing but that faculty can instruct us in the tendency of qualities and actions and point out their beneficial consequences to society and to their possessor . . .

But though reason . . . be sufficient to instruct us in the pernicious or useful tendency of qualities and actions, it is not alone sufficient to produce any moral blame or approbation. Utility is only a tendency

---

[1] In his essay 'On the Analysis of Moral Judgements', Ayer says: '. . . an action or a situation is morally evaluated always as an action or a situation of a certain kind. What is approved or disapproved is something repeatable.' (*Philosophical Essays*, p. 237.)

to a certain end; and were the end totally indifferent to us, we should feel the same indifference towards the means. It is requisite a *sentiment* should here display itself in order to give a preference to the useful above the pernicious tendencies . . .

Reason judges either of *matter of fact* or of *relations* . . . In moral deliberations we must be acquainted, beforehand, with all the objects and all their relations to each other; and from a comparison of the whole fix our choice or approbation. No new fact to be ascertained, no new relation to be discovered. All the circumstances of the case are supposed to be laid before us ere we can fix any sentence of blame or approbation. If any material circumstance be yet unknown or doubtful, we must first employ our inquiry or intellectual faculties to assure us of it, and must suspend for a time all moral decision or sentiment. While we are ignorant whether a man were aggressor or not, how can we determine whether the person who killed him be criminal or innocent? But after every circumstance, every relation is known, the understanding has no further room to operate, nor any object on which it could employ itself. The approbation or blame which then ensues cannot be the work of the judgement but of the heart; and it is not a speculative proposition or affirmation, but an active feeling or sentiment.

Enquiry Concerning the Principles of Morals
Appendix I: *Concerning Moral Sentiment* (pp. 262–6).

I have said that this account is offered as an account of practical reason and practical reasons rather than of practical rationality. But I think that we can fairly easily derive from it a conception of practical and ethical rationality. Hare certainly suggests that the existence of logical relations between practical or moral judgements and other such judgements of greater or lesser generality, and hence the possibility of logically deriving practical or moral conclusions from practical or moral premisses, makes morals a rational activity.[1] Presumably, then, a moral belief is irrationally held if it is contrary to a conclusion entailed by premisses which the person accepts. And since each major premiss is, in its turn, rationally accepted only if it can figure as the conclusion of a chain of reasoning deriving from an ultimate premiss which is the expression of a psychological attitude, we can go further and say that a moral belief is irrationally held if it is contrary to a conclusion which can be derived, by logical deduction, from an ultimate premiss which is an expression of an attitude held by the agent, together with minor premisses which express the agent's factual beliefs concerning the circumstances and nature of the actions in question. Similarly, an *action* would presumably be irrational if it were contrary to a conclusion so

---

[1] *Language of Morals*, p. 15f.; Cf. also p. 45.

derivable. To put it more simply, an action is irrational if and only if it is inconsistent with the combination of the agent's aims and attitudes and his factual beliefs. And conversely, an action is rational if and only if it is in accordance with the combination of the agent's aims and attitudes and his factual beliefs.[1]

2. SECOND ACCOUNT OF REASONS FOR ACTING

The Second Account diverges from the First at one point only. We saw that, according to the First Account, a chain of practical reasons must come to an end when one reaches an ultimate reason for which no further reason can be given; at this point one can only say: 'I cannot give any reason for performing actions of this kind; I just happen to approve of the performance of such actions.' Our Second Account can be characterized as the view that, at this point, the very fact that one has an attitude of approval towards actions of this kind constitutes one's ultimate reason for performing them.

However, we must be careful how we state this account, as will be seen if we consider the example used to illustrate the First Account:

> *A:* Why are you going to give some money to that beggar?
> *B:* Because if I don't, he may starve.
> *A:* But why should you part with your money just to stop a beggar from starving?
> *B:* Well, if I can prevent a beggar from starving, then I am preventing a great deal of unnecessary suffering.

Now if A then asks: 'Why is it right to prevent unnecessary suffering?' ('Why ought one to prevent unnecessary suffering?', 'Why should anyone prevent unnecessary suffering?', etc., etc.), B cannot offer as a reason: 'Because I approve of doing so.' Clearly B's approval of the prevention of unnecessary suffering is only a reason for *him* to prevent unnecessary suffering. So the way in which the conversation *could* continue is as follows:

> *A:* And what's your reason for preventing unnecessary suffering?
> *B:* Simply the fact that I feel approval for such actions. (or: Simply the fact that I want to do so.)

[1] An example of an attempt to work out an account of practical rationality along these lines is a paper entitled 'Rational Action', by K. A. Walton, in *Mind*, 1967. His suggestion seems to be that an action is rational if and only if it is likely to achieve the agent's intended aims and/or likely to increase his capacity to achieve his intended aims.

or:

> A: And why are you going to prevent unnecessary suffering?
> B: Just because I approve of doing so (want to do so).

Perhaps also:

> A: And why should you prevent unnecessary suffering?
> B: Just because I approve of doing so (want to do so).

And the following may also be possible:

> A: And why do you say that it is right to prevent unnecessary suffering?
> B: Because I approve of the prevention of unnecessary suffering.

In other words, the fact that I have an attitude of approval towards the prevention of unnecessary suffering is not a reason why it is right to prevent unnecessary suffering, but it is a reason for me to prevent unnecessary suffering, and it can perhaps also be regarded as a reason for me to *say* that it is right to prevent unnecessary suffering. And the difference between the First Account and the Second Account can now be put succinctly in terms of this example. According to the First Account, the ultimate reason for B to give money to the beggar is that it is right to prevent unnecessary suffering, and this is an ultimate reason insofar as it is not a principle for which any further reason can be given but simply expresses an attitude on B's part. According to the Second Account, the ultimate reason for B to give money to the beggar is the fact that B has an attitude of approval towards the prevention of unnecessary suffering.

Clearly the two accounts are very close to one another. And this close relation between them is reflected in the conflicting interpretations that have been offered of Hume's ethical philosophy. We have seen that Hume can be interpreted as an adherent of the First Account; and this is in accordance with the standard interpretation of him as an upholder of the fact/value dichotomy: when the understanding has revealed all the empirical characteristics and consequences of the action in question, there are no further facts which can be produced as reasons for an evaluative conclusion, nor is there any logical relation between these empirical facts and an evaluative conclusion; the only way of getting from the facts to the evaluation is by way of a sentiment of approbation or disapprobation. This interpretation has been challenged, most notably in a paper by Alasdair MacIntyre.[1] According to MacIntyre, Hume does not set up an unbridgeable gap between 'is' propositions,

---

[1] 'Hume on "Is" and "Ought",' in *Philosophical Review*, 1959. See also his *A Short History of Ethics*, pp. 169–75, where he is much more cautious.

stating facts discovered by the understanding, and 'ought' propositions. Rather, he is saying that the gap *can* be bridged, that there *are* logical relations between 'is' propositions and 'ought' propositions, but that the 'is' propositions must be of a particular kind, namely propositions which state facts about the human passions—human wants, desires, interests, happiness, etc. It is facts of this kind that provide the basic reasons for moral conclusions and moral actions. Thus Hume gives, as the fundamental reason for acting in accordance with justice, the fact that the observance of justice is conducive to both public and private interest. And MacIntyre suggests the following as another example of an argument which proceeds from a fact of human sentiment to an 'ought' conclusion: 'If I stick a knife in Smith, they will send me to jail; but I do not want to go to jail; so I ought not to (had better not) stick a knife in him.'

The truth of the matter seems to be that Hume is ambiguous. Passages such as those quoted above (pp. 6–7) certainly seem intended to state the view that there is a logical gap between the facts concerning an action, and the evaluation of it, a gap which cannot be bridged by offering any further facts as reasons for an evaluative conclusion, but can only be bridged by one's own sentiments. On the other hand, passages such as the following (from the very same section of the *Enquiry*) seem equally to suggest that facts about our sentiments can themselves function as the facts which constitute the basic reasons for an evaluative conclusion:

> The hypothesis which we embrace is plain. It maintains that morality is determined by sentiment. It defines virtue to be *whatever mental action or quality gives to a spectator the pleasing sentiment of approbation*; and vice the contrary. We then proceed to examine a plain matter of fact—to wit, what actions have this influence: we consider all the circumstances in which these actions agree; and thence endeavour to extract some general observations with regard to these sentiments.
>
> (Ibid., p. 265)

This close relation between the First Account and the Second Account is also reflected in a remark made by Hare at one point in *The Language of Morals*. If someone, asked why he performed a certain action, replies 'I can't give any reasons; I just felt like it', then, according to Hare, 'even in that case he had *some* reason for his choice, namely, that he felt that way' (*Language of Morals*, p. 59). However, this is a mere aside, and has no real significance for Hare's account of moral rationality. A much more important attempt to develop an account of attitudes as ultimate reasons is made by P. H. Nowell-Smith in chapter 8 of his book *Ethics*. Nowell-Smith introduces the terms 'pro-attitude' and 'con-attitude'. The following are examples of names of pro-attitudes: 'like', 'approve of', 'enjoy', 'love', 'want', 'accept', 'pleasure', 'comfort', 'desire', 'happiness'. And some examples of names of con-attitudes are: 'hate', 'dislike', 'disapprove of', 'detest', 'reject', 'decline', 'shy away from', 'pain', 'discomfort', 'aversion'. Words which name pro-attitudes and con-attitudes are called by Nowell-Smith 'pro-words' and 'con-words'. Their importance is explained in the following important passage:

> Sentences containing pro- and con-words provide good—that is to say, logically complete—explanations of choice. If you ask a man why he is gardening or why he is going to turn on the wireless and he says that he enjoys gardening or wants to hear some music, he has given a reply that makes a repetition of the question logically odd . . . In default of . . . special interpretations, it seems senseless to ask anyone why he is doing something when he has told you that he enjoys it, likes doing it, or wants to do it.
>
> Pro-words differ from each other in many ways, but they all have this in common, that they provide logically impeccable explanations of why someone chose to do something. They also provide logically impeccable reasons for deciding to do or not to do something. The 'reason for doing' which is expressed by such a phrase as 'because I want . . .' or 'because I enjoy . . .' may be counteracted by other and more weighty reasons for making the opposite choice; but each pro-sentence refers to *a* reason and, in the absence of counter-reasons, it would be logically odd not to choose.
>
> (*Ethics*, pp. 113–14)

However, Nowell-Smith's position is then made to seem more complicated when he continues as follows:

> . . . my lists of pro- and con-attitudes must be so construed that anything which could be offered as a logically good reason for or against doing anything must be included in the lists.
>
> The proposition that any statement which gives a logically complete reason for choice must include a reference to a pro- or con-attitude is thus a frank tautology. Its function is to draw attention to the existence of a class of words that have just this force. My purpose is not to prove an avowed tautology, but to show that many expressions which are normally used in giving reasons for choice do not give logically complete reasons. They are given and taken as complete explanations only because certain assumptions are involved when they are used. In particular I shall try to show that deontological

words...never give logically complete reasons for choice...
'Believing that something is the right thing to do' and 'believing that
something is my duty' are *never* good reasons for doing it and such
beliefs never explain why people do what they do.

(Ibid., pp. 114–15)

The effect of this is to make Nowell-Smith's thesis seem much less
important than it really is. For it is clearly *not* just a tautology. Nowell-
Smith says later:

A word has a pro- or con-force when it has the force of making any
further explanation of conduct unnecessary. But almost any word can
be used with this force if the context implies it.

(Ibid., p. 131)

Here there is some plausibility in saying that the claim is a mere
tautology: if the application of a particular word makes any further
explanation of conduct unnecessary, then the word is being used with a
pro- or con-force; but to have a pro- or con-force is, by definition, to
have the force of making any further explanation of conduct unnecessary. It then appears that nothing substantive is being claimed; even a
deontologist like Pritchard would surely agree that when my saying
'It's my duty to keep a promise' blocks any further question as to why
I decide to keep a promise, there is no harm in saying that the word
'duty' has a pro-force, so long as 'having a pro-force' is taken as being
equivalent *by definition* to 'making any further explanation of conduct
unnecessary'. And since Nowell-Smith adds that any word can on
occasion be used with a pro- or con-force, this helps to re-inforce the
impression that no substantive claim is being made. But so far, of
course, nothing has been said about 'attitudes', and it is as soon as we
start introducing *this* term that the thesis ceases to be tautologous.
Nowell-Smith wants to say that for a word to have a pro- or con-force
is also for it to express a direct pro- or con-attitude towards the thing in
question. Therefore an explanation or justification of an action makes
any further explanation or justification unnecessary only if it is the
expression of a direct pro- or con-attitude. For example, the statement
'one has an obligation to keep one's promises' would provide an
ultimate justification, blocking any further question 'why?', only if it
expressed a direct pro-attitude towards the keeping of promises as such.
This is obviously not a tautology, and would not be accepted by someone like Pritchard, who would presumably want to say that, whatever
attitudes one may have, whatever one may feel about keeping promises,
all this is quite independent of the fact that one has an obligation to
keep one's promises and that this constitutes the only reason that can
or need be given for keeping them.

The last example might seem to suggest that Nowell-Smith's account of reasons is equivalent to our First Account: 'One has an obligation to keep one's promises' is an ultimate reason for me to keep a promise if the sentence expresses a direct pro-attitude on my part towards the keeping of promises as such. But Nowell-Smith goes further than this; he considers the paradigmatic case of an ultimate justification to be the actual statement of a pro- or con-attitude, such as:

'Why are you spending all day working in the garden?'
'Because I enjoy gardening.'

or:

'Why are you turning on the wireless?'
'Because I want to hear some music.'

Any other ultimate justification is therefore to some degree elliptical. For example:

> ... because people, on the whole, like being amused and dislike being bored, 'because it is amusing (boring)' may be given and taken as a complete reason for reading (refusing to read) a book. But this only applies if and when the contextual background includes the relevant attitude. It would be excessively tedious if we had to give *full* explanations on all occasions.
>
> (Ibid., p. 120)

Since the difference between the First Account and the Second Account, considered as accounts of reasons for acting, is so marginal, it is not surprising to find that they both imply the same conception of practical rationality. Thus Nowell-Smith says that if a man wants X and can get it only by doing Y, then 'unless he has a con-attitude towards getting-X-by-doing-Y, it is irrational for him not to do Y' (Ibid., pp. 116–17). Here we encounter substantially the same notion of rational action as I referred to at the end of the First Account.

A second example of an attempt to work out a systematic account of the agent's pro-attitudes as his reasons for acting is that of David P. Gauthier in his book *Practical Reasoning*. However, it differs from our Second Account in two important respects. In the first place, although Gauthier argues that all practical reasoning is ultimately grounded in 'wants' (which term he uses in an extended sense, so that it is effectively equivalent to Nowell-Smith's 'pro-attitudes'), he does not consider that it is grounded solely in *the agent's own* wants. Only *prudential* practical reasoning is so grounded; for practical reasoning is divided into two major categories, prudential reasoning and moral reasoning. Gauthier's position is therefore an amalgam of our Second Account and what we shall shortly characterize as our Third Account. The second important difference in his position is that not just any wants can count as ultimate reasons. The object of one's wants must be something that can be characterized as desirable in some particular respect. For a want is intelligible only if what is wanted can be described by means of some desirability-characterization which *shows* its desirability. For example, my wanting to see a certain play at the theatre is made intelligible if I describe the play as 'amusing'. I shall argue later that, as soon as we introduce this proviso, the whole structure of 'wants as reasons' collapses. In the meantime we may notice that Gauthier's position is shared with Philippa Foot, for she too believes that wants provide ultimate reasons for acting but adds the proviso that only certain kinds of wants can fill this role:

> The crucial question is: 'Can we give anyone, strong or weak, a reason why he should be just?'—and it is no help at all to say that since 'just' and 'unjust' are 'action-guiding words' no one can even ask 'Why should I be just?' Confronted with that argument the man who wants to do unjust things has only to be careful to avoid the *word*, and he has not been given a reason why he should not do the things which other people call 'unjust'. Probably it will be argued that he has been given a reason so far as anyone can ever be given a reason for doing or not doing anything, for the chain of reasons must always come to an end somewhere, and it may seem that one may always reject the reason which another man accepts. But this is a mistake; some answers to the question 'Why should I?' bring the series to a close and some do not . . .
>
> . . . In general, anyone is given a reason for acting when he is shown the way to something he wants; but for some wants the question 'Why do you want that?' will make sense, and for others it will not. It seems clear that in this division justice falls on the opposite side from pleasure and interest and such things. 'Why shouldn't I do that?' is not answered by the words 'because it is unjust' as it is answered by showing that the action will bring boredom, loneliness, pain, discomfort or certain kinds of incapacity, and this is why it is not true to say that 'it's unjust' gives a reason in so far as any reasons can ever be given. 'It's unjust' gives a reason only if the nature of justice can be shown to be such that it is necessarily connected with what a man wants.
>
>   'Moral Beliefs' (in *Theories of Ethics*, ed. Foot, pp. 97–8)

Mrs. Foot's position here is, I think, derived from Elizabeth Anscombe's discussion of reasons for action (in *Intention*, paras. 34–41), which is in turn a development of Aristotle's dictum that in practical reasoning 'the starting-point is the thing wanted'. Miss Anscombe's own account (and perhaps Mrs. Foot's too) is closer to our First than to our Second Account, for she says:

> The role of 'wanting' in the practical syllogism is quite different from that of a premise. It is that whatever is described in the proposition that is the starting-point of the argument must be wanted in order for the reasoning to lead to any action.
>
> (*Intention*, p. 66)

In view of the fact that Hare and Nowell-Smith on the one hand, and Mrs. Foot and Miss Anscombe on the other, are usually regarded as representing the two diametrically-opposed viewpoints in recent ethical philosophy, it is interesting to find them agreeing that the chain of reasons for an action is brought to an end when one gets to the point where one has to refer to some psychological state of the agent (a pro-attitude, a want, etc.). The crucial point at issue between them, there-fore, is whether a man can be said to want absolutely anything.[1] As I have indicated, this is a question to which we shall return (chapter 3).

3. THIRD ACCOUNT OF REASONS FOR ACTING

The Third Account differs from the Second Account in identifying as ultimate reasons for an action not the agent's own wants but anybody's wants. The motive for this extension is apparently the idea that the Second Account makes all practical reasoning purely egotistical. As for the possible *grounds* for the extension, we shall consider these in the next chapter. Here we shall confine ourselves to noting that the Third Account may be proposed either as supplementing the Second Account or as being in itself a total account of practical reasoning. We have noted that the former position is adopted by Gauthier: prudential reasoning is grounded in the agent's own wants, moral reasoning is grounded in the wants of everybody, and the two kinds together make up the whole of practical reasoning. Something like the second position seems to be adopted by Hare, in his book *Freedom and Reason*, where he appears to be claiming that, if someone is trying to decide what to do, it is irrational for him not to give equal weight to the desires of everyone who

---

[1] Hare, *Freedom and Reason*, p. 110: 'It is, indeed, in the logical possibility of wanting *anything* (neutrally described) that the "freedom" which is alluded to in my title essentially consists.'

Nowell-Smith, *Ethics*, p. 115: 'It is important to notice that there are no logical limits to the possible objects of pro- or con-attitudes, other than the logical limits of language itself.'

will be affected by the actions in question. Notice that Hare is prepared to talk much more explicitly of 'desires' and 'wants' and 'inclinations' as fundamental reasons for action here than he was in *The Language of Morals*. Comparison with the earlier book, however, raises the question of how he can be said there to be proposing something like our First Account, and in *Freedom and Reason* to be proposing something like our Third Account, without being accused of inconsistency. One possible answer is to say that in any decision one has to give equal weight to the wants of everyone who will be affected; and for a large class of one's actions the only person whose wants will be affected is oneself. But the relation between the First Account and the Third Account can also be seen in the complexities of the way in which Hare states his position. Very often he seems to be suggesting that practical reasoning can be seen as a two-stage process: one first considers which action would be most in accordance with one's wants, and one then considers whether one could accept this if one were in the position of each of the other people liable to be affected. Thus Hare argues (*Freedom and Reason*, p. 89) that the content of ethical rationality is determined by the two basic features of moral judgements, 'prescriptivity' and 'universalizability'. The rules of moral reasoning are therefore two: the element of prescriptivity demands that the action which one decides on must be such that one is inclined towards the performance of it, and the element of universalizability demands that the action must be such that one can agree that others should perform it in like circumstances (i.e. even if one is then on the receiving end). We shall see in the next chapter why Hare thinks that these two demands can be synthesized into the principle that the right decision is always the one that gives equal weight to everyone's interests. So we can regard Hare's account of practical reasoning as one in which the First Account is sometimes adequate in itself, but very often has to be subsumed within the Third Account.

4. WANTING

What, now, do all three of these accounts have in common? In the first place, they all agree that there must, in principle, be a stopping-place in any moral argument—that there are always certain 'ultimate reasons' beyond which the argument cannot go. These 'ultimate reasons' could therefore be called the 'foundations' of the moral argument. Secondly they all agree that these 'ultimate reasons' must all be capable of being characterized in some one particular way. There must be some common characteristic which all these reasons possess, in virtue of which they are all capable of constituting ultimate reasons. And thirdly, this common characteristic must consist in a certain kind of relation to some particular psychological state, one which comes into the category of so-called 'pro-attitudes'. According to the Second and Third Accounts, what all ultimate reasons have in common is a certain kind of content; this common content, therefore, consists in a reference to a pro-attitude. According to the First Account, ultimate reasons do not have any one particular kind of content. An ultimate reason can have any content whatsoever, provided it is prescriptive in form. But to accept such an ultimate reason just is to have a direct pro-attitude towards the thing or action which it specifies, and, therefore, a prescriptive sentence cannot function as an ultimate reason unless it is an expression of a direct pro-attitude; being the expression of a direct pro-attitude, rather than referring to one, is thus the common characteristic of ultimate reasons according to the First Account.

It will have been seen that there is no agreement among the proponents of these accounts on a generic term to refer to the psychological states in question. The principal objection to Nowell-Smith's term 'pro-attitude' is an aesthetic one. Quite simply, the word is abominably ugly. But, in case this should be thought inadequate as a philosophical objection, it can also be pointed out that the term tells us nothing. Having been artificially coined by Nowell-Smith, it can be explicated only by words which are already part of our normal vocabulary. It is to the latter that we should look. One of Hare's candidates is the word 'desire'. He says:

> . . . if we use the word 'desire' in a wide sense, we can say that any evaluation, just because it is prescriptive, incorporates the desire to have or do something rather than something else. The wide sense in which we are using 'desire' is that in which *any* felt disposition to action counts as a desire; there is also a narrower and commoner sense in which desires are contrasted with other dispositions to action, such as a feeling of obligation (which in the wider sense of 'desire' could be called a desire to do what one ought).
>
> *Freedom and Reason*, p. 169

This 'wider sense of desire' has philosophical tradition on its side. Hobbes, for example, who may be regarded as a prominent ancestor of the theories we are considering, uses the term extensively. But, although it may be still true that the word 'desire' has this wider sense when used as a common noun, I should say that this is no longer true of it in its uses as an abstract noun and as a verb. At the present time, it is the pornographer rather than the philosopher who has staked out a claim to these. Where Hobbes speaks of 'desiring', we should probably speak of 'wanting'. The word 'want' also is popular with Hare, as with Gauthier too, and Nowell-Smith says of it:

The only ordinary English word that is sufficiently vague to be made to cover (with a little terminological ingenuity) all the cases considered is 'wanting'; but this word, just by reason of its vagueness, is far too weak to cover the more violent passions or the most permanent and deep-seated desires. (It would be absurd to talk of a Christian 'wanting' to inherit the kingdom of heaven or of a near-hysterical bobby-soxer 'wanting' to see a crooner.)

Ethics, pp. 111–12

To me, however, it does not seem absurd at all (although, of course, it would be absurd to imagine that this is *all* that can be said of the Christian or the pop-fan). I shall, therefore, speak of our three accounts as theories to the effect that 'wants provide ultimate reasons for acting'.

Two further doubts can, however, be mentioned. The noun 'want' as normally used is not precisely the noun-equivalent of the verb 'to want'. By 'a man's wants' we tend to mean his objective needs rather than his psychological attitudes and aspirations. All that I can say here is that I *shall* be using the noun 'want' as the noun-equivalent of the verb 'to want'. The second doubt concerns the relation between 'wanting' and 'liking' (with which 'enjoying' can probably be linked). 'I want x' or 'I want to x' are used with reference to a particular thing which one does not yet have or a particular action which one is not yet performing. 'I like x' (and 'I enjoy x' or 'I am enjoying x') are used either to express an attitude to a particular thing which one already has or a particular action which one is already performing, or to express an attitude to some general class of things or actions. This might seem to suggest that 'want' cannot function as the sole multi-purpose attitude-word. However, one could perhaps get round this by analysing 'liking' in terms of 'wanting'. (I am not positively advocating such an analysis, but merely suggesting that someone who wanted to defend a theory of 'wants as reasons' might make use of such an analysis as an alternative to an extended theory of 'wants and likes as reasons'.) Thus it might be suggested that 'likes' which refer to particular present things or actions can be analysed as short-term dispositions, and that 'likes' which refer to general classes of things or actions can be analysed as long-term dispositions. 'I like this' as the expression of a short-term disposition could then be interpreted as *wanting* to continue having or doing this particular thing now and *wanting* to have or do the same thing again in the same circumstances. And 'I like Xs' as the expression of a long-term disposition could be interpreted as meaning that I *would want* to have or do things of this kind in the appropriate circumstances. (The point of analysing 'liking' in terms of 'wanting' rather than vice versa is that in this way the analysis of both concepts can ultimately refer to behaviour, not to logically private inner states.)

These, then, are suggestions as to why someone might use the term 'want' rather than any other attitude-word. But we must now turn to the crucial question: why have philosophers supposed that wants, or any such psychological state, can provide ultimate reasons at all? I propose now to set out a possible argument in support of the theory of 'wants as ultimate reasons'. I do not know of anyone who has used the argument in precisely this form,[1] but I think that it indicates fairly accurately the kinds of considerations that have prompted philosophers to offer something like our First, Second or Third Account. I shall present the argument as though I considered it to be valid; in fact, of course, I do not.

5. The Argument

We have already referred to the notion of an 'extended sense' of the verb 'to want'. In this extended sense it is analytically true that, if someone intentionally performs an action, he wanted to perform it. The term 'wanting' is more often used in a more restricted sense. For example, 'doing something because one ought to do it' is often contrasted with 'doing something because one wants to do it', even though they are both cases of doing something intentionally. Someone might say: 'I don't want to own up to the fact that I broke the window, but I'm going to do so, because I know that I ought to.' But insofar as he feels the force of the fact that he ought to own up, and is thereby prompted to do so, it is necessarily the case that he becomes psychologically disposed to perform the action, i.e. that, in the extended sense, he wants to do it. For if he didn't want to do it, he wouldn't do it. We might say of him: 'He doesn't want to own up as such, but insofar as it is something that he ought to do, he wants to do it.'

Now this distinction between wanting something as such and wanting it for some further reason is very important. We can distinguish two cases of wanting something for some further reason. I may want to do X not because I consider that doing X is important in itself, but because it will have a certain consequence Y and I want Y. And secondly, I may want to do X, where the action is important in itself, but where it is important not under the description X but under the description Y. In the example on p. 4, B wants to give money to the beggar because his doing so will have the consequence that the beggar will be able to avoid starvation; this is a reason of the first kind. And he wants to prevent the beggar from starving because to do so is to prevent unnecessary suffering; this is a reason of the second kind. All reasons for wanting to do something must be of one of these two kinds. For whenever

---

[1] I am greatly indebted to Miss Ruby Meager for much of the content of the argument. It must not necessarily be supposed, however, that the argument accurately represents her own position.

anyone wants something, he necessarily wants it either as a means to some end or as an end in itself. If he wants it as a means to an end, then his reason for wanting it is that his getting it or doing it will have the consequences which he wants. And if he wants it as an end in itself, this means that he wants it for its own sake, i.e. he wants it because it is what it is; therefore the only reason that can be given for wanting X, where X is wanted as an end in itself, is that X is also Y.

In some cases a whole chain of reasons of these two kinds may be given for wanting something. I may want A because it is or leads to B, and I may want B because it is or leads to C, and I may want C because it is or leads to D, and so on. But any such chain of reasons must always come to an end. It must always be possible to reach a point at which no further reason is needed. For if some further reason can always intelligibly be demanded, then the chain of reasons will never get anchored, and consequently one will never have a sufficient reason for wanting anything. Suppose that I want A because it leads to B, and I want B because it leads to C, and I want C. If some further reason is required for wanting C, then (tautologically) I have not yet given a sufficient reason for wanting C. But in that case, if I want B because it leads to C, and I have not yet given a sufficient reason for wanting C, then I have not yet given a sufficient reason for wanting B. And if I want A because it leads to B, and I have not yet given a sufficient reason for wanting B, then I have not yet given a sufficient reason for wanting A. Therefore, if my chain of reasons for wanting A can never get to a point at which no further reason is needed, then I can never have a sufficient reason for wanting A.

The same point can be put in terms of 'knowledge' and 'certainty'. If I need to consider reasons for wanting A, this must mean that I am in doubt as to whether I want A, I do not know whether I want A. Therefore these reasons must end with something which I can know to be the case, something about which I am no longer in doubt, something about which I can be certain. For if the fact which I give as my final reason is itself uncertain, i.e. if some further reason is called for, then this uncertainty is infectious. That is to say, if I assert 'p, because q', and I do not know that q is the case, then to that extent I cannot know that p is the case. Therefore my reasons for wanting something (like my reasons for anything else) must come to an end with some fact which can be known in itself, without the need for any further reason.

The advantage of framing our reasons-for-action in terms of 'wants' now becomes apparent. For let us suppose that we arrive at the statement of some want for which no further reason *can* be given, since what is wanted is wanted neither for the sake of anything else nor under any further description. In that case, simply in virtue of the fact that it is the statement of a want, no further reason *need* be given. Let us try to explain this by means of the example we have already used. My reason for giving money to a beggar (i.e. my reason for—in an extended sense —*wanting* to give money to a beggar) is that this will, as a consequence, prevent him from starving. My reason for preventing him from starving (i.e. my reason for wanting to prevent him from starving) is that to do so is to prevent unnecessary suffering. I cannot give any reason for wanting to prevent unnecessary suffering. It is not the case that I want it because it will lead to anything else, nor is it the case that I want it under some other description, for I want it just because it is what it is. All that I can say, then, is that I want *just this*. Now, how might someone try to question the status of this as a reason?

We have seen that there is no room for the obvious question 'Why do you want this?', since *ex hypothesi* I have no further reason for wanting it. But there remain two questions which someone might try to ask. In the first place, he might ask 'Why is that a reason for doing anything?' Now I would already have shown that by giving money to the beggar I am preventing him from starving, and that in preventing him from starving I am preventing unnecessary suffering; so the question cannot mean 'Why is the fact that you want to prevent unnecessary suffering a reason for wanting to give money to a beggar?' The emphasis must therefore be on the word 'doing': 'Why is the fact that you *want* to prevent unnecessary suffering a reason for *doing* whatever is necessary to prevent unnecessary suffering (including giving money to the beggar)?' But as soon as the question is put in this form, we can see that it is absurd to ask why wanting to do something is a reason for doing it. There is a necessary connection between wanting and action. It has been said that 'the primitive sign of wanting is *trying to get*'.[1] I think that the force of the term 'primitive sign' is connected with the particular nature of 'psychological' words. The word 'wanting', even though it can in a sense be called the name of a private mental state, must have public criteria. It would be impossible ever to teach anyone what 'wanting' is if there were no public manifestations of 'wanting'. 'Trying to get something' or 'trying to do something' is one such manifestation of 'wanting' —the primary one. These public manifestations are not just symptoms, connected only contingently with wanting. Since the meaning of the word 'wanting' can be taught *only* by reference to the public criteria, the word must be linked to the criteria in virtue of its very meaning, i.e. 'wanting' and its public criteria must be *logically* connected. This does not entail that someone wants something if and only if he tries to get it or do it. But it does entail that if someone wants something but never tries to get it or do it, there must be some special explanation of why he fails to do so (e.g. that he is feeling lazy, that he feels that it is too difficult, etc.); in the absence of any such explanation, we should have

[1] G. E. M. Anscombe: *Intention*, p. 68—and widely quoted.

to say that he didn't really want it. This is what constitutes the intimate connection between wanting and action, and leaves no room for the question 'why is wanting to do something a reason for doing it?'

The second question that somebody might try to ask is: 'How do you know that you want to prevent unnecessary suffering?' or 'Are you sure it's really the case that you want to?' Once again, however, the question is out of place because of the nature of 'I want X' as a psychological statement. Philosophers have sometimes said that first-person psychological statements are incorrigible; and they have sometimes gone on to explain this by saying that the speaker knows for certain that such a statement is true, since it is a report of the contents of his own mind. Thus, it would seem to be necessarily the case that I know what I want. However, there are difficulties in this way of putting it. There are, indeed, apparent counter-instances.[1] Most of these can be taken care of simply by emphasizing that it is 'ultimate' wants, not cases of 'wanting for a purpose' or 'wanting under a different description', about which I cannot doubt. Obviously, if I want A because it is a means to B, I may be in doubt as to whether I really want A insofar as I may be in doubt as to whether A is really a means to B. But two kinds of cases might seem more recalcitrant. The first is that of Freudian 'unconscious wants'. Do these constitute examples of a person's not knowing his own ultimate wants? This is too large a problem to be properly discussed here, but two particular points can be mentioned. (a) Central to the Freudian theory is the concept of repression—the idea that unconscious wants are unconscious because one deliberately excludes them from one's conscious thoughts. Freud expresses this in the language of psychological mechanics; repression is said to be the work of certain 'psychological forces', or of the 'ego' which acts in opposition to the instincts of the 'id'. This terminology should not be allowed to obscure the fact that the concept of 'repression' implies that a person's wants remain unconscious because *he himself* represses them. We therefore seem compelled to recognize that, in order to be able to repress his unconscious wants, a person must in some sense *know* that he has these wants. (b) Freud emphasizes that no hypothesis about a person's unconscious wants is fully verified until the patient himself recognizes the wants as his own. It is not enough that he should come to accept the analyst's hypothesis as a plausible explanation of his own behaviour; he must get to the point of admitting to himself that this is what he wants and has wanted all along. He must *remember* having certain wants on certain occasions. This way of describing it is clearly linked with the importance of the concept of repression, and it too suggests that in some sense the patient must always have known that he wanted what he did want.

[1] They are usefully discussed by B. F. McGuiness in his paper 'I know what I want' (*P.A.S.*. 1956–7).

The second major objection to the claim that 'I know what I want' is an *a priori* truth is provided by the following remarks of Wittgenstein's:

'I know what I want, wish, believe, feel, . . .' (and so on through all the psychological verbs) is either philosophers' nonsense, or at any rate *not* a judgement *a priori*.

'I know . . .' may mean 'I do not doubt . . .' but does not mean that the words 'I doubt . . .' are *senseless*, that doubt is logically excluded.

One says 'I know' where one can also say 'I believe' or 'I suspect'; where one can find out. (If you bring up against me the case of people's saying 'But I must know if I am in pain!', 'Only you can know what you feel', and similar things, you should consider the occasion and purpose of these phrases. 'War is war' is not an example of the law of identity, either.)

Philosophical Investigations, p. 221e

This is important as a warning against the idea that one has some special kind of knowledge (such as that derived from 'introspection') of one's own mental states. One cannot doubt, not because one has privileged knowledge, but because doubt is senseless. On the other hand, it does not follow that 'I know what I want' cannot legitimately be used to express the fact that doubt is senseless. However, this is a question which need not be resolved here. So long as it is agreed that the doubt is senseless, this is all that is needed in order to show that, when 'I want just this' is given as an ultimate reason for acting, the question 'How do you know?' or 'Are you sure?' is out of place. Now we have already seen that the question 'Why do you want this?' and the question 'Why is that a reason for doing anything?' are also out of place. Since there does not seem to be any other question that could be asked, it follows that the status of 'I want just this' as an ultimate reason cannot be questioned. This is why basic wants are capable of anchoring a chain of reasons for acting.

To complete the argument one must show that no statements other than basic want-statements are capable of doing so. This conclusion too seems to be suggested by the preceding argument. An ordinary evaluative statement is not capable of anchoring the chain of reasons. Suppose that the statement 'It just is right to prevent unnecessary suffering' is offered as an ultimate reason, for which no further reason can be given. Here the question 'Why is that a reason for doing anything?' is out of place, because of the evaluative status of the word 'right', but the question 'How do you know?' can be asked, and no satisfactory answer can be provided. Alternatively, an ordinary descriptive statement is equally incapable of anchoring the chain of reasons. If the statement 'This action will prevent unnecessary suffering' is offered as an ultimate reason, the question 'How do you know?', whilst not out of place, can certainly be answered; given that the action is one of preventing some-one from starving, there is abundant experience to confirm that starvation is a painful, agonizing condition, i.e. a condition of extreme suffering. But one can ask 'Why is this a reason for doing anything?', and there is no clear way of answering this question, since one can without contradiction recognize that something will cause suffering without recognizing that one ought to prevent it. In the case of basic want-statements, both questions are out of place, because of the dual status of 'I want X' as both evaluation and description. If I say 'I want X', I am, strictly speaking, not describing my state of mind, but evaluating X. It is because of this evaluative aspect that the question 'Why is that a reason for doing anything?' is out of place. But at the same time my statement can function for someone else as a description of my state of mind. If someone says of me 'He wants X', he is stating the same fact which I have stated, and he is certainly making a descriptive statement. This is why the question 'How do you know?' does not create difficulties as it does with ordinary evaluative statements. And it is this duality that gives basic want-statements their unique status as ultimate reasons for acting.

6. WANTS AND PERCEPTIONS

This, then, is the argument that could be put forward in support of the three accounts of reasons-for-acting. And what now becomes apparent, I think, is that those three accounts constitute, in the sphere of practical reasoning, a position which is essentially the equivalent of an empiricist position in the sphere of theoretical reasoning. By an empiricist position I mean the idea that the ultimate grounds of one's factual beliefs about the external world are propositions about what one directly perceives. The parallels between such a position and the three accounts of reasons-for-acting are: first, the idea that in any chain of reasons there must always be a point at which one has to stop, i.e. there are always ultimate reasons; second, the idea that these ultimate reasons must all share some common characteristic(s); third, the idea that the characteristics possessed by these ultimate reasons must be such that they cannot be questioned further, and therefore no further reasons are needed, i.e. the ultimate reasons must be such that they can constitute 'foundations'; and fourth, the idea that such reasons are provided by first-person psychological statements, since these cannot be questioned further and cannot be doubted.[1]

---

[1] For a useful survey of such ideas, see Anthony Quinton: 'The Foundations of Knowledge', in Williams and Montefiore: *British Analytical Philosophy*, pp. 55–86.

There is, however, one obvious qualification that needs to be added to the argument of the previous section. Since it depends upon the supposed incorrigibility of *first-person* psychological statements, it can at best constitute an argument for supposing that *the agent's own* wants provide ultimate reasons for acting; it cannot by itself provide a sufficient justification for the Third Account. Here too there is a parallel with empiricism. Just as the empiricist account of factual knowledge has to negotiate the problem of solipsism, so, as we have seen, certain philosophers have supposed that the ultimate reasons for acting must be anybody's wants rather than simply one's own wants, since otherwise practical reasoning would be entirely egotistical, or at any rate entirely prudential. This move might, of course, be rejected. There are those who would adhere solely to the First Account or the Second Account, and who would claim either that these accounts do not make all practical reasoning egotistical, or that they do so and that this fact must simply be accepted. Nevertheless it is important that we should consider whether there is any argument which could supplement the argument of the previous section and could justify the claim that *everybody's* wants provide ultimate reasons for acting. This will be the principal concern of our next chapter.

2. Utilitarianism and the Status of Other People

The accounts of reasons-for-acting which we discussed in the previous chapter were derived principally from the work of recent ethical philosophers. But we noted also that the same views can be attributed to philosophers such as Hobbes and Hume. I now want to go a step further and argue that the notion of 'wants-as-reasons', and its various metamorphoses, form the most prominent tradition in British ethical philosophy. Between Hume's time and the twentieth century, that tradition is represented primarily by the classical utilitarian writers such as Bentham and Mill. I have previously suggested that if we are looking for a single label which can be applied to the view of ethical rationality proposed by all three of the accounts which we have considered, we can most appropriately refer to it as 'utilitarian rationality'. Although the term 'utilitarian' is sometimes reserved exclusively for Bentham and Mill and for those who have held views strictly identical with theirs, it is also frequently applied to Hobbes and Hume and other similar seventeenth- and eighteenth-century writers. The modern philosophers whom we considered in the previous chapter would, I think, be more hesitant about accepting the label for themselves. Nevertheless I believe that the similarities between them and the classical utilitarians are much greater than the differences. In the first part of this chapter I shall indicate what these similarities are.

1. UTILITARIANISM AS TELEOLOGICAL ETHICS

In the 'Three Accounts' of chapter 1, the relation between means and ends occupied a prominent place. An important element in these accounts was the idea that a reason is given for an action if it is shown that the action is a means to some end which is wanted for its own sake. This was said to be one of the two possible kinds of reason-for-acting —the other consisting in the fact that something which is not wanted as such falls under some further description, under which it *is* wanted as such. This second class of reasons might well be regarded as a subcategory of the former class; for example, if I go for a walk in order to get some exercise, it could be said that I want to go for a walk not as an end in itself, not for its own sake, but as a means to the end of getting some exercise, even though 'going for a walk' and 'getting some exercise' are alternative descriptions of one and the same activity. Our Three Accounts, then, are essentially *teleological*; and this constitutes one major point of resemblance between them and classical utilitarianism. The latter has generally been regarded as the most explicitly teleological of all ethical theories. The terms 'utilitarian' and 'teleological' have sometimes even been treated as interchangeable; and indeed, the very notion of 'utility' suggests the assessment of actions from the point of view of their propensity to achieve desirable ends. In this respect, then, it is certainly not inappropriate to call our Three Accounts 'utilitarian'.

2. UTILITARIANISM AS PSYCHOLOGISTIC ETHICS

The second main point of resemblance between classical utilitarianism and our Three Accounts is the idea that reasons-for-acting are created by certain kinds of *psychological* facts. For Bentham, the relevant psychological concept is that of 'pleasure'. The quantity of pleasure that a person or persons feel in consequence of any act is the sole criterion of the value of that act. And it is clear from Bentham's writings that the concept is not to be understood behaviouristically, as referring to a certain kind of overt reaction, nor as referring to the recognition of some objective property of the pleasure-giving thing; 'pleasure' is, for Bentham, in a fairly strong sense, a 'mental' concept, referring to a subjective attitude, and it shares the logical properties of the attitude-words which we considered in the previous chapter. Bentham particularly stresses that 'that is pleasure which a man's judgement, aided by his memory, recommends and recognizes to his feelings *as* pleasure', and that therefore 'every person is not only the best, but the only proper judge of what, with reference to himself, is pleasure, and what pain' (*Deontology*, Vol. I, p. 29 and p. 59). We have already seen that this is one of the features of first-person attitude-statements that makes it plausible to regard them as providing a sufficient basis for practical rationality (although we also noted the dangers of seeming to imply, as Bentham does, that each person is the only judge of, or has a special kind of knowledge of, his own attitudes). The other feature of such concepts which, we suggested, makes them plausible candidates for providing reasons-for-acting is their necessary connection with action. Bentham certainly sees the concept of 'pleasure' in this way. It is his constant assertion that pleasures and pains are 'the sole motives of human conduct', that 'every man's necessary impulse is towards the economy of happiness'. To his preoccupation with this theme we shall return presently.

The concept of 'pleasure' thus has, within the classical utilitarian system, a role similar to that assigned to 'wanting' in chapter 1. This similarity is increased insofar as 'pleasure' has this role by virtue of its connection with the concept of 'desire'. This is especially the case in Mill's version. Chapter 4 of his *Utilitarianism* contains the famous 'desirability' argument which Moore found so objectionable. Moore's criticisms are now thought by many philosophers to have been misplaced. Mary Warnock has argued very persuasively[1] that Mill's argument was not intended to be a deductive one, asserting a logical equivalence between 'X is desirable' and 'X is desired', but rather consisted in the assertion that the only way of showing someone that something is desirable is by pointing out to him that he does actually desire it. I would accept this interpretation as far as it goes; but what is still not sufficiently recognized is the extent to which Mill's argument is specifically an epistemological one. He says:

> The only proof capable of being given that an object is visible, is that people actually see it. The only proof that a sound is audible, is that people hear it: *and so of the other sources of our experience.* In like manner, I apprehend, the sole evidence it is possible to produce that anything is desirable, is that people do actually desire it.

The words which I have italicized are generally ignored, but are of the first importance. Their significance can be understood if one refers back to the opening sentences of the chapter:

> It has already been remarked, that questions of ultimate ends do not admit of proof, in the ordinary acceptation of the term. To be incapable of proof by reasoning is common to all first principles; to the first premises of our knowledge, as well as to those of our conduct. But the former, being matters of fact, may be the subject of a direct appeal to the faculties which judge of fact—namely, our senses, and our internal consciousness. Can an appeal be made to the same faculties on questions of practical ends? Or by what other faculty is cognisance taken of them?

This implies a direct comparison between the role of desire in practical reasoning and the role of perception in factual reasoning. Consequently the point of Mill's analogy between 'desirable' and 'visible' is not just that they are both '-ble' words; it would *not*, for example, have suited

[1] In *Ethics Since 1900*, pp. 28–33, and in her introduction to the Fontana edition of Mill's *Utilitarianism*, pp. 25–6.

his purpose equally well to use as an analogy the suggestion that, say, the sole evidence that a piece of music is playable is that people do actually play it. The relevance of the notions of 'visible', 'audible', etc., is that they refer directly to particular *sources of experience*. In using them, Mill is invoking a specific epistemological position, namely the empiricist thesis that the ultimate grounds of all factual knowledge are provided by the evidence of perception and introspection (the former providing knowledge of the external world and the latter providing knowledge of the mind). Mill's argument is then that in practical reasoning, also, there are 'foundations' consisting in certain ultimate principles which cannot be further derived by logical reasoning, and are in this sense incapable of proof, but which state the direct testimony of a particular psychological faculty. This faculty which provides the ultimate reasons for conduct is the faculty of 'desire'.

Mill's argument that practical reasoning rests on certain ultimate reasons, that these ultimate reasons are distinguished by their reference to the testimony of a particular psychological faculty, and that the relevant psychological faculty is the faculty of desire, is closely comparable to the argument which I outlined in chapter 1. But we have also noted the resemblance between the accounts considered in chapter 1 and Bentham's account of pleasure as the criterion of conduct. We must now look at the relation between these two aspects of utilitarianism—viz. the use that Bentham makes of the concept of pleasure, and the use that Mill makes of the concept of desire. Now, of course, for Mill, the connection between the two concepts is that pleasure (or 'happiness', where this is equivalent to pleasure plus absence of pain) is the sole object of desire. But this can be interpreted in two ways. It can be understood as a contingent claim: men could conceivably desire, for example, health or wealth or friendship for their own sake, but as a matter of fact they do not, since the only thing desired for its own sake is pleasure (and absence of pain). If this is the intended ground of the validity of classical utilitarianism, then the latter must be seen as a much more restricted ethical theory than the theory of 'wants-as-reasons'. It becomes equivalent to the conjunction of that theory with certain very very stringent limitations on the actual objects of human wants. On the other hand the claim that all desire is for pleasure can also be interpreted as an analytic statement. It could, for example, be argued that the relation between 'desiring something' and 'finding pleasure in something' is like the relation between 'wanting' and 'liking' suggested above (ch. 1, p. 18): 'desiring something', when the phrase is used in the context of a utilitarian ethic, is to be understood as a general label for pro-attitudes towards a particular thing which is absent, and 'finding pleasure in something' is to be understood as a general label for pro-attitudes towards a particular thing which is already present, or towards a general class of things. This would mean giving the term 'pleasure' a sense much wider than it normally has, so that it would become more or less the noun-equivalent of the verb 'to please'. Such a sense is doubtless what people have had in mind when they have talked of 'the philosophical sense' or 'the extended sense' of the word 'pleasure'; although it would perhaps have seemed less of an 'extended' sense in Bentham's own day, since at that time there still survived the usage whereby one might, for example, ask someone 'What is your pleasure?' and mean 'What do you want?'[1] If 'pleasure' is understood in this sense, it can then be asserted as an analytic truth that 'all desire is for pleasure'; and this would in no way conflict with such assertions as that men desire health, or wealth, or friendship, for their own sake. To say, for example, that one desired friendship for its own sake, and to say that one desired it simply because one found pleasure in it, would both be equivalent; each would serve the purpose of ruling out some such possibility as that one desired friendship as a means to, say, social advancement.

The question which of these two views should be ascribed to Mill has become fertile ground for philosophical exegesis.[2] One can find in the text of *Utilitarianism* evidence for either interpretation. But the attempt to determine 'what Mill really meant' is ultimately as otiose as it is futile. For, whatever Mill may have meant, there can be no doubt what he *ought* to have meant. Only on the second interpretation is utilitarianism a plausible ethical theory. If the validity of utilitarianism were dependent upon the truth of the assertion that no one ever desires any such thing as health or wealth or friendship as an end in itself, it would never have appeared and re-appeared so persistently throughout the history of philosophy. Its survival-potential can be explained only by the plausibility of the claim that 'all desire is for pleasure' when interpreted as an *analytic* statement. And in that case the thesis that the ultimate grounds of practical reasoning are provided by considerations of what is desired, and the thesis that the ultimate grounds of practical reasoning are provided by considerations of what produces pleasure, must be regarded as alternative formulations of the same theory, parallel to one another and each parallel to the thesis of 'wants as ultimate reasons for acting'.[3]

[1] Cf.: 'The public legislator, with all his powers, is generally less despotic in his phraseology than the public writer—that self-constituted legislator of the people. He makes laws without giving reasons,—laws which generally convey only his sovereign will and pleasure.' (Bentham: *Deontology*, Vol. I, p. 8.)

[2] Again, Mary Warnock provides a useful discussion. See *Ethics Since 1900*, pp. 37–9, and her introduction to Mill's *Utilitarianism*, pp. 26–7.

[3] Cf. A. J. Ayer: *The Principle of Utility* (in *Philosophical Essays*), p. 266f. A useful defence of classical utilitarianism interpreted along these lines is provided by Jan Narveson's book, *Morality and Utility*.

3. Utilitarianism and the Problem of Other People

To sum up this first part of the chapter: the theory of 'wants-as-reasons' is akin to classical utilitarianism both in being a teleological theory, and in identifying as the ultimate reason-for-acting a psychological attitude which, whether it be called 'wanting' or 'pleasure' or 'desire', is conceived of in much the same way in each case; and we are therefore justified in referring to these ethical positions collectively as 'utilitarian rationality'. We are now, however, returned to the problem which we encountered at the end of the last chapter. Utilitarianism is characteristically a theory to the effect that an action is justified if it will, in the circumstances, maximize the happiness of *people in general*. But, by the arguments which we have just been looking at, all that can be shown is that what is 'good' for each person is what he himself desires, and that, insofar as there is an analytic connection between 'desire' and 'pleasure' or 'happiness', each person necessarily desires only *his own* pleasure or happiness.[1] Some further argument is needed to show that reasons-for-acting are provided by other people's happiness or other people's wants, on an equal status with one's own happiness or one's own wants. Now, as I said at the end of the last chapter, a proponent of utilitarian rationality would not necessarily feel the need for any such argument. He might be perfectly willing to rest content with the claim that the agent's own wants, his own happiness, provide him with his sole reasons for acting. Nevertheless, a great many of these utilitarian writers *have* seen a need to extend the class of reasons-for-acting so as to include the wants of people in general, and in the rest of this chapter I want to discuss the main arguments which they have offered for doing so—first, because I want to show that none of these arguments is successful, and that therefore this generalized form of utilitarianism is, as it stands, unacceptable as a philosophical theory, but secondly, and more importantly, because I believe that certain of the arguments, when taken to their logical conclusion, will serve to indicate what is wrong with the whole project of 'wants-as-reasons'.

It is important to notice what form these arguments would have to take. The original argument for 'wants-as-reasons' was an attempt to show that the agent's own wants *necessarily* constitute reasons for acting—an argument proceeding from an analysis of the very idea of what it is to have a reason for doing something, and satisfying the conditions that reasons-for-acting must have some necessary connection with *action*, and must consist in considerations which can be *known*. Any extension of the class of possible reasons-for-acting must be

---

[1] Mill, *Utilitarianism* (Fontana ed.), p. 288: 'No reason can be given why the general happiness is desirable, except that each person, so far as he believes it to be attainable, desires his own happiness.'

justified by an argument with the same logical status and such that the
same conditions will still be satisfied. It would, for example, be entirely
out of place to adopt an intuitionist stance and suggest that one knows
intuitively that other people's wants must carry equal weight with one's
own. For if reasons-for-acting can be identified by means of this kind
of procedure, the original argument must be either illegitimate, or
unnecessary, or both. That is to say, if any claim to the effect that something constitutes a reason for acting can be established *simply* by
intuition, then it cannot be the case that reasons-for-acting are *necessarily* provided *only* by wants, since, logically speaking, one could
perfectly well recognize intuitively that anything at all constituted a
reason for acting; and as for a suggestion that wants *sometimes* provide
reasons for acting, this does not need to be demonstrated by a complex
logical argument, since, if true, it can be known intuitively. Conversely,
if one believes that an argument of the kind employed in chapter 1 *is*
necessary in order to validate the assertion that wants provide reasons
for acting, one will *a fortiori* reject the suggestion that assertions of this
kind can be verified simply by intuition.

4. Bentham's Solution

I shall look first at the way in which Bentham deals with this problem.
For this purpose it is necessary to consider the *Deontology*, a work
which is somewhat neglected but is in fact Bentham's only work dealing
strictly with ethics, that is, with individual behaviour as distinct from
political legislation. There is some doubt as to whether it constitutes a
reliable guide to Bentham's opinions, since it was compiled by Bowring
from separate and unorganized notes left by Bentham at his death.
Nevertheless, on the point with which we are concerned, there can be
little doubt that the opinion expressed in that work is Bentham's own,
since it pervades virtually everything contained in the work. This is the
assertion that the only reason a man can ever have for performing an
action is that it will produce the greatest sum of pleasure *for himself*. In
other words, Bentham does *not* extend the possible reasons-for-acting
from the agent's own wants to the wants of others.

Bentham himself tends to speak of 'motives' rather than 'reasons'.
Thus, for example, after listing all the different kinds of pleasures and
pains, he adds: 'These pleasures and pains—the obtaining the pleasure,
the avoidance of the pain—are the sole motives of human conduct'
(*Deontology*, Vol. I, p. 66). This sometimes seems to imply that the
impossibility of acting other than for one's own pleasure is a fact of
human nature, a physical or psychological fact, as when he says:
'. . . for a man not to pursue what he deems likely to produce to him the
greatest sum of enjoyment, is in the very nature of things impossible'

(Ibid., p. 13). But elsewhere, and more satisfactorily, Bentham implies that an action's being for the agent's own pleasure is a condition of its being a *rational* action. For example, he says: 'To obtain the greatest portion of happiness for himself, is the object of every rational being' (Ibid., p. 18), and he suggests that to say to someone '. . . "if you do this, you may get a preponderant pleasure, yet it is not proper you should do it", is absurdity' (Ibid., p. 60).

If the only reason a man ever has for acting is that the action will contribute to his own pleasure, how can a man ever be induced to act so as to increase the happiness of others, and how is it that men do in fact often so act? This is the question with which Bentham is preoccupied in the *Deontology*. The answer is, of course, that a man has a reason to contribute to the happiness of others when this will also increase his own sum of pleasure. Therefore, a crucial concept for Bentham is that of 'sanctions'—inducements to action, which bring considerations of pleasure and pain to bear on conduct in such a way as to counter temptations (see especially chapter VII). At one point Bentham illustrates these by means of an example intended to demonstrate 'the influence of an act upon others whose happiness is affected by it' (p. 168ff.): Suppose that a man wishes to strike a blow at another. In the first place, he will be aware of the possibility of retaliation in the form of the same or similar personal injury; this is the *physical* sanction. He risks punishment by the magistrate; this is the *political or legal* sanction. He will incur the disapproval and hostility of public opinion, since people will have been taught by experience and observation that such deeds of violence are the sources of suffering; this is the *popular or moral* sanction. And he may himself feel sympathy for his intended victim; this is the *social or sympathetic* sanction, which is strongest in relation to one's friends and family, but which in a civilized society extends much further. There remains a fifth sanction, the *religious or superhuman* sanction, which Bentham does not mention here, but which he lists elsewhere; this is the fear of divine punishment or hope of divine reward, which does not directly induce us to contribute to the happiness of other people, but which may do so indirectly if that is the kind of conduct which God chooses to reward.

These five sanctions can themselves be divided into two categories. All except the fourth refer to the possibility that one's action will have as a consequence some further event which will involve pain or loss of pleasure for oneself. On the other hand the social or sympathetic sanction refers to the pain or pleasure which one feels as a *direct* response to the pain or pleasure of another. This distinction is important for Bentham's division of virtue into two kinds: 'the production of our own happiness is prudence, the production of the happiness of others is effective benevolence' (p. 140). Prudence is itself divided into

self-regarding prudence and extra-regarding prudence, the latter being
the production of our own happiness where this can be achieved by
increasing the happiness of others. Since one engages in the production
of others' happiness *only* when this also produces happiness for oneself,
it might appear from the above definitions that extra-regarding prudence
and effective benevolence coincide, and are but two sides of the same
coin. But Bentham elsewhere seems to suggest that the difference
between them is to be found in the distinction made at the beginning of
this paragraph. The actions of effective benevolence, unlike those of
extra-regarding prudence, proceed from a direct pleasure in the happiness of others. That this is Bentham's meaning appears to be borne out
by his insistence on using the term 'effective benevolence' rather than
'beneficence'; he asserts that a man may act in a manner which is, as a
matter of objective fact, beneficent, without necessarily being at all
well-disposed (benevolent) towards those who benefit. Nevertheless, it
still has to be emphasized that benevolent actions would not be performed if they did not increase one's own sum of pleasure, as Bentham
makes clear in the following passage:

> . . . where is sympathy? where is benevolence? where is beneficence?
> Answer, exactly where they were. To deny the existence of the social
> affections would be to deny the evidence of all experience. Scarcely in
> the most brutal savage would they be found altogether wanting. But
> the pleasure I feel in bestowing pleasure on my friend, whose pleasure
> is it but mine? The pain I feel at seeing my friend oppressed by pain,
> whose pain is it but mine? And if I felt no pleasure, or felt no pain,
> where, where would be my sympathy?
>
> (Ibid., pp. 83–4)

But this is not the whole of Bentham's position. Formulations of the
kind that are thought to be typical of classical utilitarianism, as that the
right action in any circumstance is the one which will lead to the happiness of the greatest number, are certainly prominent in his writings.
How, then, can he justify them? In the first place we may notice that they
frequently refer to the activities of the *legislator* (this point has often
been made in discussions of Bentham's philosophy). The *Introduction
to the Principles of Morals and Legislation* is much more concerned with
legislation than with morals. The task of the legislator is to induce
people to act in such a way as to increase the general happiness. Since
the actions of those for whom he legislates are all aimed at private
happiness, he has to institute rewards and punishments so designed as
to make private interest and public duty coincide as far as possible. He
himself, qua legislator, does not act as a private individual, and this is
why his legislative acts are not motivated solely by his own private

happiness. To support this idea, Bentham would, I think, have to produce a theory to the effect that the legislator is *responsible to* all the members of the society, so that what counts as a reason-for-acting for each individual member (viz. conduciveness to the private happiness of that individual) must also count as a reason-for-acting for the legislator. So far as I know, Bentham does not explicitly argue this, but I think that it could be done within a utilitarian perspective.

To see how the notion of 'general happiness' extends also into the field of individual morality, we may compare the position of the legislator with that of the deontologist (a term coined by Bentham to be synonymous with 'moralist'). The parallel is frequently drawn by Bentham:

> The line which distinguishes the dominions of the Legislator from those of the Deontologist is tolerably distinct and obvious. Where legal rewards and punishments cease to interfere with human actions, there precepts of morality come in with their influences. The conduct which is not given over to the tribunals of the state for judgement, belongs to the tribunals of opinion. . . . In a word, Deontology, or Private Ethics, may be considered the science by which happiness is created out of motives extra-legislational—while Jurisprudence is the science by which law is applied to the production of felicity.
>
> (Ibid., pp. 27–8)

It is the task of both the legislator and the deontologist to make interest and duty coincide; the deontologist does this by drawing people's attention to those many cases in which one's own happiness can best be secured by contributing to the happiness of others. He also aims to influence public opinion so that it condemns or applauds actions according to their contribution to the general happiness, thereby giving weight to the moral sanction. In attempting to explain why the deontologist is concerned with the general happiness and not just with his own private happiness, we must presumably make the same kind of assumption as we did in the case of the legislator: the deontologist is responsible to the general public. In setting himself up as a moralist, he is taking upon himself the role of public adviser. He writes books and delivers discourses which are addressed to every individual, and therefore the concerns of each separate individual must all be the concern of the deontologist.

Now, it is from the point of view of the deontologist that moral judgements—judgements of right and wrong—are made. We are therefore led to the following conclusion:

> The principle, then, on which Deontology is grounded, is the principle of Utility; in other words, that every action is right or wrong—worthy

or unworthy—deserving approbation or disapprobation, in propor-
tion to its tendency to contribute to, or to diminish the amount of,
public happiness.

(Ibid., pp. 23–4)

Thus we seem required to distinguish between judgements as to whether
a person has a valid reason for performing an action, and judgements as
to the rightness or wrongness of the action; in the first case the criterion
is the agent's own happiness, in the second it is the general happiness.
But there is one further point to be made: although in any society there
are usually but few legislators, every member of a society is, at least
potentially, a deontologist. Anyone can put himself in the position of
spokesman for public opinion:

> And why should (the individual) declare his approbation of a
> particular course of conduct? Undoubtedly, because the approbation
> may lead to its adoption. And it will thus be conducive to it. Public
> opinion is made up of individual opinions; and public opinion is that
> which constitutes the popular or moral sanction. . . . Of this in-
> fluential power, every individual in the community forms a part.

(Ibid., pp. 21–2)

Our final conclusion (which, it must be emphasized, is a conjectural
interpretation of Bentham and not a paraphrase of his own words) must
therefore be that every individual can make judgements about actions
from two points of view, as agent and as deontologist. As agent, he will
make judgements as to what he himself has a reason to do, and these
will be judgements as to what will increase the sum of his own pleasure.
As deontologist, he will make judgements of right and wrong, and will
do so not as a private individual but from a public point of view, asking
of every action whether it will contribute to the general happiness. Of
this notion of 'adopting a public point of view' we shall say more
presently. In the meantime, what we find is that Bentham's position is,
strictly speaking, closest to our Second Account in chapter 1, and that
he does not provide an argument for extending it into the Third Account
and making everyone's wants reasons-for-acting.

5. HUME AND SYMPATHY

One way in which philosophers have sometimes attempted to
generalize utilitarianism is by reference to some such concept as that of
'sympathy' or 'humanity' or 'benevolence'. Hume furnishes an example
of this kind of theory. His version of utilitarianism starts out from the
characteristic principle that 'the chief spring or actuating principle of
the human mind is pleasure or pain; and when these sensations are

removed, both from our thought and feeling, we are in a great measure incapable of passion or action, of desire or volition.'[1] Hume must clearly mean by this that the 'actuating principle' consists in *the agent's own* pleasure and pain, since the status assigned to pleasure and pain here is regarded by him as following from the fact that one cannot be moved to act by anything that is indifferent to *oneself*. But within Hume's ethical theory this kind of argument from first principles is combined with a more inductive approach, involving the survey of accepted moral truths. When he adopts this latter perspective, Hume recognizes that we regard as virtues not only those qualities which are useful or agreeable to ourselves but also those which are useful or agreeable to others. In order to make this principle consistent with the earlier one, Hume finds it convenient to make very great use of the idea of 'sympathy', which he explains as follows:

> The minds of all men are similar in their feelings and operations; nor can any one be actuated by any affection of which all others are not in some degree susceptible. As in strings equally wound up the motion of one communicates itself to the rest, so all the affections readily pass from one person to another, and beget correspondent movements in every human creature. When I see the *effects* of passion in the voice and gesture of any person, my mind immediately passes from these effects to their causes, and forms such a lively idea of the passion as is presently converted into the passion itself. In like manner, when I perceive the *causes* of any emotion, my mind is conveyed to the effects, and is actuated with a like emotion.   (p. 132)

Hence it happens that 'when any quality or character has a tendency to the good of mankind, we are pleased with it and approve of it because it presents the lively idea of pleasure; which idea affects us by sympathy, and is itself a kind of pleasure' (p. 136). It is this principle of sympathy, then, that 'takes us so far out of ourselves as to give us the same pleasure or uneasiness in the character of others, as if they had a tendency to our own advantage or loss' (p. 135).

Hume, then, while making the orthodox utilitarian assertion that all action is for the sake of pleasure, wants also to put the motive of sympathy on the same logical level as the agent's desire for his own pleasure. He wants to claim at one and the same time that

> The pain and pleasure [sc. to oneself] which arises from the general survey of or view of any action or quality of the mind, constitutes its vice or virtue.

> (p. 164 *et passim*)

[1] *Treatise of Human Nature*, Book III, Part III, Section I, p. 131.

and that

> the distinction of vice and virtue arises from the four principles of
> the advantage and of the pleasure of the person himself and of
> others.
>
> (p. 153; cf. p. 145, p. 164, etc.)

Now he agrees with Bentham that the pleasure of others can be a motive
for action only insofar as one gets pleasure from the pleasure of others.
On what grounds, then, can he give this motive a special status? He
could legitimately argue that the pleasure which one gets from the
pleasure of others is of greater practical importance than, say, the
pleasure that one gets from agreeable society or the pleasure that one
gets from comfortable living—perhaps because on it depends that social
harmony which is the necessary condition of any satisfactory life. But,
as motives to action, these are all on the same logical level. They are all
sub-classes of the universal class 'acting for one's own pleasure'.
Therefore 'acting for the pleasure of others' cannot be put on the same
level as 'acting for one's own pleasure', and these two cannot be made
the twin pillars of virtue as Hume tries to make them. This criticism
applies even more to the later *Enquiry*. For, in the first place, the classifi-
cation of virtues into 'qualities conducive to the advantage or the
pleasure of oneself or of others' becomes more important there. And
secondly, the principle of sympathy is there replaced by a principle of
'humanity', which is no longer analysed as a species of pleasure to
oneself but acquires the status of an independent motive. But in that
case the whole utilitarian framework, which Hume still seems to want
to keep, necessarily collapses, since it can no longer be claimed that all
action is for the sake of pleasure.

It should be added that even if sympathy—pleasure got from the
pleasure of others—is given a central role within a utilitarian morality,
this does not provide a principle for the distribution of happiness. It
implies only that one may sometimes have a reason for producing
happiness for someone other than oneself, not that every person has an
equal claim to happiness.

Before leaving Hume, we should notice an alternative argument
which he offers, seemingly, as an optional extra, but which in fact has
far-reaching implications. I refer to remarks such as the following:

> . . . it is impossible we could ever converse together on any reasonable
> terms, were each of us to consider characters and persons only as they
> appear from his peculiar point of view. In order, therefore, to prevent
> those continual *contradictions* and arrive at a more *stable* judgement
> of things, we fix on some *steady* and *general* points of view, and

always, in our thoughts, place ourselves in them, whatever may be our present situation. . . . We consider not whether the persons affected by the qualities be our acquaintance or strangers, countrymen or foreigners. Nay, we overlook our own interest in those general judgements, and blame not a man for opposing us in any of our pretensions when his own interest is particularly concerned.

. . . When we form our judgements of persons merely from the tendency of their characters to our own benefit, or that of our friends, we find so many contradictions to our sentiments in society and conversation, and such an uncertainty from the incessant changes of our situation, that we seek some other standard of merit and demerit which may not admit of so great variation. Being thus loosened from our first station, we cannot afterwards fix ourselves so commodiously by any means as by a sympathy with those who have any commerce with the person we consider . . .

(Treatise, III. III. 1, pp. 137–9)

One may perhaps be surprised that amidst all these interests and pleasures we should forget our own which touch us so nearly on every other occasion. But we shall easily satisfy ourselves on this head when we consider that every particular person's pleasure and interest being different, it is impossible men could ever agree in their sentiments and judgements, unless they chose some common point of view from which they might survey their object, and which might cause it to appear the same to all of them . . .

(Ibid., p. 145. Cf. also
Enquiry Concerning the Principles of Morals, IX. 1, pp. 252–3)

This is reminiscent of the idea which we drew from Bentham of judging either from a private or from a general and public point of view, but Hume's version is much more interesting insofar as he makes the adoption of a general point of view a precondition of rational discourse. Although he offers these remarks as an additional account of why we concern ourselves with other people's pleasure, I hope to show in the next chapter that the kernel of truth in them provides us with the fundamental argument against any kind of utilitarian rationality.

6. MILL'S ARGUMENT

Mill, too, makes use of such notions as 'sympathy' and 'the social feelings of mankind', but like Bentham he treats these simply as 'sanctions' (see ch. III of *Utilitarianism*). The only occasion on which he appears to recognize the need for an *argument* as to why utilitarianism

D

has to be formulated in terms of the *general* happiness is at the end of chapter V. He says there that the duty of impartiality and equality is

> . . . a direct emanation from the first principle of morals, and not a mere logical corollary from secondary or derivative doctrines. It is involved in the very meaning of Utility, or the Greatest Happiness Principle. That principle is a mere form of words without rational signification, unless one person's happiness, supposed equal in degree (with the proper allowance made for kind) is counted for exactly as much as another's. Those conditions being supplied, Bentham's dictum, 'everybody to count for one, nobody for more than one', might be written under the principle of utility as an explanatory commentary.
>
> (*Utilitarianism*, pp. 318–19)

And in a footnote, in opposition to Herbert Spencer, who had said that utilitarianism requires to be supplemented with an additional principle of impartiality, Mill adds:

> . . . equal amounts of happiness are equally desirable, whether felt by the same or by different persons. This, however, is not a *pre*-supposition; not a premise needful to support the principle of utility, but the very principle itself; for what is the principle of utility, if it be not that 'happiness' and 'desirable' are synonymous terms?
>
> (Ibid., p. 319)

This argument transparently takes for granted what is precisely the point at issue. For Mill has *not* previously shown that 'happiness' and 'desirable' are synonymous terms. All that he has said is that 'no reason can be given why the general happiness is desirable, except that each person . . . desires *his own* happiness' (Ibid., p. 288—my italics). As Mill recognizes there, what this proves is that 'each person's happiness is a good to that person', in other words, that each person's happiness is desirable for that person. It is true that Mill immediately adds: '. . . and the general happiness, therefore, a good to the aggregate of all persons'. As to what this means, we are not given the least clue. It might be akin to the final point which we noted in Hume; or it might be intended to imply some conception of 'the aggregate of persons' as an agent; all that is certain is that Mill does not tell us. Therefore he has produced no ground for saying, without qualification, that 'happiness' and 'desirable' are synonymous, or even that 'happiness' is 'desirable'; and therefore his argument in chapter V cannot even get started.

But even if we allowed Mill this point, it would still not prove what he wants it to prove. He is attempting to set up a principle of equality (i.e. of *equal claims*). But the argument is fatally flawed, this time by his inconsistent use of the word 'equally'. If there are two people among whom a certain amount of happiness is to be shared, we may say that it is equally good to give happiness to either of them, or that we should distribute the happiness equally between both of them. In the first alternative, the word 'equally' has nothing to do with any positive equality; all that we are saying is that it *doesn't matter* who gets the happiness. But this is all that Mill is able to say. His words are: '. . . equal amounts of happiness are equally desirable, whether felt by the same or by different persons'. Even if this is taken as proved, it is completely different from saying that happiness ought to be distributed equally, or that everyone has an equal claim to happiness, or even that everyone's desire for happiness equally gives me a reason for satisfying the desire. All that we have here is a principle of 'indifference'.

7. SIDGWICK'S ARGUMENT

Substantially the same criticism can be directed against an argument used by Sidgwick. He argues as follows.[1] There may be different ways of distributing the same quantum of happiness among the same number of persons. What mode of distribution ought to be adopted? The utilitarian formula does not tell us. We therefore have to supplement the principle of seeking the greatest happiness on the whole by some principle of just or right distribution of happiness. Most utilitarians have in fact adopted Bentham's formula: 'Everybody to count for one, and nobody for more than one.' This principle is the only principle of just distribution which does not need a special justification; for it must be reasonable to treat any one man in the same way as any other, if there is no reason apparent for treating him differently.

This argument does at least have the merit of starting from the recognition that the principle of producing the greatest total quantity of happiness, regardless of whose it is, is not a principle of equality, and that some positive principle of equality therefore has to be found. But it doesn't really fit the bill any better than the previous candidate. Because he is intent on finding something self-evident, Sidgwick lights on what is not really a positive principle at all. If we have a quantum of happiness to distribute between A and B, and there is no positive reason for treating them differently, this does not imply a positive reason for treating them equally; and in the absence of any other such positive reason, what we should have to conclude would be that it doesn't matter how the happiness is distributed. And so we are back with exactly the same conclusion as from the previous argument. Sidgwick's mistake is to forget the category of moral neutrality. He assumes that

[1] *The Methods of Ethics*, pp. 416–17.

'ought' and 'ought not' are contradictories, whereas they are only con-
traries. That is, he assumes that if it is not positively right to treat A and
B differently, then it is wrong to treat them differently. But since it is
simply morally neutral to treat them differently, all that we have here is
in effect simply the 'principle of indifference' again.

8. HARE AND UNIVERSALIZABILITY

I want finally to look at the way in which Hare, in *Freedom and
Reason*, attempts to use the notion of 'universalizability' as a way of
generalizing from the ethical relevance of one's own desires and
interests to the ethical relevance of everyone's desires and interests.
Hare's thesis has been discussed to such an extent in recent years that
it may seem rash to suppose that anything more can usefully be said
about it. I shall not attempt to say anything very new nor shall I undertake an exhaustive treatment of the question. I want merely to draw
attention to certain points which are relevant to the present argument.

A great deal of the trouble with Hare's argument stems from the fact
that it is a conglomeration of various different ideas which are never
properly distinguished. It may therefore help if, in what follows, I try
to separate some of these different ideas and consider them one by one.

A. Like Hume in the passages quoted on pages 38–9, Hare is concerned
to argue that the move from considering one's own wants to considering
everyone's wants is in some way required by the very idea of rational
discourse in ethics. Initially this crystallizes into the demand that ethical
words have always to be used with a constant and consistent meaning.
This requirement, moreover, applies not only to their evaluative meaning but also to their descriptive meaning. According to Hare, their
evaluative meaning—that is to say, their use as expressions of approval
or commendation—is primary, at any rate in the case of the most
general evaluative words such as 'good' and 'right' and 'ought'. Such
words can be used with whatever descriptive meaning the speaker
chooses to give them. But if the word is to be used *rationally*, then that
descriptive meaning must be consistent throughout all the separate
occasions on which one uses the word. Thus it cannot be the case that
two things bear exactly the same neutral description but that one is good
and the other is not, or that two actions have exactly the same neutral
description but that one ought to be performed and the other ought not
to be performed. Now, Hare thinks that he can move from this requirement to the claim which first makes its appearance on p. 32 of *Freedom
and Reason*:

> If a person says 'I ought to act in a certain way, but nobody else
> ought to act that way in relevantly similar circumstances', then, on

my thesis, he is abusing the word 'ought'; he is implicitly contradicting himself.

What does Hare regard as justifying this transition? It seems to me to
depend upon an assumption which becomes explicit in the following
passage:

> Any judgement which has descriptive meaning must be universalis-
> able, because the descriptive meaning-rules which determine this
> meaning are universal rules. But they are not necessarily general rules.
> A descriptive meaning-rule says that we can use a certain predicate of
> anything of a certain kind. And it is obvious that in the case of some
> descriptive predicates we shall have to go into a great deal of detail in
> order to specify what kind—if indeed this is formulable in words at
> all. . . . Now universalism is not the doctrine that behind every moral
> judgement there has to lie a principle expressible in a few general
> terms; the principle, though universal, may be so complex that it
> defies formulation in words at all. But if it were formulated and
> specified, *all the terms used in its formulation would be universal terms*.
> (*Freedom and Reason*, p. 39—my emphasis)

The intention of the last sentence is presumably to rule out personal and
possessive pronouns, so that the universal rule in accordance with which
a person acts and judges cannot be one which has reference solely to his
own desires and interests. But Hare offers no grounds for saying that the
descriptive meaning-rule must be formulated entirely in universal terms.
He appears to assume that a rule is universal only if all its terms are
universal terms. In the sense in which he has been using the phrase
'universal rule', this is certainly not the case. The rule 'I call an action
"right" if and only if it is in accordance with my wants' is, in the only
sense which Hare has so far stipulated, a perfectly good descriptive
meaning-rule, insofar as it provides a perfectly consistent descriptive
meaning for the word 'right'. The equivalent rule of action, 'I ought
always to perform those and only those actions which will achieve the
ends which I want', is also a perfectly good universal rule. An even
stronger rule could be adopted: '*Everyone* ought always to perform
those and only those actions which will achieve the ends which I want';
and this would be universal in an additional sense, for it would require
not only that I should *always* act in a certain way, but that *everyone*
should always act in a certain way. All of these rules are entirely
adequate to ensure the consistent and logical use of evaluative language.

However, even if we were to allow Hare his unjustified assumption
that the universal rule has to be formulated entirely in 'universal terms',
this would still not serve to demonstrate that there is anything self-

contradictory in the position of the egoist (if we are so to call the man who acts entirely in accordance with his own wants—I have suggested previously that this need not involve an 'egoistic' way of life in the normal sense). For the egoist does not have to make a claim as extreme as those which we have just been attributing to him. His universal rule might be '*One* ought always to act in accordance with *one's* wants'. I do not know whether Hare would regard this as consisting entirely of universal terms. The following analogous case suggests that he would have to do so:

> ... 'It is illegal to marry one's own sister' means, implicitly, 'It is illegal (e.g.) in England to marry one's own sister'. But 'England' is here a singular term, which prevents the whole proposition being universal. ... It is therefore impossible to use 'ought' in such a statement. The moral judgement that one *ought* not to marry one's sister is, however, universal ...
>
> (Ibid., p. 36)

If Hare regards this 'ought' statement as consisting entirely of universal terms and therefore as legitimate, he must also allow the rule that one should always act in accordance with one's own wants. Each contains a personal reference in precisely the same degree: 'one's own sister' and 'one's own wants'. And, to develop this analogy further, if Hare wants to exclude acting out of self-interest he would also have to exclude acting out of affection or because of family ties. Here the personal reference is very important. 'It's because he's *my* friend that I want to help him.' Maybe there is no particular reason why anybody else should go out of their way to help him like this, but for me there is this most important reason—he's my friend. And the fact that he's my friend cannot be analysed into any further fact about him, statable in purely universal descriptive terms, which is the reason why he is worthy of being my friend and therefore of receiving my help. He is my friend simply because particular circumstances have brought us together. I do not claim that he is any better than anyone else, or even that he is relevantly different from thousands of other people. It is precisely this *particularity* that characterizes affection.[1]

Now it might be said that action arising out of affection is not *rational* action, and there is at first sight a certain plausibility in this suggestion. Insofar as affection is grounded in particularity in the way that I have mentioned, and there are no purely descriptive facts about a person that completely explain why he is my friend, there is something to be said for the suggestion that affection lies outside the sphere of reason (note

---

[1] Cf. J. L. Stocks, *Morality and Purpose*, especially the essay on 'Desire and Affection'.

that this is a ground for saying that it is *non*-rational, not that it is *ir*rational). But this is very different from saying that, given the fact of my affection for a person, I am being either irrational or non-irrational if I act in a certain way because of this affection. For the action is clearly in accordance with a rule, and the rule is of a kind which must surely satisfy Hare's criteria of rationality, since it is universal in *three* respects: it specifies that one ought *always* to act to help a friend; that *everyone* ought always to act to help a friend; and that one ought to help, not *my* friends, or any *particular* person's friends, but *one's* friends.

Hare might want to suggest that such an action is not a *moral* action. He states (on pp. 165–6) that the man who asks how he can best serve the interests of his family or his friends is asking a different question, playing a different game, from the man who asks what *morally* he ought to do; his use of 'ought' is not the moral use of 'ought'. I find this very difficult to accept. We might, indeed, withhold the epithet 'moral' from the reasoning of someone who deliberately *excludes* all considerations other than the interests of his family or his friends. But in a particular case it may well be that a man morally ought to act in a certain way *just because* the action is in the interests of his family or his friends.

The objections to the use of the word 'moral' may perhaps be stronger in the case of action in accordance with one's own wants. But this, even if it is conceded, does not substantially help Hare's case. He argues that someone who uses the word 'ought' morally (i.e. universalized in a strong sense, such that one necessarily gives other people's wants equal weight with one's own) and someone who uses the word 'ought' non-morally (e.g. applying it to actions which are simply in accordance with his own wants) are 'playing different games'. In a trivial sense this is obviously true. But Hare also seems to imply that the non-moral game is in some way subordinate to the moral game; that the user of the non-moral ought is, as it were, merely producing hypothetical impera-tives ('If one is concerned with one's own wants, this is what one should do') whereas the user of the moral ought is making absolute judgements (see e.g. pp. 98–9 and 165–6). This distinction is totally misleading. For the user of the non-moral 'ought' is not just playing a self-contained game which consists in answering the question 'What is in accordance with my wants?' and going no further. What he says is: '*I am going to do this* (categorically) because it's in accordance with my wants.' In the most important sense, he and the user of the moral 'ought' are both playing the same game, the game that consists in asking 'What am I to do?'

There is one further move that Hare might make. If I adopt the universal rule 'One ought to do what is in accordance with one's wants', then, insofar as my wants may always conflict with other people's wants, I am committed to saying that on such occasions someone else ought to do what is contrary to my wants. According to Hare, anyone who is willing simply to accept this conclusion is a 'fanatic'. But if this is *all* that Hare can say, it is of no great import. Unless he can find some other grounds for saying that it is illogical or irrational or self-contradictory, his use of the word 'fanatic' is purely emotive. And I do not think that he can find any such grounds. If there is a logical connection between what I want and what I ought to do, this is because there is a necessary connection between wanting to do something and doing it. But there is no such necessary connection between A's wanting B to do something and B's doing it. Therefore, there is no self-contradiction involved in my saying both that I want A not to do x and that, because it is in accordance with his wants, he ought to do x (i.e.—within the terms of Hare's argument—that he has a good reason for doing x, that he is justified in doing x). But even if what I want other people to do did logically determine what I am justified in saying that they ought to do, this still would not enable the argument to proceed in the way that Hare supposes. For suppose we allow

    (a) that my wanting something gives me a good reason for saying that I ought to act in accordance with that want;

and (what I have previously questioned)

    (b) that my use of the word 'ought' must be in accordance with a universal meaning-rule statable entirely in universal terms, such that saying 'I ought to do what is in accordance with my wants' commits me to saying that *everyone* ought to do what is in accordance with his own wants;

and (what I have questioned in this paragraph)

    (c) that *my* wanting something gives me a good reason for saying of someone else that *he* ought to act in accordance with my want.

Suppose, now, that in a particular case A's doing x would be in accordance with his own wants but contrary to my wants. It follows from (a) and (b) that I have a good reason for saying that A ought to do x, and it follows from (c) that I have a good reason for saying that A ought not to do x. Hare suggests that, in such a case, 'the natural way for the argument then to run' is for me to give equal weight to A's wants and to my own (p. 113). This phrase—'the natural way for the argument to run'—is not backed up in any way, and I fail to see why the stated conclusion should be regarded as the only natural one. One would have to say of such a case either that I *have grounds* for saying both A ought to do x and that A ought not to do x, or that I *must* say both that A ought to do x and that A ought not to do x—depending on what kind of logical relation one posited between 'want' statements and 'ought' statements. If one chose to say the latter, one would have to recognize that the three principles (a), (b) and (c) together generate a self-contradiction, and this would amount to a *reductio ad absurdum* of the whole universalizability thesis. If one chose the former option, there would be no 'natural' way for the argument then to proceed. I could give equal weight to A's and my own wants, but it would be no less natural for me to let my wants outweigh A's, or A's outweigh mine. Therefore, at this as at all the other points, Hare's attempt to generate a principle of equal consideration for everyone's wants is, insofar as it is based on the demand for consistency in the meanings of evaluative words, unsuccessful.

B. It is possible, however, that Hare's thesis could also be interpreted in such a way as to make it depend not on the nature of *meaning-rules* but on certain facts about the necessary nature of *reasons*. He can be read as saying that the relation between reasons and action, like the relation between premisses and a conclusion, cannot be person-relative, but must be an objective relation, and that this is so simply in virtue of what it is to be a reason. It would be absurd to suppose that for some people the premisses 'All men are mortal, and Socrates is a man' might be a reason for the conclusion 'Socrates is mortal', whilst not being for other people. If they are a reason, then they are a reason for anyone. And this is not just a reflection of the special kind of necessity that attaches to deductive arguments, for it is equally true of other kinds of arguments. Inductive arguments, for example (if there are such things): if the fact that the sun has risen every morning in the past is a reason for supposing that it will rise tomorrow morning, then it is a reason for *anyone* to suppose this. Therefore, it may be claimed, the same must hold for practical arguments; if p's being the case is a reason for me to do x, then it must be a reason for *anyone* to do x, because this is part of what it is to be a reason. The case can be made directly parallel to the previous ones, since reasons for acting can be reformulated as reasons for a conclusion or reasons for a belief (that one ought to do x, that one should do x, that one is justified in doing x, etc.).

Some claim of this sort must certainly be accepted, although I am not sure in exactly what form it is best stated, and there are important distinctions and cautions to be added.[1] But it still does not provide Hare

---

[1] For example, the move from 'If there is a reason for me to do x, then it must also be a reason for anyone to do x in relevantly similar circumstances' to 'If I ought to do x, then anyone ought to do x in relevantly similar circumstances' can by no means be taken for granted. For some of the difficulties, see Peter Winch: 'The Universalizability of Moral Judgements' in *The Monist*, 1965. Something like the claim here adumbrated is to be found in an interesting form in G. A. Cohen: 'Beliefs and Roles' (*Proc. Arist. Soc.*, 1966–7, especially pp. 23–4).

with a way of showing that one's reasons for acting must necessarily be based on the wants of other people equally with one's own. All that it shows is that if the fact that an action of mine is in accordance with my wants is a reason for me to perform it, then anyone must have a reason for performing an action if it is in accordance with his wants. For if the proposition 'This action is in accordance with my wants' is a reason for the conclusion 'I am justified in performing this action', then the relation between the two propositions must hold for anyone. This takes Hare no further than the position we left him in at the end of section A, where we suggested that his only possible riposte is the purely emotive charge that someone who asserts 'Everyone ought to act solely in accordance with his own wants (even where this conflicts with my own wants)' is a fanatic.

C. There remains one further interpretation that could be given to the idea that reasons-for-acting must be reasons for *anyone*. This interpretation can be found in two other writers whom we have previously mentioned as proposing some kind of utilitarian rationality, but who both feel the need for an argument which will extend the basis of that rationality from the agent's wants to everyone's wants:

> To engage in the defense of a line of action . . . is to imply that the members of one's audience have certain characteristics which make their opinions worth taking into account. It is, in particular, to assume that they can understand one's presentation, and are able to respond with intelligible criticism. But this in turn means that one concedes a potential (at very least) of practical reasoning on their parts. To see, in the light of this, why 'the dice of reason are loaded in favor of the general interest', we can reflect that it would be absurd (i.e., pointless) to raise questions and make defenses of one's acts to other people, if one were not prepared to acknowledge similar weight to similar claims on their parts. . . . There is no point in being prepared to argue if one doesn't envisage any possible terms of settlement; and one cannot hope for settlement if one's 'arguments' are going to be arbitrarily loaded in favor of oneself.
>   . . . To argue for morality at all is to claim the assent of all rational beings. But the only principle mutually acceptable to all rational beings is one which regards all of their interests as equally worth satisfying (less, therefore, those which are incompatible with others). Everyone can agree to this because everyone's interests are respected.
>   (Narveson: *Morality and Utility*, pp. 291–2)

> . . . the autonomous rational agent . . . confronted with another rational agent . . . recognizes the same factors present in this other

person as in himself. He sees this other person taking his own wants as reasons for acting, and considering himself a source of rational action.

As a rational agent, he naturally seeks acceptance, from the other, of his judgements, and correspondingly recognizes the other's claim to seek similar acceptance from him. In so far as their interests do not conflict, the two agents may be quite prepared to recognize each other's activities as fully justifiable, but conflict of interests impedes this recognition. Each sees no reason why he should give way to the other, but equally each is aware that the other sees no reason to give way to him. If they are to continue to accept each other's judgements and actions, mutual accommodation is required. Each, in his autonomy, must respect the autonomy of the other.

This respect is simply a willingness to consider the wants of the other as providing reasons for acting, and hence a willingness to accept the practical judgements of the other, in so far as they are based on consideration of all wants.

(Gauthier: *Practical Reasoning*, p. 119)

The central idea here is that the search for reasons-for-acting is essentially a search for agreement, a search for judgements acceptable to everyone, and that these can be found only when everybody recognizes everybody's wants as providing reasons-for-acting. This again is reminiscent of some of the remarks quoted from Hume. I shall discuss this argument in the next chapter, and will attempt to show that when properly developed it constitutes not an argument for considering everybody's wants, but a demonstration that reasons-for-acting cannot be based on wants at all. Meanwhile, if I can anticipate that conclusion, I suggest we must now recognize that none of the arguments for generalizing to everybody's wants is successful. And this is itself very significant. Not only does it mean that, of the Three Accounts in chapter 1, the Third Account must be jettisoned, but it also begins to raise doubts about the plausibility of the other two. The whole project depends upon the recognition of an extended sense of 'want', in which the word can be used as a generic term for all pro-attitudes. Now we noted that philosophers have felt a need to extend the class of reasons-for-acting to include other people's wants because they have assumed that otherwise the theory of wants-as-reasons would be simply a justification of egoism. But this assumption involved understanding the word 'want' in a *non*-extended sense, the limited and probably more normal sense in which 'satisfying one's own wants' is contrasted with altruistic actions (which I nevertheless perform because, in the extended sense, I want to perform them). The assumption is therefore unwarranted. One does, however, begin to suspect at this point that the assumption is made because, once one starts to treat the theory of 'wants-as-reasons' as a substantive ethical theory, one *automatically* understands the word 'want' in its normal non-extended sense. In other words, could it be that when 'I want' is understood in its extended sense, the theory of 'wants-as-reasons' really says nothing of any substance at all?

PART II
Objections

3. Rational Action

1. THE INTELLIGIBILITY OF WANTS

I have previously referred, in passing, to the question of whether absolutely anything can in principle count as the object of a want, or whether there are on the contrary certain necessary limits to the possible objects of wanting (see above, pp. 14–15). The most important discussion of this problem is to be found in Miss Anscombe's book *Intention* (especially paras. 37–9).[1] She argues that not just anything is wantable. To say that one wants something is to invite the question 'what for?'. In answer to this question, there are certain ways of describing the thing wanted which leave no room for a *further* question 'And what do you want *that* for?' Descriptions which have this effect are what Miss Anscombe calls 'desirability characterizations'. What is crucial here is that not just any description can constitute a desirability characterization. Miss Anscombe offers the following example. Suppose that someone says 'I want a saucer of mud' and, on being asked what for, replies that he does not want it *for* anything, he just wants it. In that case we would naturally try to find out in what aspect the saucer of mud is desirable.

> . . . Does it serve as a symbol? Is there something delightful about it? Does the man want to have something to call his own, and no more? Now if the reply is 'Philosophers have taught that anything can be an object of desire; so that there can be no need for me to characterize these objects as somehow desirable; it merely so happens that I want them', then this is fair nonsense.
>
> (*Intention*, p. 71)

Here the proposed answers ('. . . serve as a symbol . . .', '. . . delightful . . .', '. . . something to call his own . . .') are presumably either what Miss Anscombe would count as desirability-characterizations, or at any rate are answers which would naturally open the way to the giving of an acceptable desirability-characterization. Other examples of desirability-characterizations mentioned by Miss Anscombe are 'comfortable',

---

[1] For an opposing point of view, see Hare, *Descriptivism*, pp. 122–7.

'pleasant', 'fun', and 'it befits me' or 'it suits me'. An Aristotelian example—the description of food as 'digestible and wholesome'—is held to be acceptable on the grounds that 'wholesome means good for the health, and health is by definition the *good* general state of the physical organism' (Ibid., p. 72). The taking of pleasure in cruelty is said to be something that cannot be wanted without further explanation, but requires to be explained by reference to such notions as 'power', 'getting one's own back on the world', or 'sexual excitement', whereas 'no one needs to surround the pleasure of food and drink with such explanations' (Ibid., p. 73). This is rather a heterogeneous collection of examples, and does not make it entirely clear what would count as a desirability-characterization and what would not. We shall have to return to this question, but in the meantime I think that Miss Anscombe's position is sufficiently clear for us to consider its validity.

Miss Anscombe sometimes gives the impression that what is in question is the correct meaning of, or correct use of, the word 'want'. This is apparent in her treatment of the following example:

> Now saying 'I want' is often a way to be given something; so when out of the blue someone says 'I want a pin' and denies wanting it *for* anything, let us suppose we give it him and see what he does with it. He takes it, let us say, he smiles and says 'Thank you. My want is gratified'—but what does he do with the pin? If he puts it down and forgets about it, in what sense was it true to say that he wanted a pin? He used these words, the effect of which was that he was given one; but what reason have we to say he wanted a pin rather than: to see if we would take the trouble to give him one?
>
> (Ibid., p. 71; I presume that this last sentence means: 'But what reason have we to say "He wanted a pin" rather than "He wanted to see if we would take the trouble to give him one"?')

Now the question whether it is appropriate to use the word 'want' in describing such cases does not seem to me to be the most fruitful one to discuss. To consider the saucer-of-mud case: we can certainly imagine a man regularly making a trip to the river with his saucer and trowel at every low tide. If we asked him what he was doing and he replied 'I just want a saucer of mud', while denying that he wanted it *for* anything, this would surely be both an intelligible sentence in the English language and a possible description of what he was doing. Certainly, as Miss Anscombe says, there would be doubts as to what would count as 'having' the saucer of mud in such a case, and anything that was held to count as his 'having' it might immediately suggest some further characterization of what it was that he wanted: if he hoards all the saucers of mud in his cellar, we might say 'Ah yes, it wasn't just a saucer of mud that he wanted. He wants to acquire things, and thus to have a sense of possessing things of his own'; if he holds the saucer of mud in front of him and inhales rapturously or feasts his eyes on it, we might say 'It was that rich river-smell that he wanted' or 'what he really wanted was to admire the smooth glistening look of wet mud'. But what this seems to me to show is that what was in question was not the appropriateness of the word 'want' in the sentence 'I want just a saucer of mud', but the *intelligibility of the want*. Wanting *just* a saucer of mud is unintelligible; it becomes intelligible when it can be seen as something else, such as wanting to have a feeling of possessing something, or wanting to enjoy a certain smell or a certain visual sensation. As well as describing those wants as 'intelligible' or 'unintelligible', one could also say that they are 'rational' and 'irrational'; the relation between the two pairs of terms will have to be clarified later.

Now it might be objected that although someone's wanting, say, a saucer of mud is not intelligible to us, it may nevertheless be intelligible to him. In other words, perhaps all that can be said about such a man is that his wants are different from most people's. In that case, in giving the kind of explanation that we have been considering, all that we would be doing would be showing that his wants are like everybody else's after all. If an explanation of this kind could not be given, we should not be able to understanding his wanting what he does want, but it would not follow that his wanting it would be unintelligible, since it would be perfectly intelligible to him.

This is precisely the point that I want to contest. One *cannot* drive a wedge between 'intelligible for us' and 'intelligible for him'. I want to argue that the intelligibility of a want is essentially a matter of its relation to public, supra-individual standards and norms. This fact can be made more apparent by noting that where we have been speaking of the 'intelligibility' of a want we could equally well speak of the 'meaningfulness' of a want. The terms would, I think, be synonymous in this context. This enables us to draw an important comparison. I want to argue that it is as impossible for a man's wants and actions to have a private meaning which makes them intelligible to him alone, as it is for a man to employ a private language intelligible to him alone. Of course, a man can employ a private code which he alone understands, and similarly a particular want or action may as a matter of fact be understood only by the agent himself. But the want or action cannot be said to have a meaning at all unless its meaning can be formulated by reference to public standards, just as the private code is meaningful only because it is parasitic upon a public language. It is in this sense that the possibility of a private language has to be denied, and its denial has been one of the principal contributions of Wittgenstein to recent philosophy.

E

2. Publicity and Language

I shall not attempt a general discussion of Wittgenstein's remarks on this topic, nor of the interpretations and objections offered by other philosophers. What has already been written on the subject is probably too well known to need further elaboration, and I do not think that I am capable of adding anything new to the discussion.[1] What I want to do is to remind the reader of some of the examples which Wittgenstein uses, and to stress those aspects of the examples which make them particularly relevant to the argument of the present chapter.

I begin with the simplest example, because if taken first it may help to clarify the more complex ones. Wittgenstein refers, at one point in the *Investigations*, to the possibility of 'a case ... in which a person naturally reacted to the gesture of pointing with the hand by looking in the direction of the line from finger-tip to wrist, not from wrist to finger-tip' (I. 185). He does not develop the example there, but mentions it as one to which the surrounding discussion could be applied. I believe that the application of it would produce something like the following. If someone did react to the gesture of pointing in this way, we should naturally say that he does not understand correctly the meaning of the gesture. What are we saying here? His failure to understand correctly is not a failure to be adequately aware of some particular aspect of the gesture itself. There is no way in which we could explain to him why the gesture means what it does mean, nothing to which we could draw his attention and say 'You see, it *must* mean that you are to look in the direction of the line from wrist to finger-tip.' So his failure is not, as it were, a failure of intuition. All that we can say is that the gesture just does happen to mean this. And that is to say: this is how people in general do use it. It is because there exists a normal use, an established custom which people do in general observe, that we can talk of the 'correct' meaning of the gesture.

In this sense we can say that there exists a 'convention' which gives the gesture its meaning. We might also say that the gesture gets its meaning in virtue of a human agreement. But we must be careful how we interpret this. To say that people 'agree' may mean either that, passively, they are alike, or that, actively, they come to a joint decision. To speak of 'agreement' in this second sense would, I think, be inappropriate as a way of accounting for the gesture of pointing. The case of pointing is not like, for example, the case of people who decide on a

[1] The most important section of the *Philosophical Investigations* concerned with this topic is, roughly, paragraphs 185–280. Some of the most notable discussions can be found in the essays by Strawson, Malcolm, Ayer, Rhees and others collected by George Pitcher under the title *Wittgenstein: The 'Philosophical Investigations'*; and in Peter Winch: *The Idea of a Social Science*, to which I am also indebted for suggestions about the further application of these ideas.

password or who adopt a sign. We do not mean what we mean by pointing because of any previous decision which we or others have made. Rather, our reacting to the gesture of pointing by looking in the direction of the line from wrist to finger-tip is a 'natural reaction'. And therefore the agreement which gives the gesture its meaning is what Wittgenstein called an 'agreement in reactions'. It just is a fact about human beings that they do tend to react in this way to the gesture. Perhaps this is what Wittgenstein has in mind when, in the course of a discussion of 'meaning' and 'publicity' and 'following a rule', he says: 'What we are supplying are really remarks on the natural history of man' (*Remarks on the Foundations of Mathematics*, I. 141). If human beings did not agree in at least some reactions of this kind, there could be no such thing as human communication. And if a child did not share at least some of these reactions, it could never be taught the use of language. This is particularly apparent in the case of pointing, if we consider the role of ostensive definition in the teaching of language. If necessary, the meaning of pointing could itself be taught; but unless there were *some* natural reaction which did not need to be taught, the teaching process would never get under way. We might compare what Wittgenstein says about the role of crying in the teaching of the word 'pain'.

The second example which I want to mention is one that Wittgenstein makes considerable use of (*Philosophical Investigations*, I. 185ff., *Remarks on the Foundations of Mathematics*, I. 3ff.) Suppose that we have taught someone to write down a series of cardinal numbers in accordance with formulae of the form '+n', and have given him tests up to 1000. We now ask him to continue, for example, the series '+2' beyond 1000 and he writes '1000, 1004, 1008, 1012'. It would be natural to say that he has done it incorrectly, that he hasn't understood. But suppose that we get him to compare this way of continuing the series beyond 1000 with, for example, his way of continuing the series beyond 100, and he nevertheless still says 'But surely I *am* continuing the series in the same way. Why can't I go on in this way?' Here we would still want to insist that if one is to continue the series correctly, one *must* continue it '1000, 1002, 1004, 1006'. We want to say that the rule *compels* one to go on in this way. But what lies behind this mode of expression? In what sense does the rule 'compel' us? Clearly, in one sense the man is free to go on as he pleases. There is nothing to prevent him writing '1000, 1004, 1008, 1012'. But the claim is that he cannot *both* do this *and* be said to be following the rule. However, as Wittgenstein suggests, in such a case could we not say that it comes natural to him to understand the formula as we should understand the rule 'Add 2 up to 1000, 4 up to 2000, 6 up to 3000, and so on'? And if we see it in this way, we can understand how it might be possible to regard as rational his claim that he is going on in the same way, doing the same thing. If it is objected that there are at any rate very strict limits to the number of possible interpretations of this kind—that one could not, for example, regard '1000, 1004, 1007, 1012' as a possible interpretation of the rule 'Add 2', and that therefore the rule does at any rate compel one to remain within these limits—the answer is that the limits to what can count as 'going on in the same way' are the limits to what can count as 'regularity', and that is to say that there are no clear limits at all (cf. *Remarks on the Foundations of Mathematics*, I. 116). Is '1000, 1004, 1007, 1012' a regular sequence? No clear answer presents itself. Comparing it with '1000, 1004, 1008, 1012', we would naturally say that it was irregular and that the other was regular. Nevertheless there are an infinite number of possible ways of continuing the sequence which could all constitute it as a regular sequence, and such that one could produce a formula for determining the sequence. Therefore, however someone follows the rule 'Add 2', we can always say that it comes natural to him to understand the formula 'Add 2' in the way that we would understand such-and-such a formula.

Does this mean that there is no such thing as a 'correct' way of following a rule, and that it is never appropriate to speak of a rule 'compelling' us to go on in a certain way? Wittgenstein does say: 'It would almost be more correct to say . . . that a new decision was needed at every stage'; and: 'There is an inclination to say: every action according to the rule is an interpretation' (*Philosophical Investigations*, I. 186 and 201). But words like 'almost' are important in these remarks. What Wittgenstein is really arguing against is a misleading account of what is involved in following a rule. If, in our example, we have got the person to compare the way in which he continues the sequence beyond 1000 with the way in which he continues it below 1000, and he still says 'But isn't it the same?', there is a tendency to suppose that there is something further that he hasn't seen. We have the idea that some new intuition is needed on his part, some deeper understanding of the meaning of the rule. As against this, Wittgenstein says that when I show the man examples which I regard as demonstrating the meaning of the rule, I do not communicate to him less than I know myself. There is not anything *further* that *I* understand in the rule, and which he may fail to see. What enables me to proceed '1000, 1002, 1004, 1006' is not some deeper understanding of the rule: I haven't *got* anything more than I give to him, for every explanation which I can give myself I give to him too (*Philosophical Investigations*, I. 208–10). As in the 'pointing' example, what we have to say is not 'But can't you see?', but 'This just *is* how we do go on'. Therefore, it is only insofar as there exists a public use of the rule, a custom, that we can talk of a 'correct' way of following the rule. It is ultimately in this that the hardness of the logical 'must' resides.

Wittgenstein says: '. . . the laws of inference can be said to compel us; in the same sense, that is to say, as other laws in human society. . . . If you draw different conclusions you do indeed get into conflict, e.g. with society . . .' (*Remarks on the Foundations of Mathematics*, I. 116). This 'conflict with society' is not just a matter of disagreeing with other people, but of doing so in such a way that one ceases to give certain expressions the meaning which they normally possess. If this conflict becomes generalized, one is in effect renouncing the possibility of meaningful discourse altogether (this will become clearer in the next example).

A further point which this example shares with the previous one is the inappropriateness of saying that the 'public agreement in use' which gives a rule its meaning is established by human choice or decision.[1] There has never been any decision to the effect that the rule 'Add 2' should mean what it does. The 'agreement in use' which determines what counts as 'adding 2' in any particular case exists because men just do find it natural, for example, to regard '1000, 1002, 1004, 1006' as 'going on in the same way as' '0, 2, 4, 6'. So once again, at this level I think we have to speak of an 'agreement in reactions'. The concepts of 'choice' and 'decision' (and indeed, as I shall argue, the concept of 'wanting') are posterior to the notion of a norm. They have a place only where there already exist standards which make it possible to speak of 'rational' ways of proceeding. And the norms themselves are therefore established not by choices or decisions but by something more fundamental.

Up to now our present example and the previous example have been seen as parallel. There is also, however, an important difference between them. That the gesture of pointing has the meaning which it does have can be regarded as a fact *in isolation*. The gesture could have had a different meaning without anything else being different. It is this, especially, that makes us say that the meaning of the gesture depends upon a 'convention' (even if not one established by any decision). On the other hand the meaning of the rule 'Add 2' can be understood only by being seen as an element in a whole system of expressions and meanings. We would naturally say that if the rule 'Add 2' were to be interpreted differently, a great many other rules and expressions within the whole system of counting and computation would also have to be interpreted differently in order for the system to remain consistent. Now, of course,

---

[1] It is a misinterpretation of Wittgenstein to say as Michael Dummett does (*Wittgenstein's Philosophy of Mathematics*, p. 425f., in Pitcher op. cit.): 'Wittgenstein goes in for a full-blooded conventionalism; for him the logical necessity of any statement is always the *direct* expression of a linguistic convention. That a given statement is necessary consists always in our having expressly decided to treat that very statement as unassailable.'

everything that we have been saying about *'having to* go on in a certain way' and 'going on in *the same way'* can also be applied to the notion of a 'consistent system'. Just as one could see it as quite rational to say: 'By adding 2 I get the series of 100, 102, 104, 106, and I also get the series 1000, 1004, 1008, 1012; what is inconsistent about this?', so also we can suppose someone understanding the rule 'Add 2' in this way and not seeing any contradiction between this and, say, the fact that the series 'add 4' is also continued '1000, 1004, 1008, 1012', or the fact that whilst 2 is one less than 3 the number obtained by adding 2 to 1000 is one more than the number obtained by adding 3 to 1000. A system which differed from ours *solely* in the way in which the series 'Add 2' was continued beyond 1000 would still be a perfectly viable arithmetical system. Thus it would be quite possible to treat such a system as a *consistent* system. Nevertheless, the contingent fact that in our arithmetical system we do regard the process of adding 2 as related via the notions of 'consistency' and 'contradiction' to other moves within the system is important, and for the following reason. It would make no sense to suppose that everyone has always misunderstood the meaning of the gesture of pointing; for if everyone had always understood it to mean that one is to look in the direction of the line from finger-tip to wrist, then it just *would* mean that. On the other hand, it does make sense to suppose that everyone has always carried out incorrectly a certain arithmetical calculation (such as adding 2 beyond 1000). Even in this case there is something odd about the hypothesis (cf. *Remarks on the Foundations of Mathematics*, I. 134); but we *can* give sense to it, and we can do so primarily because we can connect this calculation with other calculations in our arithmetical system. It is this fact, in particular, that entitles us to say that the correct way of adding 2, unlike the meaning of the gesture of pointing, is not just a convention.

The third and final example which I want to look at is Wittgenstein's discussion of the suggestion that someone might invent a sign 'S' as a purely private word to refer to a purely private sensation (*Philosophical Investigations*, I. 242ff., especially 258–70). In other words, the suggestion is that he gives the sign a meaning which cannot, even in principle, be understood by another person. The purpose of Wittgenstein's discussion is to show that the very idea of such a project is incoherent and self-contradictory. To understand his argument here, it is very important to see this example as closely related to the previous one. It is often thought that Wittgenstein's argument hinges on the impossibility of verification in the use of such a word. In a sense this is true, but to put it like this can be misleading. Wittgenstein suggests that, when the man subsequently has to answer the question 'Is this an S?', he has only his own memory to go on. Therefore, there can never be, for him, any independent criterion of a *correct* memory-claim. If he wants to say that he has remembered correctly or remembered incorrectly, he would have to base this claim on some further exercise of his memory—and this, says Wittgenstein, would be like buying a second copy of the morning paper to check whether the contents of the first copy are true. Now I originally took this to mean that there can be no such thing as memory correcting a previous memory-claim. And of course that would be false. We can perfectly well imagine someone saying 'I've got that pain again that I felt last week; I know it's the same pain because I can remember exactly what it was like before', and later saying 'Oh no, it wasn't the same after all; I can remember now what it was like the first time, and it wasn't the same'. It could be perfectly legitimate to describe him as correcting a previous memory-claim solely on the basis of memory. Suppose, however, that our S-man says 'It's S again, I can remember that it was like this before', and later says 'Oh no, it wasn't S after all; I remember now that it was different the first time'. The point, I think, is this: what ground could there be for saying 'He is *correcting* himself' rather than, for example, 'First he remembers it one way, then he remembers it another way'. In the 'Add 2' example, what enables us to say that the man who continues '1000, 1004, 1008, 1012' has not understood *correctly* is the fact that there is a normal way of proceeding —and here the word 'normal' conveys both the idea that this is the usual way, constituted by what people in general do, and also the idea that this itself constitutes the proper way, the paradigm of correctness. We saw that if the man's continuing with '1000, 1004, 1008 . . .' is considered simply in abstract and in isolation, there is nothing intrinsic to it which enables us to say that it is incorrect or that he has not understood. Now, in the 'S' case, what is lacking is precisely a *normal* way of using 'S', a way in which people in general use the sign; for, *ex hypothesi*, 'S' is a purely private sign. Therefore, where one memory-claim is supposed to 'correct' another, there can in fact be nothing about either memory-claim that makes it either correct or incorrect.

But surely, it might be said, the content of any memory-experience either is or is not the same as what the man was aware of when he originally adopted the word 'S'. And similarly, the subsequent experience which is being compared with the original S must either be or not be the same as S. Therefore, it may be objected, even if there is no possible way of telling whether he is using the sign correctly or not, nevertheless when he says, on the basis of memory, 'It's S again', we can make sense of the idea of his being correct or incorrect. However, as we also saw previously, it can by no means be assumed that the notion of 'the same' always carries with it a single obvious interpretation. In the 'add 2' example, one could see it as quite rational to say that the man is 'going on in the same way' when he proceeds '1000, 1004, 1008, 1012'. It is only by reference to a normal way of seeing it that we can say that this is not 'the same'. And this is why, in the 'S' example, there is no room for remarks of the form 'He thinks that what he is experiencing now is the same as what he experienced when he invented the name "S", but it isn't really the same (or: and it really is the same).' In the 'add 2' case we have a means of marking the distinction between 'he thinks it's the same' and 'it is the same', namely by referring to what people normally say, but in the 'S' case we have no such means of marking the distinction.

'Well, doesn't he lay down what is to count as "the same" when he invents the term "S" as the name of the sensation?' But if this 'laying it down' is done in words—for example, by saying 'I shall call "S" anything which is the same as this in the respect of being an acute sensation rather like a pin-prick but without any external stimulus'— then, of course, 'S' does not belong to a private language but is simply a new term which has been incorporated into, and defined by, the existing public language. 'Then couldn't the man, without using words, just feel it as this in contrast to anything else, concentrate his attention on it under this particular aspect, and associate the term "S" with it insofar as it is felt as precisely this?' But we cannot give any sense to this notion of 'concentrating on it under a particular aspect' except insofar as we suppose him differentiating the sensation from others which he can distinguish by means of words which he already possesses in a public language. The notion of 'being aware of something under a particular aspect' is inseparable from that of 'being aware of it under a certain description'. Even if we suppose that the sensation is one which no one has ever felt before, this is itself something that a man can be aware of only if he already possesses a language. Although, in such a case, the term 'S' may not be precisely equivalent to any possible description of a sensation in the previously-existing public language, it can be given a meaning only by being contrasted and compared with these previously existing ways of referring to sensations. That is to say, it can be meaningful only insofar as it can be *situated* within a public language. Thus a great deal of stage-setting must already have taken place if we describe him as 'inventing the term "S" as a new name for a sensation'. As Wittgenstein says, the very fact that we describe him as inventing a name for a '*sensation*' is important; for 'sensation' is a word in a public language; and for the story to be plausible, it is essential for something like this to be the case.

3. EXPLANATIONS AND REASONS

Now, just as a word cannot have a logically private meaning, so a want, or an action, cannot have a logically private meaning. It is essential to the 'grammar' (in the Wittgensteinian sense) of words like 'meaningful', 'intelligible', 'rational', that the claims we make with them should be open to assessments of correctness. If someone claims to find a want or an action meaningful or intelligible or rational, we can assess the validity of his claim not just as a claim about his own psychological state (as we might look at a man's behaviour to see if he was really 'in love' or really 'felt moved'), but as an objective claim about the nature of the want or action. If a want is meaningful, it must in principle be possible to say what significance it has, what it is about it that makes it intelligible. At this point the case of meaningful wants is not simply parallel to that of meaningful language, but rather the two coalesce. For in order to be able to assign a significance to a want, one must be able in principle to characterize it in such a way as to show how it is significant and intelligible. One must be able to describe it by means of words in a public language which make it intelligible to others. And here not just any description will do. One must be able to characterize the want by using words whose role in the language is precisely to mark out intelligible and meaningful objects of wanting—in other words, by using what Miss Anscombe calls 'desirability-characterizations'. One may not be able to do this in practice. One may be relatively inarticulate. Moreover it is always possible for a particular want to have a unique significance; but still, it is significant only insofar as it can be related to, compared with, other meaningful wants whose objects can be characterized by means of desirability-characterizations.

We can now begin to see where the theory of 'wants as reasons' breaks down. I have argued that not all wants are intrinsically rational or intelligible. Those which are not can be made intelligible only if the thing wanted can be further described by means of some desirability-characterization. In other words, some further *reason* has to be given. Wants have to be backed up by reasons. Therefore, not just any assertion of the form 'I want just x' can provide an ultimate reason-for-acting. If it does so, this will be because the description 'x' characterizes the thing wanted in such a way that no further reason is necessary. And in that case, it is the fact that the thing is describable as 'x', not the fact that the thing is wanted, that constitutes the reason-for-acting. The notion of 'wanting' can be allowed to fall out altogether.

What I am arguing for, in effect, is a close connection—a qualified identity—between *explanations* of human action and *reasons* for acting. This is parallel to the connection previously made between 'intelligibility' and 'rationality'. To explain a want is to make it intelligible. Similarly, I suggest, the rationality of a man's wants depends upon the possibility of giving reasons for wanting what he wants. To want *simply* a saucer of mud is irrational, because some further reason is needed for wanting it. To want a saucer of mud because one wants to enjoy its rich river-smell is rational. No further reason is needed for wanting to enjoy the rich river-smell, for to characterize what is wanted as 'to enjoy the rich river-smell' is itself to give an acceptable reason for wanting it, and therefore this want is rational.

Now within the utilitarian tradition the notion of 'reasons' has indeed sometimes been linked with the notion of 'rationality'; but attention has primarily been paid not to 'rational behaviour' but to 'rational argument' or 'rational discourse'. 'Rationality' then tends to become equated with 'logical consistency'. In the first place this helps to explain why reasons-for-acting are identified with wants; for it is supposed that if someone wants to do x but does not do it, then he is being, if not logically inconsistent, at any rate something very like it. And secondly, it helps to explain why no other restrictions are placed on the possible range of reasons for acting; given that the reasons are grounded in wants, any giving of reasons is a giving of 'good' reasons provided only that it is comfortable to the laws of logic. And when we look at Hare's attempt to give a rather more positive content to the notion of rationality, we find the same drawback. As we saw at the end of the last chapter, he is concerned to discover what requirements are imposed on ethics by the demands for rationality; but for him this means: what requirements are imposed on ethics by the demand for rationality in our *talk* about (*argument* about) ethics. This is why Hare fails to come up with anything positive.

Having linked 'reasons' with 'rationality' and 'explanations' with 'intelligibility', we now have to make the connection between the two pairs themselves. As I have said, the relation is not one of absolute identity. The notions of 'reasons' and 'rationality' are tighter and more rigorous than those of 'explanations' and 'intelligibility'. Although I have denied that 'rationality 'is to be identified with logicality and consistency, it does nevertheless incorporate these. The considerations that move a man to action may be applied so illogically as to lead us to say that he is behaving irrationally; but by looking at his behaviour in the light of those considerations we may still be able to see it as intelligible. The important point, however, is that the characterizations of an action which explain it are *normally* the characterizations that constitute the agent's reasons for performing it.[1] The connection can be seen by looking at the examples we have already used: if I explain my wanting a saucer of mud by saying that I want to enjoy its rich river-smell, for instance, I am clearly giving a reason for wanting a saucer of mud. To

---

[1] I say 'normally' because in some cases the explanation of behaviour may consist precisely in pointing out why it is *not* to be explained in terms of the agent's own reasons. In such cases we may want to speak of 'false consciousness' or 'self-deception' or 'unconscious motivations'. The very necessity for such terms, however, implies that the primary kind of explanation of human action is in terms of the agent's reasons.

explain an action is to make it comprehensible; and in the same way, I am arguing, when we give reasons for an action what we are doing is primarily trying to make the action comprehensible. In explaining someone's action to you, I am enabling you to understand it, to see what it is about the action that makes it worth doing. This need not necessarily mean that I get you to see it as the sort of action that you yourself would perform. Suppose that I am trying to explain to you why so many people like playing Bingo. In order to explain it successfully, I do not have to get you to share their enthusiasm, nor (fortunately!) do I have to sympathize with it myself. How, then, would I explain it? I would doubtless try to bring out its connections with other kinds of activities that people go in for. I might draw attention to the elements of excitement and uncertainty, the fluctuating hopes and emotions, the tense waiting to see whether you have won, and, not least, the attraction of actually winning money. My explanations would thus consist in characterizations of the activity which show why anyone might want to engage in it. In other words, they are *reasons* which anyone could have for engaging in it. Here the word 'anyone' is important. If I had simply demonstrated that *they* have their own reasons for engaging in the activity, I would not have enabled you to *understand* the activity. The reasons must be public reasons.

It might be objected that our argument so far is inadequate as a criticism of the theory of 'wants as reasons'. For, it might be said, all that it shows is that the fact that someone wants something is not by itself a *sufficient* reason-for-acting. Admittedly, the want has to be a rational want, a want which is backed up by reasons; but still, the objection might run, these reasons are reasons for acting only insofar as they are reasons for wanting something. Moreover, the suggestion that reasons must consist in a reference to public norms might be taken to mean no more than the suggestion contained in the passages quoted from Narveson and Gauthier at the end of the previous chapter: that to give reasons-for-acting is to appeal to *what people in general want*. And in that case the reference to 'wants' would remain a *necessary* condition of giving reasons.

4. NORMATIVE CONCEPTS

At this point it is important to re-emphasize that the appeal to 'public norms' is not an appeal to generalizations about how men act or what men want in our society, but an appeal to the shared ethical and evaluative *concepts* in our common language. Thus I would claim, for example, that in our society it is rational to perform an action solely on the grounds that it is 'just', because there does exist a norm of 'justice' within our society; that to say that there exists a norm of 'justice' within our society is to say that our society possesses the normative concept of 'justice'; and that we can also express the fact that our society possesses the normative concept of 'justice' by saying that the word 'just' is a component of the normative language of our society. Now it has to be conceded that the fact that 'justice' is a *normative* concept is not simply a linguistic fact, but is ultimately a fact about how men in our society *act* in relation to the concept of 'justice'. But the relation between the two is not a straight identity; the normative force of the concept of 'justice' does not consist in any simple generalization to the effect that most men act justly, or that most men think it right to act justly. And, therefore, by bringing in the reference to concepts we are enabled to avoid a simple identification of 'norms' with 'what most men want' or 'what most men do'.

We shall return shortly to the problem of the relation between 'normal behaviour' and the normative force of concepts. But first we need to say more about how one is supposed to identify these 'normative concepts'. Their function is both to characterize an action as being of a certain kind, and at the same time to indicate that its being of that kind constitutes a reason for performing it. This suggests a similarity between words which denote 'normative concepts' and the kind of words which writers like Nowell-Smith and Hare refer to as 'Janus-words', for the latter term is supposed to indicate that the words in question both are evaluative and also have a positive descriptive content.

I might, therefore, initially state my position by describing it as the reverse of Nowell-Smith's or Hare's. They recognize that Janus-words encapsulate substantive ethical standards or principles so that, for example, one cannot agree that an action would be just without at the same time agreeing that someone would have a reason for performing it. But they consider that the fundamental ethical words are not Janus-words but words like 'good' and 'right' which, they say, simply express a pro-attitude and have no positive descriptive element. Therefore, they would argue, whenever someone attempts to justify an action by characterizing it by means of a Janus-word, such a justification is incomplete. The Janus-word must be analysed into its evaluative and descriptive elements, and one is justified in applying the Janus-word only if one has a pro-attitude towards what the word describes. Someone could perfectly well say: 'I agree that this action is "just", if the word is being used in a purely descriptive sense. However, it is not usually regarded as merely descriptive, but encapsulates an evaluative attitude and implies that one approves of the action in question. Since I do not share this attitude—since I do not have a pro-attitude towards actions which are, in a purely descriptive sense, "just"—I prefer not to use the word "just" as part of my vocabulary, but to employ instead a morally neutral periphrasis. Therefore, where an action is what people would normally call "just", this does not constitute, for me, any reason for performing it.' (Cf. e.g. Hare, *Freedom and Reason*, pp. 187–91.) In contrast to this position, I would want to claim that in a very important sense it is Janus-words rather than words like 'good' or 'right' that are the more fundamental ethical words. A pro-attitude cannot be regarded as rational unless it can be justified by showing that the object of the attitude can be characterized by means of a Janus-word. Similarly the use of a word such as 'good' or 'right', where it is being used simply to express approval, cannot be regarded as a rational application of the word unless it can be justified by means of statements employing Janus-words. And this is because in the Janus-words of a language are encapsulated the 'public norms' or 'public standards' which, as I have been arguing in this chapter, determine what counts as rational action. Now I would agree that in the case of any particular Janus-word one may refuse to admit it as part of one's vocabulary. But if this refusal is to be rational, it must itself be capable of being justified by reasons— reasons which must ultimately refer to norms encapsulated in other Janus-words. To take one of Mrs. Foot's examples, one might decide not to employ the words 'rude' and 'polite' as part of one's vocabulary. One's reason for this decision might be that adherence to the concepts of 'rudeness' and 'politeness' prevents human relationships from being natural and spontaneous and uninhibited. One's reasons, in other words, consist in appealing to the standards encapsulated in the words 'natural' and 'spontaneous' and 'uninhibited'. It follows that although one can rationally reject any particular Janus-word, one cannot rationally reject *all* the Janus-words in the language. One cannot rationally reject *all* the standards or norms of one's society, since there would be nothing on the basis of which one could reject them.

This way of stating my position is not, however, entirely satisfactory. It does not, by itself, enable one to determine what are to count as norms or standards of rational action. For, from the Hare/Nowell-Smith point of view, any word can in principle be used as a Janus-word (subject only to obvious grammatical limitations). Whether a word is being so used or not depends entirely on the attitude of the speaker and/or the listener. I think that Hare or Nowell-Smith would have to say, for example, that for Miss Anscombe's saucer-of-mud man the word 'mud' is a Janus-word, since the man happens to have a pro-attitude towards mud simply *qua* mud. The only difference between this and other instances would be that very few people happen to have a pro-attitude towards mud, whereas certain other words are much more commonly used as Janus-words because they express much more widely-shared attitudes. If this is so, it is clearly futile to try to identify norms of rational action by identifying Janus-words, for if any word with some descriptive content can in principle be used as a Janus-word, anything can count as a norm.

However, this account of Janus-words seems to me to be quite wrong. It involves putting into the same category, for example, words like 'courageous' or 'dishonest' and words like 'nigger'. These are examples actually used by Hare, and I should have thought it quite obvious that there is a vitally important difference between the two cases. The word 'nigger' does encapsulate an attitude, but it does not encapsulate a norm of rational action in the way that 'courageous' and 'dishonest' do. To say that 'nigger' is a Janus-word on the same level as 'dishonest' is precisely parallel to saying that all ultimate wants are equally rational. The case of racialism in fact provides an excellent illustration of the inadequacy of the utilitarian account of rationality. Consider Hare's treatment of racialism in *Freedom and Reason*. He has to concede there that the fanatical racialist, so long as he is consistent in applying his principles to the hypothetical case in which it is supposed that he himself is a Negro, is being perfectly rational when he discriminates against people simply because they have black skins. And this conclusion does indeed follow from the claim that wants and likes and dislikes constitute ultimate reasons. If there are no criteria for characterizing particular wants as in themselves rational or irrational, then of course it is perfectly rational to say that one *wants* to treat certain people in a certain way *simply because* they're black. It seems to me, however, that regardless of the wants and likes and dislikes of anyone, racialism is irrational if it consists in saying that the colour of a man's skin is in itself a relevant and rational ground for determining how one is to treat him. It is significant that no one ever does say that it is right to discriminate against people *just* because they have black skins. The racialist always tries to provide some further justification such as that people with black skins have a lower intelligence or are 'less highly developed' than people with white skins, or that coloured immigrants will 'destroy our way of life'. Such arguments are clearly rationalizations of a prejudice. But there would be no room for the notion of 'rationalization' here, and perhaps not even room for the notion of 'prejudice', if discrimination against people because of their skin colour were perfectly rational in itself.

Because Nowell-Smith's term 'Janus-word' fails to suggest any distinction between words like 'dishonest' and words like 'nigger', I think it better not to use the term. One could perhaps talk instead of 'ethical characterizations' or more generally of 'evaluative characterizations'. In calling words like 'dishonest' evaluative or ethical one may distinguish them from words like 'nigger' which are merely emotive. And the term 'characterization' distinguishes words like 'dishonest' from words like 'good' and 'right', for the former evaluate actions *qua* actions of a specific kind (this is the idea of a combination of evaluation and description which the term 'Janus-word' was supposed to convey). The reference to 'characterizations' is deliberately reminiscent of Miss

Anscombe's 'desirability characterizations'. I prefer not to use Miss Anscombe's own term, first because it carries precisely that suggestion of a necessary connection between desire and action which I wish to reject, and secondly because it is purely positive whereas we require one which includes both positive words and negative words, i.e. words like 'honest' and words like 'dishonest'.

We are now faced with the following problem. Reference to the notion of 'Janus-words' seemed at first to offer us a way of identifying those social norms which determine what is to count as rational action. But we now find that we have to distinguish between genuine ethical or evaluative characterizations and other Janus-words, and as yet our only basis for the distinction is that the former alone embody rational norms. The question therefore arises: can we find any independent criterion by which to identify genuine evaluative characterizations and thence to identify the 'social norms'?

We might begin by noticing that according to writers like Hare and Nowell-Smith the evaluative element in Janus-words is part of the *meaning* of those words. This is hardly a suitable accompaniment to the suggestion that whether a word is or is not a Janus-word depends on the attitudes of the people who use it. The conjunction of the two claims is dangerously reminiscent of crude attempts to identify the meaning of a word with the accompanying idea. Therefore, we can perhaps distinguish between evaluative characterizations and emotive Janus-words by separating the two claims. Only in the case of genuine evaluative characterizations is the evaluative element part of the actual meaning of the word. In a word like 'nigger', on the other hand, the so-called evaluative aspect is merely an emotive veneer. In the *Concise Oxford Dictionary* the entry under 'nigger' begins: 'Negro (usu. derog.: . . .)'. It would be absurd to suppose that one might similarly refer to a word like 'dishonest' as 'usu. derog.'. If someone calls Negroes 'niggers' and does not intend the word to have any derogatory force, he is simply unaware of the *associations* that the word has. But if someone does not realize that to call an action 'dishonest' is to provide a reason for not performing it, he does not understand the *meaning* of the word 'dishonest'. Thus we are led back once again to the idea that we can understand the nature of rational action by connecting it with the nature of meaningful language, and to the general question of what it is to say that something is part of the meaning of a word as distinct from being part of the association that the word carries. It should be noted that this distinction is not just one between the meaning of the word and the attitude which an individual user might express by means of it; for the emotive association which a word carries may sometimes be taken for granted by a whole community, as is perhaps the case with the word 'nigger'. Since we have previously noted that there is a close relation between the meaning of a word and the way in which people in general use it, it is clear that the distinction we need to make here is a very fine one. The remainder of my remarks in this section will be merely a couple of tentative suggestions as to how one might make it.

According to the Nowell-Smith/Hare thesis, one can separate the 'descriptive content' and the 'evaluative content' of Janus-words. This sounds plausible with a word like 'nigger', where it could be maintained that the word's 'descriptive content' is its equivalence to the word 'Negro' and its 'evaluative content' is its derogatory force. But it is much more questionable whether this neat bisecting operation is possible with a word like 'dishonest'. The possibility that suggests itself here is that the evaluative content of a word is part of the meaning of the word when it is inseparable from its descriptive content. What could possibly count as a purely descriptive, totally neutral equivalent of the word 'dishonest'? Dishonesty is not just a matter of making false statements. For a start, it involves other kinds of falsehood besides that of the spoken or written word. But not even a more general formulation such as 'deliberately causing other people to hold false beliefs' is adequate. It includes too much: jokes, for example, could hardly be called 'dishonest'. It also includes too little: it is quite possible to be dishonest without creating any beliefs which are, strictly speaking, false. Clearly some such notion as that of 'deceit' is involved. The word 'deceit', however, is as inseparable from its ethical implications as the word 'dishonest' is. Nor can one explain the difference between 'creating false beliefs' and 'deceiving people' in purely neutral terms. I do not see how one can explain it without bringing in some such idea as that of 'trust', i.e. without referring to inter-personal relations which cannot be indicated except by means of ethical concepts. Thus any attempt to explain the meaning of 'dishonest' either does not bring out the meaning fully, or uses ethical terms. How do we in fact explain to a child the meaning of the word? By examples, clearly. And the child cannot learn which actions are dishonest, cannot come to see what is common to all these actions, without learning a great deal about ethics.

What we have found, then, is that the meaning of 'dishonest' can be explained only by indicating its position within a whole nexus of ethical concepts. This suggests a further criterion of any genuine evaluative characterization, namely that it is integrally related to a *system* of ethical and evaluative concepts. We noted the importance of the idea of a system in our discussion of language and publicity (see above, pp. 59–60 and p. 62). We saw there that, if one brings in this notion, it then becomes possible to say that even though the meaning of the words in a language is ultimately determined by the way in which people in general do actually use them, nevertheless it can be the case that most people are mistaken about a particular meaning. So also here, the notion of a system can be put to similar use. The idea of dishonesty can be related to the idea of honouring the trust that other people place in us. This in turn can be seen as part of the wider idea of respecting the autonomy of other human beings, or of treating others as ends rather than as means. We thus arrive at the consideration of certain fundamental kinds of relationships between human beings—relations of community and co-operation, their connection with ideas of fairness or justice or fraternity or solidarity, and their contrast with relations of exploitation or oppression. What is the nature of the connection between different concepts within such a system? It is not necessarily one of logical equivalence or entailment. One could without inconsistency accept certain of these concepts and reject others. Nor is it a matter of causal connections. It is not to be supposed, for instance, that 'honesty' is related to 'respect for the autonomy of others' as the means to an end. We *can* say, however, that it is possible to show more clearly the *point* of one such concept by relating it to other concepts within the system. This kind of connection is a two-way one. We can see more clearly the point of honesty—that is to say, we can see more clearly what honesty *is*—by bringing it together with other concepts under the more general notion of 'respecting the autonomy of others'. And we can also show what is involved in 'respect for the autonomy of others', and show why it is important, by showing that it can be instantiated in things like honesty (although respecting the autonomy of others doesn't necessarily *entail* being honest). The only general remark I can make about inter-connections of this kind is that the different concepts together make up a meaningful way of life. But this is what we *cannot* say about the evaluations implicit in the use of the word 'nigger'. Of course, racialism can be, in one sense, a whole way of life. But the notion of colour has, in itself, no connection with any of the concepts which are relevant to the question of how one is to treat other people. Not only is it totally unrelated to any concepts of the kind we have just been looking at, but it is equally unrelated to any of the concepts one might counterpose to them—the concept of self-interest, for example. The notion of the colour of a man's skin simply has no place here. The only way in which it can have any evaluative significance at all is by being set in the context of a system of aesthetic considerations. It could be said, for example, that black is a gloomy colour; but that, of course, is not what racialists have in mind.

5. The Relation between Public Standards and Private Wants

I suspect that my discussion still leaves the notions of 'norms' and 'normative concepts' and 'evaluative characterizations' imprecisely

F

defined. Subsequent chapters may help indirectly to make them clearer. But I think that I have said enough to enable us now to return to the question raised earlier (see above, p. 65). The question was: if reasons are necessarily public, if they necessarily refer to social norms, might this not simply mean that reasons-for-acting are ultimately grounded in facts about what all men or most men want? And in that case would we not be recognizing that it is, after all, *wants* that constitute ultimate reasons-for-acting?

The simplest version of this suggestion is to be found in the quotations from Hume on pp. 38-9. Central to Hume's version is the idea that private standards and public standards are *alternatives*—alternative points of view from which one might form one's judgements. In that case the distinction could be illustrated by the following example. A proposed road scheme might be very much to a particular individual's own disadvantage, involving the destruction of the whole of his front garden, thus depriving him of the opportunity to engage in his favourite hobby of gardening, destroying his beautiful rose beds, ruining the whole appearance of the front of the house, and bringing the noise and the fumes of the traffic right up to his front doorstep. But if asked for his assessment of the merits of the scheme, he might nevertheless say that he thought it was the best possible one in the circumstances, since it would enable people to travel more easily and in greater comfort, cut down the number of accidents, and cause the least overall inconvenience. In the first case he would be described as looking at the matter from a personal or private point of view, and in the second he could be described as looking at it from a general or public point of view. Hume's suggestion is that our normally adopting the latter point of view is a matter of convenience; we would always be contradicting one another if we judged from the former point of view. One can indeed observe from our example the truth of this claim. There could be no rational discussion as to what would be the best road scheme if all the participants in the discussion spoke purely from the former of the two points of view. This, however, is not what I have been referring to in emphasizing the necessary publicity of standards. In my sense, the man is employing public standards just as much when he adopts the former of the two points of view. This can be seen from the kind of vocabulary he might use. Insofar as he refers to the notion of 'peace and quiet', disturbance caused by noise, the choking stench of traffic fumes, the enjoyment of a hobby, the beauty of flowers, etc., he is invoking publicly-shared concepts and public standards of evaluation. It is because he does so that we can describe as 'rational' his potential objections to the road scheme from the point of view of his private wants and interests.

The suggestions made by Narveson and Gauthier (see above, pp. 48-9) differ slightly from Hume's. They would involve saying that, in the above example, the man's judgement of the road scheme is *rational* only if it is made not from a private point of view but by taking into account the wants and interests of *everyone* affected by it. In one sense this suggestion is closer to my own position. It is at any rate an attempt to link the two notions of *publicity* and *rationality*. But since the notion of publicity is still the same as that employed by Hume—namely, that of public interest—this position is in another way even further from my own. For I want to say that, in the above example, both points of view are rational because they are both public in my sense, even though one of them is the point of view of private interest and the other is the point of view of public interest.

What might now be claimed is that these public norms—in the sense in which *I* am using the term—are themselves constituted by facts about what most men want. It might be said that, in the above example, the notion of 'peace and quiet' constitutes a public standard of evaluation only because most people do as a matter of fact want peace and quiet. In other words, although people's private wants do not themselves constitute reasons in the full sense, people do nevertheless want things independently of any reference to public reasons, and insofar as people with these private wants encounter the same wants in other people, the wants become legitimized as rational general standards. Just as, according to Wittgenstein, the meaningful use of language presupposes 'agreement in judgements', so also—the suggestion might run—meaningful action, and the existence of public concepts for evaluating it, presupposes agreement in wants.

However, in my earlier remarks on Wittgenstein I argued that this talk of 'agreement in judgements' should not lead us to suppose that the correct use of language is laid down by any previous *decision*. As Wittgenstein says, the kind of agreement that is involved is not 'agreement in opinion' (*Philosophical Investigations*, para. 241). I have suggested that the notions of 'decision' and 'choice' are logically posterior to the notion of public norms which determine what counts as 'correct' or 'rational' language-use. Similarly I want to argue that public norms of rational action are prior to the notion of 'wanting'. Now although the question is one of logical priority, it is not entirely separable from considerations of chronological priority. And, of course, I would agree that a child does want things before it ever learns general standards of evaluation. Obviously we can say, for example, that the baby wants the breast simply on the basis of the fact that it reaches for it or cries until it is satisfied. Moreover its wanting the breast is one of those shared 'natural reactions', like crying or reacting to the gesture of pointing, which are a precondition of the possibility of rational behaviour, such that a baby which shared none of these natural reactions could never learn the use of a public language or the application of impersonal public standards. But for all that, it remains true that in a very important sense the child *learns* how to want things. It learns the normal uses of the phrase 'I want . . .'; and this is very much more than just a matter of learning to use a particular word.

There are two especially important ways in which this is so. In the first place, not every physical movement that a child makes is an occasion for teaching him that he wants something, nor even every physical movement which is identifiable as a movement towards something. Out of all the many such movements which a baby makes, only those like reaching for the breast which we can understand in terms of existing human norms of intelligible action do we treat as wants and respond to as such. Therefore, for the baby, the process of learning to use the words 'I want . . .' is inseparable from the process of learning to act *rationally*. And although we ascribe wants to the baby prior to its having learnt this, we do so only because we can see certain elements in its behaviour as *potentially* the actions of a rational agent. Now I suggested earlier that irrational wants can still count as wants (pp. 54–5) and what I have just said should not be regarded as contradicting this. The man who claims to want a saucer of mud may perhaps rightly be said to want it even if his wanting it is completely irrational. But this is because the physical expression of the want, his trying to get it, can be seen as not just an incomprehensible physical movement but an *attenuated version* of a recognizably rational action. The want is clearly parallel to fully rational wants such as, for example, wanting a saucer of milk to drink, but fails to fit at some vital point. We can think of all sorts of accounts of the want which *could* make it rational, but it so happens that all of them are rejected. What enables us, then, to see this want as a want is the fact that we can relate it to a background of rational wants. Unless this background is presupposed, there is no room for the concept of wanting to operate at all.

The second important point is that in learning to use the words 'I want . . .' the child learns that in some cases he is the final authority on what he wants and in others he is not. He discovers that it is he himself who has to answer such questions as 'Do you want to go to the toilet?' or 'Do you want a drink of milk?', and if he says 'Yes', then whether he is right to give this reply is simply a question of how he subsequently behaves. His assertion that he wants a drink of milk is questioned only if, when offered the milk, he doesn't drink. On the other hand, his tentative essays in the use of the phrase 'I want . . .' soon show him that if he says 'I want it' with reference to many other things, he will be asked 'What for?' and may well be told 'Don't be silly, of course you don't'. And thus, what is most important, he learns when '. . . because I want to' counts as a reason and when it doesn't. He learns that this form of words has a specific use.

More precisely, I think that there are four main uses which the phrase could have. It may be used to rebut the suggestion that one has an *ulterior* motive for performing an action. For example, someone might ask: 'Why are you inviting him to dinner? Is it because you want him to invite you back to his in return?', and the reply might be 'No, I just want to.' This reply means that there is no further result which I hope that his coming to dinner will help to bring about. But it does not mean that there is no further reason for having him to dinner. It may be that I think that I will enjoy his company, or that I just like entertaining in general, reasons which can themselves be unpacked into further specifications of what it is that I will enjoy in the situation. So '. . . because I just want to' does not here act as an ultimate reason, it simply indicates what kind of further reason can be given.

Secondly, 'I just wanted to' might be used to rebut the suggestion that one has any conscious reason at all. Suppose we are walking along the pavement, and I stop and look in a shop window; you ask 'Why did you stop to look in that window?' and I perhaps reply, 'Oh, I don't know, I just wanted to.' This is in place as a reply to a request for reasons not because it states a reason but because it implies that I had no reasons. My action was not the outcome of any reasoned intention on my part. We might call it 'acting on impulse', though the phrase is perhaps a bit too strong, too dramatic, for the case I have imagined.

Both these uses of 'because I want to' might be called elliptical; they do not mean simply and literally that my wanting something is my reason for acting. The two remaining uses are more central. There are the cases, such as those which I have already referred to—the child's wanting to go to the toilet or wanting a drink of milk—where the wanting is the expression of what is little more than a physical sensation, a biological stimulus. And finally there are the cases which could be referred to as 'matters of taste'—preferences which can be recognized as purely subjective. The paradigm of these is 'taste' in the literal sense. Suppose someone asks me why I take four spoonfuls of sugar in a cup of tea. There might be some reason such as that I want to replenish lost stores of energy or that I want to get fat; but if it's just a question of taste I might reply 'I just want my tea that way'. (More likely would be 'I just like it that way', but the difference is not important; we have seen that the two can be linked.) Why can we not give any further reason for wanting or liking the taste of ultra-sweet tea? Because there are no possibilities of any further characterization of the taste. It is a simple sensation, not allowing of any alternative modes of description. We cannot see the thing wanted in different ways, see different aspects of it. To use a slightly dated philosophical terminology, sweetness is simple and unanalysable. We can compare one taste with another, but beyond that there are no further possibilities of description. Something similar could be said of the previous case. There, it is not that one wants to experience a sensation, but that the wanting *is* the sensation. So, again, there are no possibilities of re-description. A sensation of hunger just is a sensation of hunger, and therefore if 'I want to eat' means no more than 'I am hungry' there is no room for further discussion as to whether and why I want this (although there may very well be other considerations relevant to the question of whether I ought to satisfy my hunger).

Compare these cases with, say, the question whether I want to live in the house where I was born and brought up. Here there is a very great deal that can be said which is relevant to my assessment and definition of what I want, for there are various different ways in which I can see the house. I can see it as 'home', or I can see it, perhaps, as 'a rather ordinary nineteenth-century terraced house badly in need of repair'. And each of these characterizations sets my attitude towards the house within the context of a great many other connected concepts and values, so that by examining the relations between these I shall find various further considerations which will help to form my attitude. Now the typical example of practical reasoning is surely the 'home' example, not the 'ultra-sweet' example. The range of 'matters of taste', and the extent of 'wants as biological stimuli', are very limited, because most of the things we want are things of which one can see different aspects and give further descriptions, and we want them because we see them in a certain way. In these latter cases, therefore, there can be no question of a norm being constituted by pre-existent wants. As we have said, it becomes possible to want the thing only when one has already learnt to see it in the relevant way; I can value my house as a 'home' only because I have already learnt the concept of a 'home', and in learning the concept and its place within a form of social life I have learnt an evaluative norm.

We are now in a position to draw our conclusions from the two points which I have tried to make about the way in which one learns the use of 'I want . . .'. From this second argument we can conclude that, in that majority of cases where the possibility of wanting something is dependent upon already having learnt to see the thing in the relevant way, the norm is both logically *and* chronologically prior to the existence of the corresponding want. We have conceded that the more limited kinds of wants, on the level of tastes and biological stimuli, can be regarded as in one sense prior to rational norms. But what emerges from our earlier argument (p. 74) is that, even here, the notion of a norm has a logical priority. For we suggested that what counts as a want, even at this biological level, is determined by the system of rational norms within a culture, and that one is able to ascribe wants to a baby at all only because one can see its actions as potentially those of a rational agent. Our paradigm of wanting is not wanting at the biological level of stimulus and response, but wanting at the level of rational reflection and assessment. Thus, when we describe animals as 'wanting' something, we do so only in a secondary sense; for, as in the case of the young child's behaviour, what separates the animal's 'wants' from other physical movements is not something intrinsic to the physical movements as such, but simply the fact that certain of them can be seen as analogous to human 'wants' in the full and primary sense.[1]

6. THE ROLE OF REASONS

In this chapter I have been attempting to undermine the thesis of 'wants as reasons' by showing the inadequacy of its conception of rationality. We must now turn back to the original arguments of chapter 1, and try to see what went wrong. The argument started out from two assumptions: (a) that any account of practical reasons must be such that there is a necessary connection between the reasons and *action*; (b) that any fact which is to constitute an ultimate reason for acting must be something that can be *known*, without standing in need of further proof or evidence. Let us look at each of these assumptions in turn.

(a) In a sense it is clearly true—or perhaps a truism—that there must be some kind of connection between practical reasons and action. What I have been suggesting is that the fact that certain kinds of considerations have an essential bearing on action is a *cultural* fact. Consequently if we want to show what gives reasons their 'force', we have to show— as I have in effect been doing—how action in accordance with or contrary to reasons is connected with one's standing in a certain specific kind of relation to other human beings (*qua* rational agents and *qua* language users), and with the possibility of one's actions possessing a meaning or intelligibility. The assumption behind the thesis of 'wants-as-reasons', however, is that the connection between reasons and action is a much stronger one than this. It amounts to an idea of reasons as considerations which *impel* one to action. Any particular consideration cannot have the force of a reason-for-acting, it is supposed, unless it is such that one *must* act. And this 'must' is assimilated to the status of a logical 'must'. Now although it is not logically impossible that someone might want something but not act in accordance with the want, the connection is at any rate of this order. In default of certain specific kinds of explanation (e.g. the existence of a conflicting want), the man's failure to act must be regarded as indicating that he doesn't really want what he is supposed to want. Therefore a want is, almost by definition,

---

[1] In this section, and indeed in this chapter as a whole, I have found very useful an article by A. Phillips Griffiths and R. S. Peters: 'The Autonomy of Prudence' (*Mind*, 1962).

something that *impels* one to action, makes one *bound* to act. And this is why wants are thought to provide the ultimate reasons for acting.

We can trace here the influence of the traditional empiricist picture of a radical distinction between man as a spectator or as a thinking being, and man as an agent. This involves a suggestion that action is something other than the 'natural' state of a man. The idea is of action as something a man can 'go in for' on particular occasions; and it is on such occasions that 'reasons' play their role. A man is normally in a condition of inaction, and something is always required to *move* him from this condition of inaction to a condition of action. It is the task of reasons to provide this motive force.

Now we *could* challenge this account with an alternative description. We could say that in a sense a man is always 'doing something', even if in some cases the most appropriate way of specifying what he is doing is to specify what he is refraining from, or to say that he is just relaxing or being idle. And, what is very important, the sense in which a man can be said to be always doing something is closely connected with the fact that we can always raise questions about what *reasons* there are for a man's doing what he is doing, even when he is primarily refraining from something or being idle. True as this is, however, it would be wrong to ask which is the *correct* account of action: the account of it as something that men engage in when there is something to detach them from a state of inaction, or the account of it as something that men are engaged in all the time, the only variation being a change from one kind of action to another. Each way of describing has its own uses, and it would be absurd to suppose that we can never properly describe someone as 'doing nothing' or reproach someone with being 'inactive'. The mistake is to generalize one of these forms of description into a total account, an absolute account which is offered as the *only* possible way of describing human action. It is on the basis of such a procedure that philosophers have insisted that reasons *must* ultimately consist in something like 'wants'. As a way of questioning this 'must', it is legitimate to point to an alternative way of describing, to the possibility of saying that in a sense a man is always performing *some* kind of action. We thus remove the supposed difficulty of explaining how reasons could ever induce a man to act unless they were ultimately grounded in wants. But this is not to say that we are basing an alternative account of reasons on this alternative account of action; for the latter is not offered as an 'account' at all, but merely as a further way of talking about human behaviour.

Here it may be objected that, even if the connection between reasons and action is not of the 'impelling' kind, there does exist this logical connection between wanting and action; and therefore, if a particular reason is to lead to action, it must refer to something that the agent wants.[1] For example, the fact that a particular action is 'fair' may be a reason for performing it; in that case it is a reason for acting, regardless of whether the agent wants to do what is fair; but his recognition that the action is fair will not lead him to perform it unless he wants to do what is fair. This claim appears to depend upon making the notion of 'an action which a man performs because he wants to perform it' equivalent by definition to the notion of 'an intentional action'. In that case the claim is tautologous. As it stands, it is a fairly harmless tautology. But it is liable to be re-interpreted. Thus we find Mrs. Foot apparently starting out from a position such as this and arriving at the conclusion that, since a reason-for-acting must refer to something that can be wanted, considerations such as pleasure or interest provide ultimate reasons for acting whereas considerations such as justice do not (*Moral Beliefs*, p. 98). It is easy to see how this conclusion becomes plausible. The assertion that 'reasons refer to things that are wanted', taken out of context, would naturally suggest considerations such as pleasure or interest rather than considerations such as justice. But if 'want' is being used as a piece of philosophical terminology in accordance with the above definition, such a restriction of the objects of wanting is impermissible. There can perfectly well be such a thing as an action which is performed intentionally insofar as it is just, and therefore, if 'intentional' and 'want' are interdefined, it is perfectly possible to perform an action because it is just and because one wants to do what is just. Thus the claim that reasons must refer to something that is wanted if they are to lead to action is either a true tautology which tells us nothing about reasons-for-acting, or else it is a claim which does say something concrete about the nature of reasons but which is, however, false.

(b) Something like the following might be said: 'We don't normally push our reasons back further than, for example, "... because it's fair".' But the status of this as a reason *can* always be called in question. It does make sense to ask 'Why should I do what is fair?' If someone suggests that the reason '... because it's fair' can't be called in question, because 'One ought to do what is fair' is an analytic truth, then we have to unscramble the descriptive and prescriptive elements in 'fair' and ask 'Why should I do what is fair$_1$?' (where 'fair$_1$' is purely descriptive). Therefore, to halt one's reasons at some 'public norm' such as that of fairness is, in philosophy if not in everyday life, to leave one's reasons open to doubt, and therefore to leave one's justification hanging in mid-air. And if we try to justify this reason by deriving it from other

---

[1] Cf. Anscombe, *Intention*, p. 66: 'The role of "wanting" in the practical syllogism is quite different from that of a premise. It is that whatever is described in the proposition that is the starting-point of the argument must be wanted in order for the reasoning to lead to any action.'

public reasons of the same sort, this process can continue *ad infinitum* and, therefore, the justification will still never get anchored. We therefore have to push back the justification until we get to something that is no longer open to doubt—and this is done by referring ultimately to basic wants.

Now perhaps it is true that one can always ask 'Why should I do what is fair?', and that the same goes for any other norm of this kind. But it is important to look and see exactly what someone might mean by this. One should not assume that just anything can count as 'questioning the reason'. One possibility is that someone who asks this question might genuinely not understand why 'because it's fair' can provide a reason for acting. I have argued above that someone of whom this was true would not really understand the meaning of the word; he wouldn't really understand what fairness is. This is the sense in which a child might ask 'Why should I do what is fair?' Therefore we would answer this question by teaching him to comprehend the meaning of the word. We could do this by showing him the connections between fairness and other concepts, showing him the place that fairness has in our ways of seeing our relations with other people. At a fairly fundamental level, for example, we might help a child to understand what is meant when it is said that an action is unfair by getting him to imagine himself in someone else's position, asking him 'How would you feel if someone did that to you?', and so on. This is, of course, a very familiar move. But it is vitally important to recognize what we are doing here. We are not giving a *further reason* for being fair, nor are we *deriving* the notion of fairness from anything else more fundamental, nor are we going further back to anything that is 'less open to doubt'. We are explaining the meaning of 'fairness', showing what fairness is.

Someone who asked 'Why should I do what is fair?' might, however, understand perfectly well what fairness is. He might, instead, be expressing a reluctance to act fairly, in view of, say, the difficulties involved. 'It's much easier and simpler to be unfair; what is so important about "fairness", that it should outweigh these considerations?'—this might be the gist of his query. We could answer it in much the same way as in the previous case; we could attempt to show how the notion of fairness is connected to a whole system of other ethical concepts, and perhaps indicate its importance by showing how fundamental its position is within the system. We could, for example, point out that some such notion as that of fairness is central to the very idea of a human *social* existence or a human *community*. Once again it is of crucial importance to recognize what kind of argument this is. It is not the act-utilitarian argument that a particular agent ought to act fairly because his doing so is a necessary condition for the continuing viability of the community (a useless argument, since no act-utilitarian has ever succeeded in making the factual conditional claim at all plausible). Nor is it the rule-utilitarian argument that one ought to act fairly because if everyone acted unfairly human social life would cease to be viable (an invalid argument, since no rule-utilitarian has ever succeeded in demonstrating how a factual claim about the consequences of everyone's acting in a certain way can provide utilitarian grounds for any particular person's action). It is not, in fact, any kind of attempt to derive reasons for acting fairly from considerations other than those of fairness. It is an attempt to show the *importance* (i.e. the significance) of the *concept* of fairness.

Alternatively one might reply to this query by offering *incentives*. One might very well do this by attempting to prove to the agent that his acting fairly is a way to getting something that he wants. One might, for instance, argue that if he acts fairly towards the other person, then the other person will be more likely to act fairly towards him. But this has nothing to do with any attempt to show why fairness is important, nor is it an attempt to show the agent that he should perform this action because it is fair. The fairness of the action has become completely incidental. And the fact that we do often get people to perform actions by means of incentives of this kind indicates only that people are more likely to perform an action of it will lead to something they want. It does not indicate that wants have any logically superior status as reasons-for-acting.

A third possible interpretation of the question 'Why should I do what is fair?' is as a way of *objecting* to the notion of fairness. According to writers like Hare, one can always reject reasons of this kind, because one can always refuse to accept the concept—of fairness, or whatever—as part of one's ethical vocabulary. This is true. But as I have argued previously, it is also true that if one's objection to the concept is to count as a rational objection, then it must itself be capable of being backed up by a reason, a reason of the same public and normative kind. Someone who said 'Why should I do what is fair?' could not mean simply 'I just refuse to accept the concept of fairness—I just *don't want* to accept it, and that is all there is to be said'; or at any rate, if he did mean this, his position would not be a rational one. And that is why, although a reason like '. . . because it's fair' *can* always be called in question, it does not *normally* stand in need of any further justification. It does not normally leave the matter open to doubt. If a positive and rational objection to the concept is made, then there may very well be a great deal more that can be said, on both sides; but in the absence of any such positive objection, it is not the case that anything more *needs* to be said. 'Because it's fair' is in itself a perfectly adequate and self-sufficient reason for doing something. It does not provide us with 'certainty' (of a logically absolute kind), but since *any* reason (including reference to wants as reasons) can always be questioned, the quest for that kind of certainty is illusory. Reasons of this kind ensure not certainty but rationality, and that is what we should be looking for.

Writers like Hare have connected the possibility of saying, for example, 'I just refuse to accept the word "fair"' with a particular conception of freedom. Hare says, in *Freedom and Reason*: 'It is . . . in the logical possibility of wanting *anything* (neutrally described) that the "freedom" which is alluded to in my title essentially consists' (p. 110). And so it seems to him to follow that, if 'because it's fair' is offered as a reason for performing an action, a man must be 'free' simply to reject this as a reason-for-acting without anything more needing to be said.[1] Now we might react to this suggestion simply by denying the factual claim and asserting that we are not, in fact, absolutely free to form our own evaluative or moral opinions. But I think that it is also important to challenge Hare's conception of freedom. That conception is epitomized by the fact that 'freedom' is contrasted with 'reason'. Although Hare's aim is to show that the demands of freedom and the demands of reason are not incompatible, what is more significant is not this conclusion but the fact that Hare sees a problem here, i.e. that he sees freedom and reason as even potentially in conflict. It seems to me, on the contrary, important to recognize an essential connection between freedom and reason. For a start, the notion of freedom is inseparably linked with the concepts of 'choice' and 'decision', and I have argued previously that to speak of 'choosing' or 'deciding' implies the existence of rational norms by reference to which one chooses or decides. Notice the typical phrases with which we talk about freedom: 'freedom to form one's own opinions', 'freedom to act in accordance with one's own beliefs and convictions', 'freedom to do what one thinks right'; forming an opinion, holding a belief or a conviction, thinking something right, are essentially rational activities, and it is precisely insofar as they are rational that we can give sense to the notion of ownership here—to talk of *a man's own* beliefs etc. Even if we define freedom in terms of wanting —'doing what one wants'—I have been arguing that, although there can be such things as irrational wants, to say that one wants something is in most cases not to report a felt psychological state but to invoke rational standards. There is, indeed, a sense of the word 'free' such that to say that one is free to do x means no more than that it is possible for one to do x. And in this sense Hare is trivially correct in saying that a man is free to reject, without further explanation, any reason-for-acting whatsoever, even though he is being completely irrational in doing so. But insofar as it is something of value, something important in human life,

---

[1] Cf. pp. 1–2, and pp. 187–91, where Hare insists that we cannot be compelled to accept any particular evaluation by 'the mere existence of a certain conceptual apparatus'.

freedom is essentially connected with the kinds of rational activities I have been mentioning. A man is, in a trivial sense, free to emit any vocal sounds whatever, but if he engages in mere babbling or utters a totally arbitrary sequence of words he could hardly be said to be exercising freedom of speech, and if we try and get him to stop talking nonsense we can hardly be said to be restricting his freedom. Similarly if a man engages in purely arbitrary physical movements he is not exercising freedom of action. And it also seems to me that, with regard to Hare's man who simply and without further explanation refuses to accept reasons, if we say that he is being irrational we are not, properly speaking, setting any limits to his freedom to make his own ethical or evaluative judgements. For what he is saying or doing will not count as 'making ethical or evaluative judgements' unless it can be seen to have at least some reference to standards of rationality and, therefore, to public norms. The freedom of the abstract individual, divorced from a culture and therefore from a concrete rationality, is a totally empty freedom (in this respect I feel very much inclined to agree with a writer like Hegel). This is the crux of the disagreement between the thesis I have been defending in this chapter and the position I have been attacking. The utilitarian account of reasons-for-acting is essentially individualistic and psychologistic. I want to argue that the nature of human action and human reasons cannot be properly understood unless it is seen primarily in social terms.

4. Ends and Means

1. THE RESTRICTIVENESS OF TELEOLOGICAL ETHICS

At the beginning of chapter 2, we identified two essential characteristics of utilitarian rationality: first, its *psychologistic* character, and second, its *teleological* character. In chapter 3, I criticized the psychologistic aspect, and I shall now turn to criticism of the teleological aspect. But before I embark on this criticism, there is an initial problem to be mentioned, the question of how this aspect of utilitarian rationality is properly formulated. There are two basic possibilities here, offered by the vocabulary of 'ends and means' and by the vocabulary of 'actions and consequences'. We can say that reasons-for-acting are provided solely by the ends to be achieved, and that there are reasons for or against the use of particular means only insofar as the means will lead to certain ends; or we can say that reasons-for-actions are provided solely by the consequences of the actions. The drawbacks of the vocabulary of ends and means are represented by the following kind of case: A wants to bring about situation s, and this can be done only by means of performing action x; therefore, A has a good reason for performing action x; but by performing action x he will also bring about situation t, which is a situation which he would want to avoid. Any utilitarian would certainly say that the latter fact provides the agent with a good reason not to do x, and that if there are no other relevant considerations the question whether he has a better reason for doing x or for not doing x is to be determined by comparing the relative desirability of s and t. Now strictly speaking only s would normally be said to be relevant as an end; we would tend to say of t not that it is relevant as an end but that it is relevant as a consequence. By dint of a certain sleight of hand, we might be able to accommodate the case to the vocabulary of ends and means. We could say that, once he recognizes that his doing x will lead to t, the avoidance of t becomes an end for him. However, if he does x without recognizing that it will lead to t, we still want to say that he has a good reason for not doing x, even though the avoidance of t has not acquired the status of an end. Therefore, in order to retain the vocabulary of ends and means, we would have to resort to some complex locution such as that A has a good reason for not doing x because doing x would lead to t and the avoidance of t would be an end for A if he recognized that doing x would lead to t.

On the other hand the awkward cases for the vocabulary of actions and consequences are those where A has a good reason for doing x just because he likes doing x. In the vocabulary of ends and means we can say that doing x is an end in itself. Any utilitarian moralist would surely agree that in such a case A would have a good reason for doing x: in traditional utilitarian terms he would have a good reason because x would increase the sum of his happiness, and in more contemporary terms he would have a good reason because he wants to do just x. But the only way in which the action can be said to be 'justified by its consequences' is by saying that A has a good reason for doing x because doing x will have as its consequences the satisfaction that A will get. Now if the teleological aspect of utilitarian rationality consists in this, then it is identical with the psychologistic aspect. I shall, indeed, be stressing that the two aspects are linked; but if they are so closely linked as to be entirely identical, then, in the present thesis, there is nothing further to be said on the teleological aspect. However, I believe that the plausibility which attaches to the teleological case amounts to more than this; and, therefore, we are still left with the problem of how best to formulate it.

Having stated this problem, I intend to leave it unresolved. By pointing out the difficult cases which would have to be incorporated within a satisfactory formulation, I have sufficiently indicated what is included in the position that I intend to attack. I shall refer to it in terms both of 'ends' and of 'consequences', and I shall seek to show that the whole enterprise, however formulated, is misconceived.

In chapter 3 I criticized the psychologistic aspect of utilitarian rationality principally on the score that it produces too permissive an account of practical rationality. In effect, it makes any felt ultimate want immune to rational criticism other than on grounds of incompatibility with other wants. My criticism of the teleological aspect is the reverse: it produces too *restricted* a view of practical rationality. I want to suggest that a teleological standpoint in ethics is in itself a perfectly possible and rational one, but that it is not the *only* rational ethic. My argument will depend upon the points which I attempted to establish in chapter 3. I shall assume it to have been demonstrated that a particular ethic is rational if it is grounded in the ethical concepts of our language. Using this as a criterion, I shall argue that the utilitarian teleological view of ethics, if put forward as the only correct view, rules out other ethics which are in point of fact perfectly rational.

Now, of course, the teleological view, if correct, would naturally rule out other *philosophical theories* about the nature of ethical reasoning.

What I am mainly concerned with in this chapter, however, is the question whether acceptance of the teleological view would commit one to regarding as irrational any particular *concrete values* which men actually adhere to. In order to determine whether it is *intended* to do so, I want first to consider what are the features of the teleological view that have led philosophers to advocate it.

2. The Plausibility of the Teleological View

(1) We have already, in this chapter, mentioned the close connection between the teleological and the psychologistic aspects of utilitarian rationality, and in chapter 1 we saw that the teleological aspect needs to be introduced as part of the requirements of the argument for 'wants as reasons'. The claim that ultimate reasons consist in wants could not, we saw, be plausibly made without distinguishing between actions which consist in doing or producing x because x is a necessary means to something else that is wanted and actions which consist in doing or producing x because x is wanted for its own sake. Now, of course, it may often be the case that a man's reason for doing x is that x is a necessary means to something that he wants, but it by no means follows that his reason-for-acting consists in *the fact that he wants* what he does want—this is the gist of what I have been arguing in the previous chapter. I suggested that the temptation to identify reasons with wants stems from the mistaken notion of a reason as that which impels a man to act—this being one particular aspect of the ubiquitous and misleading identification of reasons-for-acting with causes of action. The same view underlies the primacy that is attached to 'ends'. If something is an end for an agent, it is essentially that which he aspires to, that which attracts him, and the idea that ultimate reasons must involve reference to ends is a product of the idea that reasons are what *move* a man to act.[1] Of course, a man will not intentionally perform an action unless it is the case that, in some very general and largely vacuous sense, there is something about the performance of the action that makes it a thing worth aiming at in his eyes. But this does not mean that its being, in this sense, an 'end' for him *is his reason* for performing it.

Something of the same confusion infects the use of the word 'purpose', and indeed of the term 'teleological'. Much recent work on the explanation of human action has contrasted the causal model of explanation with 'teleological explanation'. Various writers have argued that the primary form of explanation relevant to human actions is 'teleological' in the sense that it states the agent's purposes and intentions in performing the action. With this I would largely agree. But we then have to beware of the slide from the suggestion that 'to understand why an

[1] On this aspect of teleological ethics, see Winch: *Moral Integrity*.

action is performed we need to discover what the agent's purpose was' to the suggestion that 'the reason for performing any action always consists in its being for the sake of some purpose (end)'. Similarly, although we may allow that the primary kind of explanation of human action is teleological explanation, this in effect means only that such explanations are in terms of the agent's reasons, and does not entail that those reasons are themselves 'teleological'.

The arguments which I have previously urged against 'wants as reasons' can, then, also be directed against the teleological view of ethical rationality insofar as this is said to be either demanded by, or parallel to, the role assigned to wants. But there are other features of the teleological view that add to its plausibility, and to these I now turn.

(2) In recent controversies between teleologists and anti-teleologists,[1] the line between them has been drawn at a point which makes the argument much easier for the teleologists. The argument has been over whether there are any cases where it is legitimate to say not only that an action is right or wrong just because it is the kind of action that it is, but also that any consideration of the further consequences of the action is bound to be irrelevant to the appraisal of the action. The question has been posed in the form: can there ever be an action which is right or wrong 'whatever the consequences'? Now if the teleologist's claim is merely that, when we are considering whether an action is justified, it is always appropriate to investigate its consequences, this claim is much simpler to defend than the more strictly teleological claim that the appraisal of an action *consists simply in* the wieghing of its consequences. Even when the argument is defined in the former terms, there may be something to be said against the teleological viewpoint; I shall subsequently suggest that from a certain moral standpoint it may sometimes be appropriate to say of an action that it is right (or wrong) 'regardless of the consequences'—and in such a case we could also use the phrase 'whatever the consequences' as a synonym. But still, this does not mean that we can ever say in advance that no conceivable consequences of a particular action could possibly be relevant to the appraisal of the action. This can be simply shown. It is a much-noted fact that an occurrence can often be described equally as a man's action and as a consequence of his action. For example, we can say 'A stabbed B, and as a result B died' or we can say 'A killed B'. From the existence of such possibilities of redescription it follows that until we know the consequences of an action and the way in which those consequences are connected to the action, we cannot be certain that there is not room for further discussion as to *what kind of action* it was.

[1] E.g. in G. E. M. Anscombe's 'Modern Moral Philosophy,' Jonathan Bennett's 'Whatever the Consequences', and subsequent comments by other writers, mostly in *Analysis*.

G

The 'teleological view' that I am attacking in this chapter is not the easily-defensible claim that consideration of consequences is always appropriate, but the stronger claim that the appraisal of an action *always* consists *simply* in the weighing of consequences. The latter claim, through being confused with the former claim, acquires a plausibility that is entirely unwarranted.

(3) I come now to the most important argument for the claim of the teleologist, and this is, quite simply, that the claim is virtually a tautology. It is suggested that the teleological view is equivalent to the assertion that, if x is valued, then necessarily it is valued either as a means to an end or as an end in itself; and from this it seems to follow that any attempt to justify an action must consist in showing that it is either an end in itself or a necessary means to something which is an end in itself.

It is here that we need to raise the question whether the teleological view is intended to exclude any of the concrete values that men adhere to. I would suggest that it is normally regarded as doing so and that this is what makes it a significant ethical theory, but that it is a plausible theory only if it does not do so, since its plausibility depends upon its being in effect true by definition and applicable to any conceivable ethical values. The plausible interpretation of the teleological view is such that, if something is valued, and is not valued as a means to something other than itself, then it is, by definition, valued as an end in itself. And the teleological claim then seems to become unfalsifiable. Suppose, for instance, that someone offers the following counter-example: 'The importance of "fairness" is not a matter of ends and means; the reason why I ought to act fairly is not that it will necessarily produce beneficial results either for myself or for people in general, but simply because one has an *obligation* to deal fairly with people.' Here the teleologist can reply: 'But this is only to say that fairness, if it is not a means to any other end, is important as an end in itself; therefore your case is no exception to my rule.' This kind of move could as well be made against any other conceivable counter-example, and it is the awareness that the teleologist always has this move up his sleeve that contributes most to the plausibility of the teleological case.

If the notion of 'being valued as an end in itself' is understood in this way, there is little point in questioning the dictum that 'whatever is valued is valued either as a means to an end or as an end in itself'. What we need to examine is the legitimacy of this negative use of 'valued as an end in itself' such that it simply *means* 'valued other than as a means to something else'. Now I am willing to allow that we can always raise questions of ends and means in relation to any particular action, and that *when* we do so, we *can* always use the phrase 'end in itself' in this negative way. Suppose A says to B: 'What was the point of your keeping your promise? What good did you think would come of it?', it is legitimate for B to reply: 'I didn't keep my promise because I saw it as a means to anything; it was an end in itself.' Such a reply, though it may at times sound strained, is possible whatever the nature of the action. But the dangers arise when this possibility is exalted into a *theory of ethics*. It is then supposed that this relation of ends and means is what ethics is essentially about. In the case just imagined, it is supposed that if B gives this reply, we can understand his sense of an obligation to keep his promise by considering it as an end for him.

I want to stress two pernicious consequences that follow from this supposition. The first is that, having grouped together under the heading 'ends in themselves' all those cases where something is valued other than as a means to some further thing, one tends to imagine that there is some one kind of value that all these things possess, namely 'intrinsic value', and that there is some one kind of judgement or attitude that can be termed 'valuing something as an end in itself'. One then proceeds to ask what kind of judgement or attitude this is. One candidate which gets chosen is the notion of an 'intuition'; the connection between this notion and a teleological scheme is readily apparent in Moore's *Principia Ethica*, in his 'intuitive judgements of intrinsic value'. When this notion is seen to be epistemologically inadequate, an alternative candidate is found in the notion of 'wanting (or desiring) something for its own sake'. Thus the teleological aspect of utilitarian rationality once again leads back to and reinforces the psychologistic aspect. But both of these notions, and any other candidate that might be found, seem to me to be mere fictions. There is no single attitude or judgement that corresponds to the phrase 'valuing something as an end in itself.' As I argued in chapter 3, there are cases where we can say 'I just like it, that's all' or 'I just want to' and where such assertions simply report a felt psychological attitude or intuition; but these are exceptional cases, not the normal cases of valuing something for its own sake. The kinds of cases that are covered by the latter phrase in its most general sense are, considered psychologically, extremely diverse, and in most cases the fact that the thing in question is not valued as a means to something else does not mean that one does not value it for a reason, as distinct from simply feeling it to be valuable. The attempt to single out some privileged psychological concept and to define ethics in terms of it has vitiated much of the ethical philosophy of this century. The notion of 'intrinsic value' has been equally disastrous. Moore says that, in order to decide what things have intrinsic value, 'it is necessary to consider what things are such that, if they existed *by themselves*, in absolute isolation, we should yet judge their existence to be good' (*Principia Ethica*, para. 112). But according to this criterion, nothing has intrinsic value; indeed, in the case of any of the things that men actually value, it is surely logically impossible to conceive of them as existing 'in absolute isolation'.[1] I have already intimated that any genuine ethical or evaluative concept has its sense only in the context of a system of ethical concepts. On the plane of action, correspondingly, a man's ends have value only as part of a meaningful way of life, and therefore only within a given setting. (Ironically, Moore's own principle of 'organic unities' is relevant here.) These facts become submerged and confusion arises when it is supposed that things which are valued in themselves all have some one kind of value which is 'intrinsic value'.

The second consequence of exalting the relation of ends and means into a theory of ethics is much more general. I have allowed that any action *can* be considered in terms of ends and means. But in a great many cases, this will not be the most appropriate way of looking at it. Consider our earlier example of acting fairly. A man may quite rationally believe that he ought to act fairly, while not believing that his doing so will contribute either to his own greater good or to the greater good of people in general. We can, if we wish, look at such a case in terms of ends and means, and say that for him fairness is an end in itself. But if we *start* with a perfectly general principle that all practical reasoning takes the form of determining what things are ends in themselves and what means are necessary to the achievement of those ends, and if we *then* turn to consider what form practical reasoning should take in particular cases, the possibilities which this general principle implies will not include the idea that in certain cases one rational way of deciding how to act would be to ask what is the fairest course to take, but rather will appear to be limited to certain alternative kinds of reasoning. To assert that an action is to be evaluated in terms of ends and means is to suggest that it should be evaluated by reference to the state of affairs which it will bring about. The point here is not just that to see the man's acting fairly in teleological terms is liable to be misleading. What is important is rather that, although we can if we wish apply to the man's action the categories of ends and means, nevertheless in order to bring out what is significant and distinctive about his action it is necessary precisely to *contrast* it with actions performed from a teleological point of view. And if we are guided by the general principle that all practical reasoning is about ends and means, the possibility of making this contrast is no longer available.

This point becomes even more important when we recognize that not only a man's particular actions, but his whole ethical view of life, may need to be described primarily by being contrasted with the teleological viewpoint. For then it is not just that the vocabulary of ends and means is less appropriate in some cases than in others. If it were simply a matter of this, then it might still be plausible to suggest that the teleological

[1] Cf. R. F. Holland: 'The Autonomy of Ethics' (*P.A.S.S.V.*, 1958).

account is useful as a general description of practical reasoning, even if in the cases of some actions there is more to be said. But for a man whose whole ethic of life is non-teleological, it is *qua* general description that the teleological account is inadequate. For such a man, *the whole* of practical reasoning is non-teleological.

In the remainder of this chapter I offer examples of various kinds of non-teleological ethic. These are important, then, not because they suggest particular actions as counter-examples to the teleological account, but because they offer *alternative general descriptions* of ethical reasoning. I shall argue that these ethics are all rational, since they are grounded in the ethical concepts of our language, but that the effect of adopting a teleological account as a total description of ethical reasoning is to deny their rationality.

3. THE ETHIC OF ACTION AND THE ETHIC OF ACHIEVEMENT

We have mentioned that the notion of an end is primarily that of a 'state of affairs' or a 'situation' which is brought about by an action. Thus we may be led to formulate a contrast between actions and their ends insofar as the former are 'dynamic' and the latter 'static'. The paradigmatic cases of 'action for the sake of an end' are actions aimed at producing a state of *satisfaction* (for example the satisfaction of some need or deficiency such as hunger or thirst) and actions which consist in *making* something—for example producing some material object such as a building or a piece of furniture or a machine. (And it is because these cases are paradigmatic that utilitarianism inevitably becomes 'materialistic'.) In such cases the action gets its value solely from the value of the state of affairs which has been brought into existence when the action is over and completed. Therefore an ethic in which such cases are paradigmatic is what I would call an 'ethic of achievement'. The contrast between this and an 'ethic of action' can be illustrated by the example of artistic activity. It is not the case that the activity of the writer or painter or sculptor or composer, let alone that of the musician or actor or dancer, has value and significance solely insofar as it is the bringing into existence of a finished 'work of art'. The grappling with the materials, the application of skill and technique, the surmounting of difficulties, the total physical and intellectual involvement in the activity—all these are what give artistic activity its value. We might say that the artist *identifies himself with* the activity. It can quite well be the case that once the work of art is completed, the artist ceases to have any further interest in it. Thus, although the activity is in one sense to be defined teleologically, since it is essentially *creative* and aimed at *producing* something, the kind of value that it has is not necessarily teleological value. An insistence here on the application of a teleological ethic carries with it also a particular and limited aesthetic. The teleological ethic outlined by Moore in *Principia Ethica* is perhaps the supreme example of an ethic in which aesthetic values are paramount. Yet intrinsic value is assigned only to the *contemplation* of works of art; and this is because Moore, operating with a vocabulary of 'ends', is thereby predisposed to concentrate on static situations rather than on dynamic activities. He is thus led into a very limited view of art, excluding both the idea that creative artistic activity is itself important and also the idea of works of art as essentially prompting an active response rather than simply being contemplated.

In accordance with what has been said previously in this chapter, we can expect a predictable response from the teleologist. He is likely to point out that, although the teleological vocabulary has misled Moore, it is not bound to be misleading, since it is quite possible to assert that creative artistic activity is an end in itself. In order to meet this response, I want to consider a further example.

Within the Marxist ethic, two contrasting traditions are discernible, both of which can be traced back to Marx's own writings. Marx uses the term 'alienated labour' to refer to the condition in which a man's labour becomes a mere means to the satisfaction of his need to maintain his physical existence. Thus 'life itself appears only as a *means of life*', for a man's labour is his 'life-activity', it is that which defines his relationship to the external world and his nature as a human being, but in the condition of alienation it ceases to be this (*Economic and Philosophical Manuscripts*, pp. 101–2). It becomes something 'external to the worker', something imposed on him as an unavoidable necessity, so that 'he does not fulfil himself in his work but denies himself' (Ibid., p. 98). This comes about as a consequence of the economic division of labour, for then his labour is not his own but labour for another, and the product of his labour, since it belongs to another, becomes an alien object. Alienated labour is thus the precise opposite of typical artistic activity as we have characterized it, and indeed Marx himself and later Marxist writers have treated artistic activity as the paradigm of free non-alienated work. The contrasting element in the Marxist ethic is to be found in Marx's characterization of exploitation not in terms of the relation of a man to his work, but in terms of the *possession* of the products of labour. From this point of view, exploitation is measured by the notion of 'surplus value'. Now these two ideas are by no means incompatible with one another; they can be seen as two aspects of the same condition of exploitation, and this is how Marx presents them in the *1844 Manuscripts*. Nevertheless it has often happened that different traditions within the Marxist movement have emphasized one or the other of these aspects. One representative of the former tradition is William Morris, who explicitly makes artistic activity central to a socialist ethic. The ethic of action is also prominent in the syndicalist tradition, exemplified by Sorel, who contrasts the 'ethic of the producers' with the 'ethic of the consumers', and who also speaks of the artist as an instance of the former. Other instances of a Marxist ethic of action are the 'socialist humanism' of the 'new left', and the 'existentialist Marxism' of Sartre. On the other hand, the idea of a Marxist ethic as being concerned with the redistribution of the products of labour is prominent in the Bolshevist and the Fabian traditions and constitutes virtually the sole ethical content of Stalinism.

We saw that a possible teleologists' rejoinder to the example of artistic activity was that, although the teleological vocabulary is perhaps less suited to this example than to others, nevertheless the example can be accommodated within a teleological framework. But we are now dealing with a contrast not between two particular activities but between two complete ethics. And the way in which this contrast needs to be described just *is* that the one ethic is teleological and the other is not. My particular reason for choosing this example is that, within a Marxist perspective, the notion of free non-alienated activity is of course a notion of something to be brought about; the purpose of revolutionary action is to create a society in which non-alienated activity is possible. Therefore, the example might at first seem favourable to the teleologist's case. But although both forms of the Marxist ethic allow room for teleological action, the difference between them emerges when we ask of them the basic question 'What kind of ethic is it?' The answer to this *must* be that the one is a teleological and utilitarian ethic, the other is not. If the terms 'teleological' and 'utilitarian' are to have any significant use at all, they must be used to mark this contrast. To look for a way of saying that both of these ethics are teleological and utilitarian is to rob the terms of their point.

4. INTEGRITY AND UTILITY

In the previous section we referred to the possibility of a man's 'identifying himself with' a certain kind of activity. This idea can be developed further. Consider again the example which we have just been using. The Marxist 'ethic of action' (as contrasted with the 'ethic of achievement') itself admits of two possible emphases. Such an ethic could be taken to specify the kind of action that is to be made possible by means of the revolutionary creation of a new society, while leaving entirely open the question of what form the revolutionary action itself is to take. Alternatively, however, the same ethic could be taken as a specification of the kind of action which the revolutionary himself is to engage in. Someone who adheres to this ethic may take the view that revolutionary action is itself the supreme example of free non-alienated

activity, activity which is no longer defined by the imprisoning categories of existing social relationships and therefore is no longer imposed as something alien, but is genuinely creative and involves authentic
and truly human relationships with one's fellow-agents. It is in such a
case that we may be able to speak of a man 'identifying himself with' the
kind of activity which is valued within this ethic. It may be that his life
is endowed with a meaning precisely through his participation in such
activity. His commitment to the value of such action is what goes to
make up for him his personal and ethical identity. For, in general, the
unifying principle of any particular ethic may consist not only in its
providing an answer to the question 'What is the best kind of world that
could exist?' (which, from the utilitarian point of view, is the *sole* basic
question of ethics), but also in its providing an answer to the question
'What is the best kind of life for me to live?' These two points of view
need not necessarily supply a different content to the ethic which a man
adopts. Most existing ethics can be seen as providing an answer to either
question (e.g. the best kind of world is one in which there is as little
human suffering as possible, and the best kind of life to live is one which
minimizes human suffering). But, if we look again at the case we have
been considering, we can see that the two points of view may conflict.
For suppose it should appear to a Marxist more likely that a socialist
society can be brought into existence by means of the kind of action that
is condemned by the Marxist ethic—for example, by means of repression and exploitation and an élitist form of organization—than by
means of the kind of action that is valued within the Marxist ethic.
From a teleological point of view, the use of repressive methods would
be justified if it were likely to produce in the long run a condition of
greater freedom than could otherwise have been brought into existence,
since the long-term increase in freedom would outweigh the short-term
increase in repression. But someone for whom the Marxist ethic is not
just a commitment to a certain ideal of human society but a commitment
to a certain kind of life might look at the matter differently. He might
say that to use such methods would be to go against everything he
stands for and everything to which he is committed. He might perhaps
express it by saying that, even if such action offers a greater chance of
success, he *could never bring himself to do it*. What stands in the way is
the kind of life he is committed to, the way in which he is committed to
it, and the way in which this kind of commitment gives his life its point.
From this point of view, it is perfectly rational to assert that one has no
choice but to commit oneself to authentic and ethically-acceptable
revolutionary action while accepting the fact that it may offer a lesser
chance of success.

We should note incidentally that we are here committed to a qualitative distinction between actions which are futile and actions which *may*

succeed against all the odds, the distinction being one to which utilitarianism need give no special significance. From a utilitarian point of view, there can be only a quantitative distinction between the probabilities of consequences. The degree of probability of such-and-such consequences following from action x has to be *weighed against* the degree of probability of such-and-such consequences following from action y; and the case where certain consequences are entirely improbable simply constitutes one extreme on the same spectrum. But from the point of view which we have introduced, a qualitative distinction has to be made. If the Marxist thinks that a certain kind of revolutionary action has *no* chance of success, then the suggestion that a revolutionary should nevertheless engage in it so as to remain true to his principles would be incoherent (unless he were deliberately adhering to an 'ethic of the absurd' of the kind that Camus speaks of—but that would be a completely different kind of ethic). But if he thinks that a certain kind of revolutionary action has *some* chance of success, then it *can* be rational for him to declare that he ought to engage in it even though it has less chance of success than an alternative form of action.

Underlying all this is the idea that a man's actions, by virtue of being *his* actions, have a unique kind of significance for him which they do not have for anyone else. This looks like a truism. But from a utilitarian point of view it is not really even true. All that a utilitarian can say is that I should be more concerned about my own actions than about other people's because I have more control over the results of my own actions than over the results of other people's actions. The difference is simply one of degree. It is not the difference in kind which consists in saying that my actions are important to me just because they are mine and therefore define what kind of man I am.

This point becomes especially important when it acquires moral dimensions. The utilitarian can give no distinctive sense to such concepts as 'conscience', 'guilt', and 'remorse'. He may perhaps employ these concepts, but he will have to define them simply as heavily-charged versions of 'regret'. For the account which he gives of moral praise and blame is in terms of their utility: when other people do wrong we blame them to make them better, and when we ourselves do wrong we blame ourselves even more because there is more that we can do about it. The utilitarian may call this 'guilt' or 'remorse', but then he is hardly giving these concepts their full sense. What is really constitutive of remorse is not the thought that evil has occurred, but that it has become part of oneself. It has 'entered into one's soul', as it were.

Giving the notion of 'conscience' its full force may now lead to a further departure from utilitarian ideas. It enables us, I think, to make some sense of what might be expressed in the words 'Though evil may come, let it not come through you'. This idea may well appear suspect.

An example of such suspicion is to be found in Jonathan Bennett's article 'Whatever the Consequences' (*Analysis*, 1965–6). Bennett imagines a case where a surgeon is faced with a choice between operating on a woman who is in labour so as to save her life at the cost of killing the unborn child, or not operating, in which case the woman will die and the child can be delivered alive by post-mortem Caesarian section. The choice is between the woman's life or the child's. Bennett is here concerned not so much to defend a particular decision as to attack a certain way of making the decision which would consist in saying 'If the surgeon operates he will kill the child, whereas if he does not operate the woman's death will be simply a consequence of his refraining, and since it is always wrong to kill an innocent human being it would be absolutely wrong to operate, whatever the consequences.' Bennett argues that there would be no way of distinguishing between 'action' and 'consequences' here which would support the relevant moral distinction. One of the candidates which he considers is the notion of 'immediacy': someone might argue that there is an immediate connection between the performance of the operation and the death of the child whereas there is a lesser degree of immediacy between the surgeon's refraining from operating and the woman's dying, and that this is why operating would be 'killing' and therefore wrong, whereas refraining from operating would not be 'killing' and would therefore not be wrong. Bennett comments:

> Suggestions come to mind about 'not getting one's hands dirty'; and the notion of what I call 'immediacy' does help to show how the literal and the metaphorical are mingled in some uses of that phrase. In so doing, however, it exposes the desire to 'keep one's hands clean', in cases like the obstetrical example, as a symptom of muddle or primness or, worst of all, a moral egoism like Pilate's.

This charge of 'moral egoism' might be thought an appropriate comment on any application of the idea considered at the beginning of this paragraph. But we should look first at just why we are entitled to make the accusation in the obstetrical case. Here it is very important that the surgeon clearly *would* be responsible for the woman's death. Therefore, if he said 'My conscience forbids me to kill, whatever the circumstances' this would very likely be simply a way of trying to evade responsibilities which he does have. This is why the comparison with Pilate is appropriate. But we can also imagine other kinds of case. It might be, for example, that the refusal to kill a man is likely to lead to undesirable consequences not because of an inevitable chain of physical events but because of the probable subsequent actions of the potential victim or of some other human agent (a contemplated political assassination might be a case in point). This difference is relevant not because the intervention of human agency makes the consequences less dependable—for the subjective probabilities could well be just the same. Rather, one's own individual responsibility takes on a different kind of significance. There is then room, for example, for the notion that the moral failings of others do not license one to employ immoral means oneself. This is one possible interpretation of the idea 'Injustice is stronger than you are—but let it not be committed through you.'[1] We might usefully refer to the notion of 'integrity' here; the term is sometimes used to indicate a fidelity to any ideal, but I think that it can also legitimately be used to indicate one particular way of seeing moral demands, in contrast to the standpoint of utility.

Again, in the obstetrical example it is important that the reasons for killing the child are moral reasons. We could imagine a different case where the reasons for killing someone or causing some other harm were reasons of personal advantage. It could very well be that from a utilitarian point of view the good outweighed the harm—think of Raskolnikov in *Crime and Punishment*, for example. Here, I think, it would make sense to say that what utility prescribes, conscience forbids. Certainly this could not count as 'moral egoism'. But though there are cases which are indubitably one or the other, the line between 'conscience' and 'moral egoism' is hard to define. The difficulty may be illustrated by an example from Conrad's novel *Lord Jim*.

In the central incident of the novel, Jim is mate of the ship *Patna*, carrying a boat-load of 800 pilgrims across the Indian Ocean. In the middle of the night the *Patna* collides with something, probably a submerged hulk, and is holed. Only a single rusty old iron bulkhead keeps back the water. But it is bound to give way, and then the ship will sink immediately. When that happens, there will be boats enough for half the pilgrims, perhaps, but no time for them to be of the slightest use. As Jim sees it, there is no help, they are as good as dead already: 'before he could shout three words, or make three steps, he would be floundering in a sea whitened awfully by the desperate struggles of human beings, clamorous with the distress of cries for help.' The other four officers decide to abandon ship, and save their own lives at least. Jim knows that it is his duty to stay, until the ship sinks. Firmly resolved, he stands watching as the other four put out the boat. As they are struggling with it, one of the four, who has a weak heart, collapses. The other three manage to get the boat over the side, and clamber into it. They call to the fourth man, desperately, to jump. Jim's mind goes blank, and he himself jumps into the boat. And this one action, which he has neither premeditated nor truly intended, subsequently brings him into total disgrace.

[1] Cf. Alexander Solzhenitsyn: *The First Circle* (Fontana), p. 418.

What is clearly relevant to the ethical assessment of Jim's action is the fact that he has failed in his duty. It is an officer's duty not to abandon ship. But though this may be agreed, its significance may differ according to whether or not one considers it from a utilitarian point of view. Now, of course, in order to understand the point of defining the duty of a ship's officer in this way we have to bring in utilitarian considerations. The point of having skilled officers in charge of a ship is to ensure that the voyage is completed safely, and that when dangers arise the ship is brought through them without loss of life; and this object is bound to be defeated if, in dangerous circumstances, the officers use their position of authority in order to abandon ship. But the question is: is the significance that the officer's duty has *for him* exhausted by its utilitarian rationale? If so, then it is always possible that the demands of duty may be outweighed by other utilitarian considerations. Thus Jim, if he had been a utilitarian, might have estimated that if he stayed on board he would not be able to do anything to help save lives or relieve suffering. There were so few boats and he would have so little time that if he tried to get the pilgrims into them there would be complete pandemonium and the result would be just as bad as if he had done nothing. On the other hand, by abandoning ship he and the other officers would at least make sure that four lives were saved, and would therefore in fact be marginally increasing the total number of survivors. This, from a utilitarian point of view, might be taken as justifying Jim in abandoning ship; and even if such consequences should be thought insufficient to outweigh the demands of duty, nevertheless for the utilitarian it must be conceivable that more extreme consequences of the same kind would at some point do so. But a totally different attitude towards the idea of duty would also be possible. A man might identify himself with the attempt to fulfil his duty. His commitment to the duties of a ship's officer might provide him with his idea of his own moral identity; it might constitute the overall meaning that his life has for him, the whole moral 'point' of his life. In that case the demands of duty would simply not be the kind of thing against which utilitarian consequences could be weighed. The very idea of such a comparison would be inappropriate, since the notion of fulfilling his duty constitutes the whole framework of his moral life. Certainly it would always be appropriate for such a man to consider what would be the respective consequences of abandoning or not abandoning ship. But the consequences can justify him in abandoning ship only if they are such as to make it his *duty* to do something that involves abandoning ship. (For example, suppose that the only conceivable way in which the lives of the passengers can be saved is by someone's rowing the boat to the shore to fetch help, and he is the only man capable of doing this; he might decide that his duty as an officer to save the passengers is more stringent than his duty not to leave the ship.)

This second attitude towards duty is the one that Jim takes in the novel. But his version of it is profoundly ambiguous. What weighs upon him subsequently is the disgrace, the shame, the 'acute consciousness of lost honour'. Now if by this 'loss of honour' were meant simply the loss of other people's good opinion of him, then Jim would be ethically uninteresting. However, what really concerns Jim is not how other people see him but how he sees himself. His sense of dishonour is of the kind that could be expressed by saying that he can no longer face himself, no longer live with himself. Marlow, the narrator of the tale, speaks of 'those struggles of an individual trying to save from the fire his idea of what his moral identity should be' (Penguin edition, p. 66); and when, towards the end of the novel, Jim seems to have salvaged something, Marlow refers to 'the belief in himself snatched from the fire' (p. 206). This might seem to bring Jim's case closer to the kind of thing we have been talking about. We could then attribute to Jim an over-riding concern for his own moral integrity, which outweighs all considerations of mere advantage. His moral ideal is the preservation of a clear conscience. But what Conrad's novel brings out very clearly is that this would in fact be a perversion of the notion of moral integrity. He shows us that the notion cannot *by itself* give a *content* to the ethical life, and that it is, above all, when it is made to do this that it gets distorted into moral egoism. Moral integrity involves fidelity to a moral ideal, and this ideal must be independently specifiable. In Jim's case the ideal is that of devotion to duty; but the ambiguity in Jim's conduct consists in the fact that his aspiration towards moral integrity, instead of being simply an expression of the kind of importance which the fulfilment of his duty has for him and the kind of steadfastness with which he adheres to it, tends to become the pursuit of something over and above it. Since his youth, Jim has been inspired by day-dreams of heroism.

> He saw himself saving people from sinking ships, cutting away masts in a hurricane, swimming through surf with a line ... He confronted savages on tropical shores, quelled mutinies on the high seas, and in a small boat on the ocean kept up the hearts of despairing men—always an example of devotion to duty, and as unflinching as a hero in a book.
>
> (p. 11)

Accordingly he tends to see his failure to stay on board the doomed ship not just as an abandonment of duty but as 'a chance missed' (p. 67). What is significant here is not just the crudity of his youthful vision of heroism, but something more deep rooted. After his failure on the *Patna*, Jim's effort to rehabilitate himself takes the form not of an attempt to strengthen his self-control so that he can devote himself more rigorously to the fulfilment of his duty, but rather of an active search for an opportunity to prove to himself his selfless devotion—just as, previously, he had wanted not simply to do his duty but to be 'an example of devotion to duty'. Marlow says of him: 'He made so much of his disgrace while it is the guilt alone which matters' (p. 136). I implied above that the notions of 'disgrace' and 'honour' can help to illuminate that of 'integrity'; but when the consciousness of disgrace has become something separate from the consciousness of guilt, then correspondingly integrity has become something separate from the identification of oneself with a moral ideal. It has become an autonomous ideal in itself. And when it is pressed into service in this role—when a man sets up for himself a positive 'ethic of integrity'—then it degenerates into a perversion of itself. Thus Marlow speaks of Jim's attitude as 'a sort of sublimated, idealized selfishness' (p. 136) and as an 'exalted egoism' (p. 313).

But this does not mean that moral integrity in its true form is mere moral egoism. Nor, on the other hand, is the concept merely equivalent to that of consistency (which is the kind of account that a utilitarian writer would tend to give of integrity). It is a distinctive moral concept, one which may sometimes conflict with a teleological approach, and which is so deeply embedded in our ethical language as to guarantee that in such a conflict it constitutes a rational position.

5. The Religious Ethic and the Humanistic Ethic

The distinction between 'integrity' and 'utility' may (though it need not) coincide with another distinction. I shall presently attempt to show the connection between the two pairs of opposites, but the second pair must first be independently introduced.

Consider the notion of 'reverence'. The term undoubtedly denotes a recognizable attitude towards the world or towards some particular thing in the world. It is characteristically an attitude towards something which one feels to be greater than oneself, something before which one feels humble. It can be identified with a 'sense of awe', in that it is principally evoked by the encounter with something which is seen as in some sense mysterious, even incomprehensible, beyond man's understanding or beyond man's control. One example would be the Wordsworthian attitude to nature, which is trivialized if it is thought of merely as an aesthetic recognition of beauty in the natural world. One might very well question the appropriateness of Wordsworth's extension of it into a kind of pantheistic philosophy, but the appropriateness of the actual 'sense sublime' is not in itself something that one would question, even if one did not share it. As a second literary example, consider the following passage from Lawrence's *The Rainbow*. Tom Brangwen's wife is in labour; he feels helpless to comfort her or assist her—

> When her pains began afresh, tearing her, he turned aside and could not look . . . He went downstairs, and to the door, outside, lifted his face to the rain, and felt the darkness striking unseen and steadily upon him. The swift, unseen threshing of the night upon him silenced him and he was overcome. He turned away indoors, humbly. There was the infinite world, eternal, unchanging, as well as the world of life.
>
> (p. 81)

The first comment which I want to make is simply that such an attitude is a coherent and intelligible one. When Brangwen recognizes that 'there is the infinite world . . .' this cannot on any grounds be dismissed as an 'irrational belief'; indeed, only in a very limited sense is it a belief at all. Moreover, the attitude of reverence and awe is intelligible not just as an attitude towards some particular thing or situation but as a generalized attitude towards the universe. It is at the heart of any religious view of the world. In describing it as a 'religious' attitude I do not necessarily mean to imply that it is theistic. A theistic view of the world—by which I mean a belief in the existence of a superhuman power which is in some degree anthropomorphic and to which certain definite quasi-human characteristics are attributed—is a theory, a hypothesis, which can be true or false. But in itself the religious attitude, the sense that man is not the most important thing in the universe, and that therefore the world is not to be used by men simply for their own benefit, cannot be true or false, although in any particular case in which a person feels led towards such an attitude it may be possible to point to features of the situation which render it appropriate or inappropriate.

My second point is that such an attitude is not just an emotional response, but a *moral* attitude. Although the attitude of reverence does not entail any specific moral beliefs or principles, there is more than just a contingent relation between it and certain characteristic moral points of view. This may become more apparent if we introduce a new concept—the idea of 'the sacred'. The connection between this and the attitude of reverence is clear; to regard something as sacred is the typical expression of such an attitude towards it. Equally clearly, 'sacred' is a value-word, and to call something 'sacred' is to ascribe a certain kind of value to it. But a non-teleological value. If one regards x as sacred, this does not mean that it is valued as an end, for this is not the kind of value that can be increased by producing more of x. Indeed, it is not the kind of value that can be produced or increased at all. To take a rather crude example, if someone believes that life is sacred we should not expect him to act on this belief by begetting as many children as possible (though the belief might very well mean attaching a special kind of importance to the act of procreation). This does not mean that the religious attitude, the idea that something is sacred, is in itself incompatible with teleological moral beliefs. For example, the sense that life is sacred may find expression in activity devoted to preserving human life by feeding the hungry, healing the sick, and so on, and these are certainly activities which involve the use of techniques, means, to achieve a desired end. But the religious attitude is also a possible basis for characteristically non-teleological moral beliefs. The idea of the sacred is the idea of the unapproachable, that before which one draws back in awe; it indicates a sphere in which it is wrong for man to bend everything to his own will. Thus we may arrive at the moral belief that a man's duty is not to fashion the universe according to his own fancies, but to respect it for what it is. Therefore, the idea of the sacred is a possible basis for an ethic of constraints, of 'Thou shalt nots' directed to ensuring that one does not abuse certain things. For example, it is against such a background that the ethic of pacifism gets its force. The pacifist's claim is not just that the taking of human life is unlikely ever to have consequences which could outweigh the evil done, but that no consequence could conceivably outweigh it. From a teleological point of view, this is absurd. But the pacifist's belief is that the value which human life has is not of a kind to be weighed against alternative desirable states of affairs—it does not, for example, reside in the happiness or satisfaction which the man himself or other people get as a result of his being alive—and this can make sense if we associate such a belief with an attitude of 'reverence for life', a sense that life is sacred. This phrase 'reverence for life' is given very great prominence in the ethical writings of Albert Schweitzer, whose moral beliefs illustrate very well the two ways in which I have said that a sense of the sacredness of life may be expressed. His attitude of reverence for life led him to devote himself to medical work in equatorial Africa, but it also found expression in his refusal even to kill the insects which might be flying around his operating room, a refusal which might appear medically absurd and, from a teleological point of view, completely irrational. As a third example, I instance a broadcast discussion on the ethics of heart-transplant operations.[1] Most of the participants were doctors, whose perspective was a desire to reduce human suffering, and they were somewhat perturbed to hear Malcolm Muggeridge pronounce his disapproval of such operations on the grounds that the human body is made in the image of God, that as such, like all creation, it deserves our deep respect, and that it is therefore not to be pulled apart and patched up like a piece of machinery. It is not necessary for someone who shares Muggeridge's point of view to believe literally that man is made in the image of a

[1] See *The Listener*, 15 February 1968, p. 203.

divine but semi-anthropomorphic Creator; but what is at the bottom of such an attitude is an inclination to view the human body with awe and wonder, and to believe that such a creation is essentially degraded when it is treated as what Muggeridge calls 'a collection of spare parts', simply the means by which men can satisfy their physical needs. Now one can certainly argue that Muggeridge is wrong to take this view of transplant-operations, and one can advance reasons for saying so. One may argue that it is inappropriate to look at such an issue from such a perspective; and one might attempt to justify this by, for instance, suggesting that such a perspective involves an insensitivity to the suffering which can be relieved by heart-transplants, or by pointing to considerations which make the human body other than an appropriate object of reverence.[1] Or one may argue that disapproval of such operations is wrong even within a religious perspective, and that the sacredness of the human body is more appropriately respected if medical skill is used to preserve one human life where otherwise two would be lost. But one cannot dismiss as completely impossible Muggeridge's whole approach, and the kinds of considerations he regards as relevant.

By now the connection between this and the previous section will perhaps be apparent. I made a contrast there between the notion of an ideal *world* and the notion of the good *life* as alternative frameworks for an ethical standpoint. I suggested that each of them is, in itself, equally possible. Now, although the second of the two can therefore stand on its own, the religious attitude can give it a further foundation, by fitting it into a wider context. From a religious point of view, one might well want to say that it is not for man to determine what the world should be like; rather, a man's task is to do the work that falls to his lot, and above all to do it well. Therefore, such an ethic would be particularly likely to emphasize individual integrity rather than successful or effective action. With the religious attitude may go the idea of a man's being 'on trial' in the world (which of course need not imply an anthropomorphic judge), the idea that a man is at every moment answerable for what he is—whereas he is not answerable for the state of the universe.

In 'Whatever the Consequences', Bennett suggests that religious considerations do not present a serious challenge to a teleological theory of ethics. He implies that where a religious point of view is offered as a contrast to a teleological point of view, it amounts to an opting out of moral reasoning altogether. An aside on 'conservatives' who 'say something like "I must obey God's law, and the rest is up to God"' is followed by the comment that 'because this suggests a purely

---

[1] Thus one participant commented that 'if man is made in the image of God, then God must have a great many malformations'.

H

authoritarian basis, it lies beyond my present scope' (p. 93). Now although certain kinds of religious ethic may take the form of an appeal to divine authority, this is not the case with the 'religious attitude' that I have been speaking of. The latter could, in a sense, be seen as a recognition that human authority is not absolute. But this does not mean that it is necessarily an appeal to any alternative (divine) authority. The actual content of such an ethic is not determined by referring to any pre-ordained law. In the sense in which I have been speaking of it, the 'religious ethic' springs from a particular view of the world and of man's relation to it. How this attitude is to express itself in concrete actions is something which the agent still has to decide. Therefore this religious ethic does not involve any diminution of human responsibility, and is in no sense authoritarian.

6. THE ETHIC OF COMMON INTERESTS AND THE ETHIC OF OBLIGATIONS

The concept of 'the sacred' may also help to elucidate another ethical position—the morality of 'obligations'. In turning to this, we finally arrive at the classical opposition between teleological and deontological ethics. The traditional objections to utilitarianism have largely been lodged on the grounds that it cannot account for the normally-accepted notion of 'obligations'. This in itself is an insufficient objection, since it is by no means clear that utilitarianism is *intended* to account for it. The utilitarian theory is most plausibly presented as providing a logic-ally-derived foundation for ethics, which can serve as a *corrective* to our normally-accepted notions. However, most utilitarian writers have in fact taken up the challenge and tried to show that there is no incom-patibility between utilitarianism and the normal ethical concept of obligations. They have not been very successful. I do not want to review here the long history of this controversy.[1] My own view, which I will not attempt to justify, is that act-utilitarianism can never provide grounds for seeing anything *distinctive* in the notion of 'obligations' and thus for making anything more than a peripheral distinction between statements of the form 'A has an obligation to do x' and statements of the entirely general form 'A is justified in doing x'. This means, for example, that in attempting to explain an obligation to keep a promise, a utilitarian may provide all sorts of reasons why one should keep the promise, but can never allow simply that one has an obligation *because one has promised*. And rule-utilitarianism is even less successful, for every formulation of it either collapses into act-utilitarianism or ceases to be genuinely utilitarian. The one utilitarian formulation that does offer a real

---

[1] The most recent statement of the anti-utilitarian case, together with a summary of the literature, is David Lyons' book, *Forms and Limits of Utilitarianism*.

possibility is what has been called 'contract-utilitarianism'.[1] The 'social contract' tradition and the utilitarian tradition have been closely linked, most obviously through the person of Hobbes, and it does seem to me that the former theory presupposes the latter (though not necessarily vice versa—Bentham was an outspoken opponent of the social contract theory). Now if the social contract theory is taken to assert that all obligations are created by promises, it is plainly false. But I believe that the notion of promising is best taken as a paradigm, rather than a necessary condition, of the creation of obligations. The real point of the theory is the idea that obligations are essentially things which one voluntarily enters into, places oneself under. It is not necessarily the case that the carrying out of any particular obligation is always justified by being conducive to the interests or satisfactions of oneself or others; but men agree (tacitly or explicitly) to regard themselves as bound by obligations to one another because it is in their interests to live together on these terms. The obligations are created by this tacit or explicit agreement, by one's voluntarily consenting to participate in and accept the conventions of a society. The connection between obligations and the utilitarian justification is thus at one remove. Utilitarian considerations explain the point of such obligations, and the advantage of entering into them; they do not necessarily justify each particular case of having an obligation to do something, for what justifies each particular case is the fact that *one is already bound* by the obligation. At the heart of contract-utilitarianism, then, is a certain view of social relationships: men consent to be bound by obligations and to impose limits on their freedom because it is in their mutual interests to do so. The model of society which is at work here is that of a cooperative enterprise, a 'joint-stock company'; and although this is not the only way in which men are related to one another within a society, it is claimed to be the only way that is relevant to the concept of obligation.

In contrast to both act-utilitarianism and rule-utilitarianism, this does seem to me to be a viable teleological account of obligation. It does justice both to the distinctive nature of the notion of obligation and to the idea that considerations of obligation are ultimately subordinate to considerations of interest and want-satisfaction. I believe that it is a rational ethic (though some philosophers have denied this) and that it in fact corresponds on the theoretical level to the attitude that many people adopt in practice to social obligations. But it is not the only rational view. The basic difference between the teleological and the deontological view of obligations is that the former makes obligations subordinate to considerations of interest and want-satisfaction whereas the latter makes them primary and independent. Against the so-called 'unattached ought' of deontological obligations it has been argued that

[1] See R. Grice: *The Grounds of Moral Judgements.*

obligations attach always to a particular social role, and therefore require to be justified by reference to the usefulness of the particular role within the society.[1] Now certainly if the concept of obligations is limited to those obligations imposed by a particular social order, then it is both logically and ethically reprehensible to refuse to allow the possibility of raising questions either of the value of the social order itself or of the fulfilment of one's obligations within it. If this is what the deontologist is claiming, he is rightly cast in the role of one who advocates unquestioning obedience to authority. But insofar as the deontologist claims that obligations are primary, he is *ipso facto* claiming that they are prior to any particular social order. The deontological view, properly interpreted, is one which, instead of seeing men as first living together in a society, and consequently having to recognize certain obligations to one another in order to meet the needs which arise from their living together, claims rather that the relations in which a man stands to other human beings can themselves only be described in terms of the concept of obligation. It can be plausibly claimed that obligations are prior to interests only if the notion of obligations is used not to indicate a set of rules but to indicate the way in which one sees oneself as related to other human beings. It is a measure of the kind of importance that one attaches to the existence of other human individuals. Understood as a view of human social relations, the ethic of obligations is no less rational or plausible than any other view. And if it is understood in this way, there can be no possibility of, and no necessity for, deriving the statement that one has an obligation to every other human being from any other principle or giving it any further justification. To support such a statement one can only appeal to how one sees other people.

The 'ethic of obligations' stems from the kind of attitude towards inter-personal relations which is also expressed by saying that the human individual has an absolute value, or that the human individual is sacred. Something of the difference between this and a teleological view of human relationships is stated in the following example. In Koestler's novel, *Darkness at Noon*, Rubashov, an 'old guard' revolutionary, has been arrested in one of the Stalinist purges, and is being interrogated by Ivanov, who says to him:

> There are only two conceptions of human ethics, and they are at opposite poles. One of them is Christian and humane, and declares the individual to be sacrosanct, and asserts that the rules of arithmetic are not to be applied to human units. The other starts from the basic principle that a collective aim justifies all means, and not only allows,

[1] Cf. MacIntyre in *A Short History of Ethics*, pp. 84–7, 93–4, 172–3, 196–7, et passim.

but demands, that the individual should in every way be subordinated
and sacrificed to the community.

(p. 128)

The second of the two ethics is presented rather unfairly. It is not
necessarily inhumane, not necessarily a matter of 'subordinating and
sacrificing' the individual to an abstract 'community', but simply of
aiming at the greatest happiness of the greatest number. The difference
between the two ethics, however, is aptly summed up when the former
is said to assert that 'the rules of arithmetic are not to be applied to
human units'. This is what Rubashov himself comes to feel at the end
of the book. He reflects on the fact that the purpose of the revolution
is to abolish senseless suffering, and that this has turned out to be
possible only at the price of a temporary enormous increase in suffering.

So the question now ran: Was such an operation justified? Obviously
it was, if one spoke in the abstract of 'mankind'—but applied to 'man'
in the singular, the real human being of bone and flesh and blood, the
principle led to absurdity.

(p. 202)

Neither of these viewpoints—that of the good of mankind and that of
the sacrosanctity of the individual—is any more or less rational than the
other. One's adherence to the one or the other is determined—as it is
for Rubashov—simply by what is significant in one's own experience.

The example of Rubashov also makes it clear in what way the ethic
of 'absolute obligation towards every human individual' is anti-
teleological. Detailing the 'temporary increase in suffering' which is
required by the attempt to eliminate the senseless suffering of future
generations, Rubashov says:

We have been so consequent, that in the interests of a just distribution
of land we deliberately let die of starvation about five million farmers
and their families in one year. So consequent were we in the liberation
of human beings from the shackles of industrial exploitation that we
sent about ten million people to do forced labour in the Arctic
regions and the jungles of the east, under conditions similar to those
of antique galley-slaves . . . Acting consequently in the interests of
coming generations, we have laid such terrible privations on the
present one that its average length of life is shortened by a quarter.
In order to defend the existence of the country, we have had to take
exceptional measures and make transition-stage laws, which are in
every point contrary to the aims of the Revolution. The people's
standard of life is lower than it was before the Revolution; the labour

conditions are harder, the discipline is more inhuman ... our leader-worship is more Byzantine than that of the reactionary dictatorships ... We whip the groaning masses of the country towards a theoretical future happiness, which only we can see ... These are the consequences of your consequentialness.

(pp. 129–30)

The real ethical dilemma arises here if we suppose the estimation of consequences to be accurate, and that the aimed-for happiness of future generations really can be achieved by these and only these means. In that case there can be no doubt that, if these political actions are to be evaluated solely by reference to the total sum of consequent happiness and suffering, they are in fact justified. The point of this example is that the sufferings imposed on the present generation are of precisely the same kind as those which are to be for the first time abolished for countless future generations. Therefore, from the very fact that one generation is to be set against innumerable others, it follows that the total decrease in suffering will far outweigh the temporary increase. This would be the teleological view. But if one regards oneself as bound by an absolute obligation to each of one's fellow human beings, if one regards every human individual as inviolable and sacrosanct, then one will not regard oneself as justified in using them for the sake of however exalted an aim, even if it be the happiness of innumerable other people. One easily falls into Kantian language here: one's obligation to another human being demands an absolute respect for the autonomy of that person, and therefore one is debarred from seeing other persons as units to be added or subtracted in an equation of potential happiness, since this is to treat them as mere means. But Kant himself confuses the matter when he sets in opposition to the notion of 'treating persons as means' that of 'treating them as ends'. For in reality this is simply the other side of the same coin. What is characteristic of the utilitarian conception of human relations is that it does involve seeing other persons as, at most, 'ends'—that is to say, as possible units of happiness or satisfaction to be brought about. The real contrast is between this and seeing other people as neither ends nor means. To suggest that the relation in which one stands to other people is to be measured solely by one's tendency to regard or disregard their interests, to make them happy or unhappy, indicates an extreme impoverishment of the vocabulary of human relationships—albeit an impoverishment which is indeed taking place within our own society.

7. The Complexity of Ethical Concepts

The effect of this chapter has been not only to show how drastically over-simplified is the utilitarian account of ethics, but also to complicate the picture which we ourselves presented in chapter 3. The idea which emerged there was that of a set of norms embodied in the language of a society. We can now see more clearly that our own language, at any rate, embodies not just one but a number of rational ethical viewpoints. There is no simple one-to-one correlation between a particular society and a particular ethic. At the same time it is important that the different ethics which we have been looking at are all situated within a single normative language. Could we, indeed, see them as 'alternative' ways of life if this were not the case? It would seem that, although a particular language does not impose a particular ethic, it does impose a context within which there can be intelligible ethical disagreement. There are, then, important questions concerning the relations between ethical points of view and social units, and we shall have to devote some attention to these questions in our remaining chapters.

The present chapter has also served to give further content to the concept of an ethical 'system' which we employed in chapter 3. Faced with the difficulty of how to identify what can count as 'normative concepts', we suggested that a possible test might be their belonging to an ethical system. We have now encountered some examples of such systems. I certainly do not wish to imply that I have exhaustively enumerated all possible ethical systems; any attempt to offer a finite list would indeed involve a fundamental misunderstanding. But, having provided ourselves with some examples, we are at any rate in a better position to consider whether any general remarks can be made about the nature of an ethical system as such. To this problem also we shall return.

PART III

Counter-Objections

5. Varieties of Ethical Relativism

In this last third of the book I want to consider some criticisms that might be made of my argument in chapter 3. It might be thought that the position sketched in that chapter, by relating practical rationality to social norms, begs a number of substantive ethical questions: that it makes the only rational ethical position one of devotion to society and its values; that it rules out *a priori* the possibility of ever rationally dissenting from or changing the values and norms of a society; and that it makes ethical values completely relative to a particular society, depriving them of any absolute status. These criticisms might appear particularly appropriate from a utilitarian point of view, for it could be said that the utilitarian principle provides a criterion for assessing the value of devotion to any particular society instead of giving it a complete and unquestionable value; that it provides a criterion for judging the current values of a society and determining in what ways they need to be developed or changed; and that, although men's wants may vary from society to society, the actual notion of want-satisfaction or happiness constitutes an absolute standard applicable to any human society, so that rational evaluative judgements can be made which transcend any particular community. My aim will be to show that these criticisms all rest on misinterpretations of the view I am defending.

1. DURKHEIM ON 'COMMITMENT TO THE GROUP'

I shall begin this chapter by attempting to clarify the sense in which rationality is necessarily 'social'. A convenient way of doing this will be by means of a comparison with a position which is in many ways similar but also exhibits important differences. I have in mind Durkheim's account of the nature of morality and its connection with social solidarity, as presented in the first part of his lectures on *Moral Education* and in his lecture on *The Determination of Moral Facts*. The essence of this argument is as follows:

1. Moral conduct is characteristically *regular*, rule-guided. But this is not just the regularity of habit; the rule is seen as imposed from

outside, by *authority*. These two ideas, regularity and authority, coalesce in the conception of *discipline*, which is, therefore, the *first element* of morality.

2a. All human objectives are either *personal* (those which concern the agent himself) or *impersonal* (those which concern something other than the agent). Behaviour aimed at personal objectives is universally regarded as having no moral value. Therefore morally valuable behaviour must be directed at impersonal ends. What are these impersonal ends? Not the interests of some other person, for another person is not so different from myself as to be in a generically different category, possessing moral value where I have none. Not the interests of a plurality of other individuals, for the sum of zeros is still zero. Therefore the impersonal goals of moral action must be supra-individual; but moral action must serve some living, sentient being; now, this supra-individual sentient being can only be society, i.e. any human group (if we set aside the hypothesis of a divine being). We have thus proved incidentally, by an argument similar to Kant's argument for the existence of God, that society must be more than a collection of individuals, since without this postulate morality is unintelligible. This can also be proved on independent grounds.

2b. But society, as well as being beyond the individual, must also have some organic connection with the individual, if it is to inspire moral action. This connection does exist. For the individual is not truly himself unless he is involved in society. Whatever is best in us comes from society. Language is social in the highest degree; and language is not just a system of words, but implies a mentality, a system of ideas; principal among these are the ideas of religion and science, both of which are social institutions. Thus, just as our physical organism gets its nourishment outside itself, so our mental organism feeds itself on ideas, sentiments and practices that come to us from society. Egoism is therefore self-contradictory. In order to realize ourselves, we must put ourselves in touch with that source of our mental and moral life, viz. society; *commitment to the group* is the moral duty par excellence, and this constitutes the *second element* of morality.

3. These two elements are two aspects of the same single reality. For, what gives moral rules their authority? The considerations which have just shown that morality is made *for* society, show also that it is made *by* society. It is impossible for the individual to be the author of morality. This is confirmed by the fact that morality varies from society to society; history shows that the morality of each people is directly related to its social structure. Society is well fitted to produce in us a sense of its authority, for it infinitely surpasses the individual not only in possessing incomparably greater power but in

being the source of that intellectual and moral life to which we turn to nourish our thought and morality. It also possesses the necessary aura of mystery, since it is never completely comprehensible to us. The two elements of morality are thus two aspects of its relation to society: as discipline, society commands us; as attachment to the group, society attracts us, constituting an ideal to be realized. And this explains the distinction traditionally made by moralists between the good and the necessary.[1]

Durkheim is in effect making a two-fold claim: that society is both 'the source and the end of morality' (*Sociology and Philosophy*, p. 59). And these two aspects—society as the source of morality, and society as the end of morality—are, for Durkheim, very closely connected. He believes that the considerations which support the one claim support also the other. It is this, above all, that I want to deny.

Durkheim's arguments in 2b and 3 to the effect that society is the source of morality come closest to my own position. What is particularly important is that he emphasizes the role of language in this respect. It is essential to be clear about what this role is. It is not simply a causal role; not just that without language we could never express our moral judgements or formulate our moral beliefs. Durkheim sometimes seems to be in danger of reducing his thesis to a very obvious claim of this kind, as when he says, for example, that 'without language, essentially a social thing, general or abstract ideas are practically impossible' (*Sociology and Philosophy*, p. 55). In discussing certain other aspects of intellectual life, Durkheim describes their relation to society in terms which are almost explicitly causal. His claim concerning the social origin of science, for example, is that the separating-off of science from religion 'occurred because society, as it became more complex, made such a development imperative'. This is extended into a general theory concerning not just our intellectual life but all our other faculties, all those activities which endow our life with value: 'If we have an ever more compelling need for various activities, if we are less and less satisfied with the rather slow and dull life that man leads in less developed societies, it is because our society requires more and more intensive labours and more and more industry, so that it has become habitual, and, through time, habit has become a need' (*Moral Education*, p. 70). But I think that we can also find in Durkheim's argument indications of a more subtle view of the inter-relationship of society, language and morality. He says of language that it is 'not merely a system of words; each language implies a particular mentality, that of the society which

---

[1] The numbering of these paragraphs is my own. Roughly speaking, paragraph 1 corresponds to Chapter 2 of *Moral Education*, paragraph 2a to Chapter 4, paragraph 2b to Chapter 5, and paragraph 3 to Chapter 6.

speaks it . . . and it is this mentality which provides the foundation for individual mentality' (*Moral Education*, p. 69). This comes very close to the sort of thing which I want to say—that our language encapsulates standards determining what can count as rational moral discourse.

Durkheim's failure to make this vitally important distinction between the two differing kinds of inter-relationship between language and morality leads directly to a corresponding ambivalence in his account of the relation between society and the individual. On the one hand, passages such as the following suggest a view which I would endorse:

> Society . . . is outside us and envelops us, but it is also in us and is everywhere an aspect of our nature. We are fused with it. Just as our physical organism gets its nourishment outside itself, so our mental organism feeds itself on ideas, sentiments, and practices that come to us from society.
>
> (*Moral Education*, p. 71)

This is consonant with the view which I have proposed, but not with a purely causal account of the relation between society and mental or moral life. It implies that the 'ideas, sentiments and practices' which provide the content of our mental and moral life are *necessarily* social in origin; thus the very possibility of there being a moral concept of 'justice', for example, is *inconceivable* without public agreement in the use of the concept and in the understanding of its normative force. On the other hand, Durkheim seems to imply elsewhere that it is a purely contingent matter whether any particular instance of human activity has this social character or not. To support the claim that 'the individual . . . is not truly himself, he does not fully realize his own nature, except on the condition that he is involved in society', Durkheim refers to the fact that when society loses its power of promoting the identification of individual wills with itself, when the individual dissociates himself from collective goals in order to seek only his own interests, the suicide rates go up (*Moral Education*, p. 68). Clearly the possibilities of 'being involved in society' and 'not being involved in society' here mark a totally different distinction—a distinction between two different kinds of activity in which men actually engage. The point of the previous distinction between being involved and not being involved in society was to bring out the fact that the meaning which attaches to *any* human action is *necessarily* a social meaning; and therefore this would be equally true not only of the individual who identifies himself with the pursuit of collective goals but also of the individual who seeks only his own interest. Durkheim's failure to resolve (or even recognize) this ambiguity between different senses of 'being involved in society' is directly responsible for the inadequacy of his transition from the claim that 'society is the source of morality' to the claim that 'society is the end of morality'.

Durkheim attempts this transition in part 2b of the argument: the individual is not truly himself unless he is involved in society, ... therefore commitment to the group is the moral duty par excellence. Now, this is not just an attempt to show that society, since it is so important for the individual and so enriches his life, is worthy of his devotion. A much stronger claim than this is being made. Durkheim seems to be suggesting that individualism, a failure to commit oneself to the group, is in some way self-contradictory, since all the important human activities are necessarily social. This emerges quite clearly from the following passage:

> The self-centred person, the egoist, ... goes contrary to nature ... He lives as though he were a whole, one who has in himself his raison d'être and who is sufficient unto himself. But this is an impossibility, a contradiction in terms. In vain do we sever—or attempt to sever— the bonds that connect us to others. We find ourselves unable to do so. We cling necessarily to the milieu surrounding us. ... One can even say that the absolute egoist is an unrealizable abstraction. In order to live a purely egoistic life we would have to strip away our social nature, which is quite as impossible as escaping our shadows. All we can do is to approximate more or less to this abstractly conceived limit.
>
> (*Moral Education*, pp. 71f.)

This kind of move in moral philosophy is by no means uncommon. We can describe it as an attempt to derive a substantive moral position from a definition of the necessary nature of morality. I do not wish to imply that such a move is impossible; but, very often, it trades upon an ambiguity in the use of some term or set of terms, which is used in one sense in the statement of analytic truths about morality, and in another sense in the making of substantive moral claims. An error of this kind lies at the heart of Durkheim's argument.

Consider the case of a hermit who lives in complete physical isolation. He has chosen this way of life because it has a particular meaning for him; he sees it, perhaps, as a rejection of worldly temptations for the sake of an intimate communion with God. Now, the very possibility of his seeing his life in this way, or in any other way, is dependent upon the availability to him of a shared culture and a shared language. This is as true of him as it is of any other rational agent. And therefore, of course, in the sense in which any rational agent is necessarily involved in some pattern of social life, the hermit himself is so involved. In choosing solitude he has not made a choice which is in any way self-contradictory.

And yet, in the sense in which Durkheim understands 'social solidarity' and 'commitment to the group', these are values which the hermit has repudiated. According to Durkheim, 'the only question that a man can ask is not whether he can live outside society, but in what society he wishes to live' (*Sociology and Philosophy*, p. 55). But in the most natural sense of the words, a hermit is precisely a man who has chosen to live outside society.

What is true of the hermit is true also of the egoist. How would the egoist describe his way of life? He might say, for example: 'It's every man for himself in this world. If you don't look after yourself, nobody else will. If you go around spending all your time worrying about other people's troubles and trying to help them out, you soon find yourself being exploited and made use of. That's a mug's game. So I'm out for all I can get. I'll do somebody else a good turn if I think there's something in it for me. But I keep my eyes open; no one is going to make a fool of me.' This is a perfectly rational description—indeed, it is in a sense a perfectly rational justification—of a particular way of life. As such it invokes shared concepts and shared patterns of thinking, just as does the advocacy of any other way of life. Three points in particular can be stressed:

(a) The very existence of the concept of self-interest is possible only within a public language; it is not just 'given'. An animal which instinctively acts in a way which ensures its self-preservation is not acting out of self-interest. To categorize a mode of behaviour as 'self-interested' is to see it as attaching to one among a number of possible ways of life; it is to give it a meaning.

(b) One can give reasons for being an egoist to the same extent as one can give reasons in support of any other way of life. And what I have said about the relation between reasons and the normative concepts of our public language applies equally in this case.

(c) The notion of egoism has to be given a *content*, and this content is provided by the particular culture. What is to count as 'self-interest', 'benefit', 'gain', etc.? The answer is not self-evident; it is necessarily related to a particular scheme of values.

The upshot of all this is that the egoist, like the hermit, is no less involved in a social existence, in the sense in which any rational human existence is necessarily a social existence. There is nothing irrational about egoism; it is not an 'impossibility', or a 'contradiction in terms', or an 'unrealizable abstraction'. In making it appear as such, Durkheim is trading on the ambiguity of the notion of 'being involved in society'. If this is a necessary characterization of rational action, then it applies equally to the egoist. If it is a contingent possibility, then it is one which the egoist rejects, but in that case he does so without self-contradiction. Notice also, in this connection, the unusual way in which Durkheim characterizes egoism. The egoist is, according to Durkheim, one who believes that he 'has in himself his raison d'être and . . . is sufficient unto himself', who attempts to sever the bonds that connect him to others, and who has to strip away his social nature. If this were really what egoism amounted to, then the claim that it is a contradiction in terms would be slightly more plausible. But the egoist does not act as though he were sufficient unto himself; on the contrary, what is absolutely typical of him is that he makes use of other people. What he effectively denies is not the existence of other people, but the importance of their interests.

I would add that there are a great many other possible attitudes to society between the extremes of egoism and commitment to the group. Rejection of existing society and existing social ties, and devotion to the cause of creating a society which would be worthy of the individual's commitment; solidarity with a particular class or group within society, perhaps in opposition to the rest of society; a contempt for contemporary social life and a consequent commitment to the values of intimate personal relationships—these are some of the possibilities. No one of them is a 'commitment to the group' of the kind that Durkheim advocates. But none of them is, on that account, incoherent. Like egoism, each of them is a meaningful way of life, and therefore in the necessary sense socially meaningful.

These are my reasons for saying that the considerations which support the claim that society is the source of morality cannot also be made to support the claim that society is the end of morality. A possible objection might be made here. I have said that the ambiguity of the notion of 'being involved in society', which enables Durkheim to say both that society is the source of morality and that society is the end of morality, is already present in the very arguments for the claim that society is the source of morality (see above pp. 115–16). It might be objected, therefore, that the sense in which Durkheim thinks that society is the source of morality is in fact precisely parallel to the sense in which he thinks that society is the end of morality, and has nothing to do with the thesis which I am trying to put forward and which I have read into his argument. Perhaps the claim that society is the source of morality *is* just a contingent causal claim—for example, that a man cannot properly feel the force and authority of moral demands unless he is, in the strong sense, fully committed to the group, i.e. to society as a specific political institution or set of institutions, as a territorial entity, etc. Here I can only repeat that Durkheim *is* ambiguous—that there *are* indications in Durkheim of the kind of connection I want to make between social existence and ethical rationality, and that, to the extent that Durkheim makes it, his argument is important.

Section 2a of my summary of Durkheim constitutes an independent argument for the claim that society is the end of morality. As such, it

I

must also be taken into account. A crucial *non sequitur* in this particular argument is the suggestion that, since action aimed at the agent's self-interest has no moral value, action aimed at the interests of some person other than the agent can have no moral value either, because there is no significant difference between any two human beings which could account for the possession of moral value by one and not the other. Part of the trouble here is Durkheim's preoccupation with ends. One can see the plausibility of saying that there is no morally significant difference between the benefit of one human individual and that of another. But between the two kinds of *action* there is all the difference in the world. I think it could reasonably be suggested that the morally significant difference between the two kinds of action just *is* that the one is self-interested and the other is altruistic. What greater difference could there be?

There is also a more general point to be made in connection with section 2a, quite apart from the detail of the argument. It may be that the distinction between moral and non-moral action is linked in some way with the distinction between individual ends and social ends. For my own part, I think that Durkheim's scheme is much too simplistic, just as I think that the more common identification of the moral/non-moral distinction with the self-interest/altruism distinction is equally a glib over-simplification of a highly complex concept. However, a case could be made for Durkheim's identification. But the point is that this would simply be a characterization of the concept of 'morality', whereas the case that I want to make concerns the necessarily social nature not just of moral action but of any rational action. This is equally true of section 2b of Durkheim's own argument, which is intended to show not just that society is the source of morality but that it is the source of our mental life in general, of all our 'ideas, sentiments and practices'. And it does not follow from *this* that either moral action or rational action in general is bound to be aimed at social ends.

The ethic of 'commitment to the group' is also fostered by section 3 of Durkheim's argument. Durkheim there talks about the nature of moral 'authority', and seeks to show that this conception can be explained so long as we recognize that the source of moral demands is society. The following passage is particularly important:

> Even that element of mystery that seems inherent in all conceptions of authority is not lacking in the feeling we have for society. . . . We constantly have the impression of being surrounded by a host of things in the course of happening whose nature escapes us. All sorts of forces move themselves about, encounter one another, collide . . . yet we go without seeing them until that time when some impressive culmination provides a glimpse of a hidden and mysterious event

which has occurred under our noses. . . . There is above all one fact that constantly re-enforces this feeling: it is the pressure which society continually exerts upon us. . . . Whenever we deliberate as to how we should act, there is a voice that speaks to us, saying: that is your duty. . . . Because it speaks to us in an imperative tone we certainly feel that it must come from some being superior to us. That is why, in order to explain this mysterious voice that does not speak with a human accent, people imagine it to be connected with transcendent personalities above and beyond man. . . . It is our task to divest this conception of the mythical forms in which it has been shrouded . . ., and to grasp the reality beneath the symbolism. This reality is society. . . . When our conscience speaks, it is society speaking within us. The tone with which it speaks is the best demonstration of its remarkable authority.

(Moral Education, pp. 89–90)

It is easy to see how, once this account is accepted of the manner in which society is felt to be the source of morality, it becomes plausible to suggest that, to the extent that we are moral agents, our relation to society is necessarily that of 'servants and instruments' to a 'superior end' *(Sociology and Philosophy,* p. 53). Durkheim's account calls for a nice assessment. On the one hand, it is important to stress the objectivity of values, the fact that they are not just created by the will of the individual. In this sense it is true to say as Durkheim so often does that 'social facts' are not just the sum of facts about the behaviour of individuals. And we can legitimately say also that the social status of values is what gives them their 'authority'. On the other hand, the conception of society as a complex of alien forces set over against men is one that ought to be resisted. It seems to me to be an extrapolation from particular, purely contingent, kinds of social organization. At one point Durkheim says:

. . . we have viewed morality as a system of rules, external to the individual, which impose themselves on him from outside. . . . It is not we, in effect, who create morality. Doubtless, since we constitute part of the society that elaborates it, in a sense each of us collaborates in the development giving rise to morality. But the part played by each generation in the evolution of morality is quite restricted. The morality of our time is fixed in its essentials from the moment of our birth; the changes it undergoes during the course of an individual's life—those in which we can share—are infinitely limited. . . . Furthermore, each of us is only one among innumerable units who collaborate in such a change.

(Moral Education, p. 107)

It is notable that the viewpoint here is that of 'the individual'; the possibility of collective control by men of their social life, including the collective re-assessment of their ethical values, is not considered, or at least is not thought relevant. This restriction is, in effect, a restriction to the consideration only of one particular and limited type of society. In a society where human action is primarily individual action, it is natural that the actions of other individuals, and hence the practices of the society as a whole, should be seen as alien, as empirically given. And therefore, in turn, it is natural that Durkheim should conclude that

> of all that which transpires in the vast moral milieu constituted by a great society like ours, amidst the infinite number of actions and reactions reciprocally involving millions of social units at each instant of time, we sense only the few repercussions that reach our limited personal spheres. . . . All that makes up the very substance and continuity of collective life—all this is beyond our purview, all this escapes us.
>
> (*Moral Education*, p. 86)

It then seems to follow that, if society is the source of morality, we can act morally only by putting ourselves in touch with an external force, committing ourselves to that which is outside us and dominates us—'the group'. Of course I do not mean to counterpose any suggestion that, once we postulate collective action, we can talk of men creating ethical values *ex nihilo*. As I have already mentioned, we still have to emphasize the notions of 'objectivity' and 'authority'. At the same time, however, we have to remember that the norms of a society are ultimately constituted by the practices of actual human beings. By refusing to limit ourselves to Durkheim's initial preconceptions, we can see the relation of men to society and to 'social facts' as something other than that of 'servants and instruments', and consequently we can see the possibility of being involved in a social form of life without the necessity of being 'committed to the group'.

What Durkheim says about authority and 'mystery' is connected with what he says elsewhere about ethical relativism (*Moral Education*, pp. 86ff.) and about the possibility of ethical criticism and change (*Sociology and Philosophy*, pp. 59–62). These are both topics which I am bound to consider also in relation to my own position. I shall deal with the second in my next chapter. At this point I want to use Durkheim's comments as a way of leading into a general discussion of the first topic, that of ethical relativism. The connection of ethical relativism with my suggestions about the nature of ethical rationality is, I imagine, obvious enough. I have argued that standards of rationality are provided by the concepts and norms of a particular society or culture. Given a plurality of different cultures, it seems to follow that what is right in one culture may be wrong in another. I shall argue that a certain form of cultural relativism, when stated with all the necessary reservations, does follow from my position, and that there is nothing objectionable about this. At the same time I shall disclaim any allegiance to any of the various over-simplified and even naïve forms in which relativism has often been propounded.

2. THE CONCEPT OF 'SOCIAL STRUCTURE'

Durkheim's own remarks are concerned with the relation of morality to social structure. He believes it to be a matter of historical fact that 'morality varies from society to society. . . . That of Greek and Roman cities is not ours, just as that of primitive tribes is not the morality of the city.' He quite rightly argues that this variation is not to be explained as 'the result of errors', as though 'Roman morality was different from ours . . . because human intelligence was then veiled and obscured by all kinds of prejudices and superstitions since erased.' But he then goes on to say:

> If there is one fact that history has irrefutably demonstrated it is that the morality of each people is directly related to the social structure of the people practising it. . . . Given the general character of the morality observed in a given society . . . , one can infer the nature of that society, the elements of its structure and the way it is organized. Tell me the marriage patterns, the morals dominating family life, and I will tell you the principal characteristics of its organization. The notion that the Romans could have practised a different morality is really an historical absurdity. . . . Suppose that through some miracle they opened themselves to ideas such as those that are the basis for our present-day morality: Roman society could not have survived. . . . Each social type has the morality necessary to it. . . . A moral system is built up by the same society whose structure is thus faithfully reflected in it.
>
> (*Moral Education*, p. 87)

This is a common way of describing the relation between moral beliefs and social life. What I wish to criticize in Durkheim's formulation is the suggestion that a relation of this kind is a necessary one; for this means, in effect, that the moral ideas of a society have no independent status, but are always dependent upon and relative to the social structure of that society. Social structure is then seen as an aspect of social reality which has a special privileged status, above criticism. The very term 'structure' encourages the idea that this is some kind of objective framework within which men act and which is to be accepted by them as something given, a part of the natural order. And if morality is regarded as a reflection of it, it is easy to see how this strengthens Durkheim's view that society, as an independent reality, imposes a morality upon its members.

It is therefore important to stress that social structure is itself constituted by particular patterns of behaviour within a society. Take Durkheim's own example: as instances of the morality of a society he refers to 'the marriage patterns, the morals dominating family life', and suggests that these reflect the structure of the society. But it could equally well be claimed that they *are* an element in the structure of the society. Is the distinction between monogamy and polygamy, for example, a distinction between two different moralities or between two different kinds of social structure? And how about the distinction between matriarchy and patriarchy? Either account of it is equally valid. And just as these instances of moral ideas can also be seen as elements of a social structure, so too a social structure can be seen also as a complex of ways of acting and of evaluating actions. Durkheim does not specify here what he would regard as instances of social structure; but from his treatment of the subject elsewhere I think we may take it that he would regard the 'division of labour' as a prime example. Now it is surely a truism that the concept of the 'division of labour' functions as a description of certain ways in which men act—not of their moral behaviour, certainly, but at any rate of their economic behaviour. If we wanted a primitive model by which to illustrate the notion of division of labour, we might describe a hypothetical society where, instead of each man dividing his time between hunting, fishing, and tilling the soil, some men are hunters, others are fishermen, and others are farmers, and they therefore exchange with one another the products of their labour. In other words, in order to elucidate the nature of this social structure we describe how men act, what their patterns of behaviour are. My purpose in emphasizing this truism is to bring out the fact that social structure cannot be given a privileged status as the determinant of the evaluative concepts of a society and, therefore, as itself immune from evaluation and criticism. Of course, the concept of social structure is not otiose. Not every aspect of men's behaviour in a society goes to make up that society's structure, and the distinction between social structure and other kinds of behavioural patterns is important. But at the same time we have to bear in mind that the social structure is just as liable to regulation and change by reference to our evaluative concepts as are those activities which take the social structure for granted. It is notable that the structure of a society cannot even be fully described and understood without bringing in the evaluative concepts of the society. Durkheim, for example, in giving an account of the division of labour, makes great use of the concept of 'organic solidarity', and something like this is clearly necessary in order to distinguish between a mere multiplicity of human beings engaged in various different kinds of work, and a *community* based on the division of labour. But the term seems to me to be very clearly an evaluative one, and this in its very essence, not just because most people happen to approve of solidarity. It immediately brings in notions of men's duties and obligations to one another, and considerations of justice and fairness, and so on. Hence we can see how it is quite natural both that the morality of a society should provide us with an indication of its social structure, and that changes in the social structure should necessitate changes in the morality. But this is only to say that the activities and evaluations of men in a particular society constitute a meaningful whole, not that the social structure is always and necessarily the determinant of everything else.

Now, of course, it *may* happen that changes take place in the social structure which are not consciously willed by the members of the society, and which then necessitate a further adaptation in the form of changes in men's ethical assumptions. But this is always a contingent historical phenomenon, which, in any particular case, calls for an explanation. This is very relevant to the interpretation of Marxism, which may therefore serve as an illustration of my general point. Marxism has often been interpreted as a simple economic determinism. On this interpretation, it would be necessarily true of any historical epoch and any society that its moral and intellectual values, its political and legal institutions, and so on, would all be reflections of an under-lying economic class structure, which could itself be changed only by the pressure of economic forces. But, according to what I have said above, this 'class structure' and these 'economic forces' are themselves constituted only by certain forms of human activity and can therefore in principle be consciously evaluated and changed, and in that case it is incumbent upon Marxism to explain why, in certain historically specific societies, the economic structure exercises a predominance over other aspects of social life, determining them without being itself deter-mined by them. It is at this point, I would suggest, that the Hegelian concepts of 'reification' and 'alienation', and their connection with the economic division of labour, acquire a crucial significance within Marxist theory. Through them, Marx is able to argue that in a class society the products of human labour take on the appearance of some-thing alien which rules men instead of being ruled by them. This is true not only of the product of the individual worker's activity, but also of the economic structure itself; this too is a product of human action, but 'the social relations between men assume in their eyes the fantastic form of a relation between things'. And thus it is possible to explain how in such a society the economic structure exercises a determining influence on other aspects of human life without being itself fashioned and formed in accordance with men's conscious purposes and values. I am not suggesting that Marx himself always presents the matter in this way. At times he does in fact do so explicitly (as, for instance, in his reference to the 'fetishism of commodities'); but the economic determinists can equally well find support in Marx's own writings. What I want to insist on, however, is that Marxism requires this kind of interpretation, as does Durkheim's theory and any other attempt to make ethical values derivative from something like 'social structure'.

Thus, to return to my own argument, in accepting some kind of ethical relativism I do not mean that ethical concepts are bound to be relative to *something else* within the culture. I have agreed that the different aspects of a culture are inter-related, since the culture constitutes a meaningful whole. But to claim that ethics is relative *to*, say, social structure is to suggest that it stands in a *subordinate* relation, and this is what I want to deny. 'But still,' it might be said, 'any form of cultural relativism necessarily implies that an ethical system is at any rate relative to the particular culture, and therefore relative to something other than itself.' But to me it seems precisely that the culture is *not* something other than the ethical system. Not that the two terms are synonymous; but still, to say that ethical norms are culturally relative is simply to say that some men act within one normative system and others act within another, and that this is what makes us say that they inhabit different cultures.

3. BELIEFS AND CONCEPTS

I hope I have also made it plain by now that the sort of cultural relativism which I want to maintain is not to be formulated primarily in terms of ethical beliefs, but rather in terms of ethical concepts. I do not wish to say that standards for evaluating action are provided by what all or most people in a society happen to approve or disapprove of. For these beliefs can themselves be judged in accordance with the concepts possessed by that society. Formulating our theory in terms of 'concepts' rather than 'beliefs' immediately eliminates the problem which usually bedevils ethical relativism, of deciding *whose* beliefs are to constitute the standards of a society. (Everyone's? Impossible, since unanimity does not exist. A particular sub-group, then? But why any one rather than another?...) Moreover it enables us to point out as we did in the previous chapter that within any one society or culture there are likely to be a number of different sets of ethical beliefs, which are not reducible to a uniform moral consensus. And it will also help us to deal with certain arguments which have traditionally been thought to rule out the viability of any kind of ethical relativism. I have in mind principally an objection which G. E. Moore formulates as follows. Ethical relativism is seen by him as the view that when someone says 'This is wrong' he is merely making a judgement about the norms of his own society. But in that case, if A says 'This is wrong' and B says 'No, it isn't', and if A is referring merely to his society and B to his, and their societies are different, then they are not differing in opinion at all. So on this view, it is impossible for two men belonging to different societies ever to differ in opinion on a moral question. And this is a view which Moore finds 'hard to accept' (*Philosophical Studies*, p. 336). I think that substantially the same objection has also been formulated as follows: if an action X is wrong according to the norms of one society but right according to the norms of another society, then, since there is no way of saying that either society is mistaken, it will follow that 'X is both right and wrong'. The theory would imply that this statement is not a contradiction, but surely it must be one.

Moore's argument rests on the interpretation of ethical relativism as a claim that the statement 'This is wrong' *means* 'This is contrary to the norms of my society'; or, as Moore puts it, that 'This is wrong' is a judgement *about* the norms of the speaker's own society. But I do not think that any version of ethical relativism is bound to involve such a claim. The essence of ethical relativism is that judgements of right and wrong are *intelligible* only within a particular culture; criteria on the basis of which one makes a judgement of this kind can be provided only by a particular culture, i.e. by the norms that constitute that culture. So when A and B, from different societies, say 'This is wrong' and 'No, it isn't', they are not making a judgement about the norms of their respective societies, but simply about the rightness or wrongness of the action in question. They do not mean 'This is (not) contrary to the norms of my society'; they mean what they say. All that does follow, at the most, is that if the norms of their respective societies differ, then there may be no way of resolving the disagreement.

However, I do not want to leave the matter there. I think that Moore's objection also raises more fundamental issues. In brief, I do not think that it *is* necessarily intelligible to speak of ethical disagreement between two persons who judge from within two radically different cultures. The view which Moore finds 'hard to accept' may nevertheless be one which has to be accepted. I would suggest, to begin with, that when Moore sets up this hypothesis of A and B, from different societies, saying 'This is wrong' and 'No, it isn't', we need to spell out in more detail what sorts of case he might have in mind. In any imagined case it must be possible to raise and to answer the question 'What are they disagreeing *about*?' The answer might seem obvious: 'they would be disagreeing about whether this action is right or wrong, whether this man is good or bad'. But it is a mistake to suppose that such phrases as 'this action' and 'this man' have an unambiguous reference in statements of this kind

An action is right or wrong, a man is good or bad, only under a certain description; and where the ethical concepts of two cultures differ, the same possibilities of ethical description will not be available in both cultures. Consider an imaginary ethical 'disagreement' with an inhabitant of Periclean Athens. Suppose him to say of a particular individual that the latter is a good man insofar as he is *sophron*, that is to say, insofar as he possesses the virtue of *sophrosyne*. I choose this example because there is within our ethical vocabulary no precise equivalent of the concept of *sophrosyne*. We might translate it as 'moderation' or 'temperance', but these do not have the same kind of moral significance as is possessed by '*sophrosyne*'. Sometimes the latter is mere prudence, but it does not invite the kind of response which would be appropriate to the merely prudent avoidance of excessive self-indulgence, for the effect of the concept is to link such behaviour with more fundamental moral issues. *Sophrosyne* is the virtue which the intemperate drinker stands in need of, as does the man who is so impatient for pleasure as to ignore his own long-term benefit, but it is also that virtue the lack of which may assume tragic dimensions when it takes the form of pride or anger or presumption (as, for example, in the plays of Sophocles). In its debased form, the idea of avoiding excess was grounded in the fear that the gods might be jealous of human extravagance; but it also had a more profound form, whereby any kind of excess was seen as a transgression against a moral order in the universe which sets to everything its limits. This finds expression in the saying of Heraclitus that 'the sun will not overstep his measures; otherwise the Furies, the ministers of justice, will find him out'. Thus, though each of the elements covered by the concept of *sophrosyne* may find a parallel among our own ethical concepts, the importance of the concept is that in bringing all these elements together it made it possible to see them as a unity and thereby to give to each of them a particular moral force. The philosophical significance of all this is not simply that, since '*sophrosyne*' is untranslatable, the disagreement between us and the Athenian cannot be stated. It is that the concept of *sophrosyne* raises moral issues which cannot be raised in our culture. Therefore, *a fortiori*, we and the Athenian cannot disagree about them.

Now it might be said that, after all, Greek moral concepts in general are not so very different from our own, so that even if we have no precise equivalent of *sophrosyne*, by explicating its relationship to other concepts we can make it comprehensible—indeed, this is what I have just been trying to do. It might even be urged that I have exaggerated the difference between the Greek concept and our own. But this is no matter. For if it is the case that we and the Athenian have sufficient ethical concepts in common to be able to debate about the importance of *sophrosyne*, this still illustrates my claim—that ethical disagreement is possible only between persons who *do* have some ethical concepts in common. In other words, there can be meaningful disagreement only where there is some measure of agreement.

The fact that not just anything can count as a meaningful evaluative question is connected with the fact that not just anything can count as a meaningful evaluative judgement. To take one of Mrs. Foot's examples: 'Clasp your hands three times an hour' is not, as it stands, intelligible as a piece of advice. It becomes meaningful only when it is set against some kind of background which is capable of giving it a meaning—if the clasping of one's hands, for example, is to be seen as a gesture of piety, a symbolic act of prayer. It follows that the question 'Ought I to clasp my hands three times an hour?' equally requires to be put in some kind of context if it is to be a meaningful question. And since the question will be given a *different* meaning within *different* systems of values, it follows that if A and B both ask this question from within different cultures, the question may not necessarily mean the same for each of them. Therefore, it may not necessarily make sense to speak of them as 'disagreeing' in their answers.

Moore's objection gains its plausibility because the sort of situation it naturally suggests is one where the action does have a meaning in both cultures. When we talk of 'cultural differences' we think first of cases where what is regarded as right in another culture seems totally wrong to us. For example, A and B may be a European and a Polynesian talking about polygamy. If polygamy is normal in the Polynesian's culture, and the European regards it as immoral, it does at first sight seem plausible to say that they are engaged in ethical disagreement rather than that the question 'Is polygamy right?' has a different meaning and raises different issues for each of them. But, to recur to our earlier example, suppose that the action which A and B are considering is a man's clasping his hands three times an hour, and that this does have a meaning in B's culture. If A is a twentieth-century European, it is likely that, if asked whether this action is right or wrong, he simply will not know how to start answering the question. He will have no idea what to make of it. So in this case, when the two men do not agree, there is less of a temptation to suppose that, therefore, they disagree, and we can more easily see the point of saying that the question of agreement or disagreement simply does not arise.

What, now, of the objection that cultural relativism leads to the assertion of 'X both is and is not right' as a claimed non-contradiction? Here again, we need to ask in what context this is supposed to be said. Clearly, within a particular culture there will be no grounds for saying 'X both is and is not right'. What the objection refers to is the possibility of saying this where a certain action is in accordance with the norms of one culture but contrary to those of another. Now this *might* perhaps be said—by an anthropologist, as a paradoxical way of pointing out the existence of cultural diversity. But he wouldn't *just* say this. He would have to go on to spell out what he meant, viz. that he *was* speaking as an anthropologist, and was pointing out the existence of different norms in different societies. And he would thereby have shown that he was not making a moral judgement, and have re-interpreted his statement in such a way that it was no longer a contradiction; just as someone who says 'At the present moment it is both summer and winter' removes the appearance of self-contradiction if he goes on to explain that he means 'At the present moment it is summer here and winter in Australia'. Now our objector might say that this is precisely what he is objecting to—that cultural relativism does make 'This is right' like 'It is summer', i.e. that on any occasion when it is said, either it does not claim the assent of anyone outside the speaker's own culture, or, if it does, then 'right' must be understood as an incomplete predicate needing to be completed in the form 'right in such-and-such a society'. But to make *this* the objection is, I think, to beg the question.

The standpoint from which these objections are made is one which also finds expression in the idea that ethical relativism 'weakens the force' of moral obligations and demands. Now in one sense this may be true. Someone whose ethical position is, say, that of a Platonist, or a theistic one, may find greater difficulty than an ethical relativist in giving any sense to the idea of attempting to change certain of the moral principles of one's society. I do not say that such a person would *necessarily* find such obstacles; he may, for example, believe that the absolute moral standards laid down by God or inscribed on the walls of the universe must find different expression in different historical epochs. But, on the other hand, he may find the idea of ethical change incompatible with the idea of absolute timeless standards, whereas the ethical relativist, believing that moral standards are rooted in paradig-matic patterns of human behaviour, will not encounter the same meta-moral obstacle to value-change. However, this can constitute an objection to ethical relativism only if there are independent grounds for believing the theory to be mistaken.

But the suggestion that ethical relativism weakens the force of moral demands is probably intended to imply something stronger than this— something that might be put by saying that ethical relativism makes morality 'merely conventional'. In other words, the idea is that moral demands would then have *none* of their characteristic force *at all*. They would have to be seen simply as conventions which happen to be observed in a particular society, but might perfectly well have been otherwise. As soon as we start developing the content of this notion of 'mere convention', however, we begin to see what is wrong with the objection. In chapter 3 (pp. 59–60) I argued that the essence of a convention is that it is completely arbitrary, and that to say this is to say that it is completely self-contained and could therefore be changed without our having to change anything else. It is a convention of our society that we shake hands with one another as a form of greeting. This 'might perfectly well have been otherwise'; that is to say, if it were customary to embrace one another Russian-style instead of shaking hands, this would make no difference, it would not involve any further change in our norms or values or in our way of life in general.[1] Now if this is the distinction between the conventional and the non-conventional, then it is one which a 'cultural relativist' position by no means precludes us from making. We can recognize without any difficulty the difference between the case of 'shaking hands' and, for example, the notion of 'gratitude'. The latter is so embedded in our conceptual scheme, so closely tied up with so many other ethical notions, that a society which did not possess the notion of gratitude would have a completely different way of seeing human actions and human relationships. Could we, for example, do without the notion of gratitude and still retain in the same form the notion of 'generosity' or 'kindness'? Looked at from this point of view, the concept of gratitude is clearly not an 'arbitrary convention' which 'could perfectly well have been otherwise'. And it is true not just of 'gratitude', but of our moral concepts generally, that they are embedded in a system, and that it is this which distinguishes them from 'mere conventions'.

What, then, could be meant by someone who said that ethical relativism 'weakens the force' of moral demands? What is this 'force' which moral demands ought to have but would not have? So far as I can see, there is no other possible answer except to say that it just is the force that moral demands do have. For example, it might be claimed that if ethical relativism were to be accepted, it would no longer be possible to see how the demands of justice could have such importance that someone might be prepared to die for the sake of justice. But the reason why the demands of justice have this force is quite simply because of the possible meanings that can be given to the idea of death and to the idea of justice by their relation to other normative concepts— because of the way in which the concept of justice is tied to the very idea of a human community and therefore lies at the root of all our most important values, and because of the way in which political causes and political movements which transcend the individual can give sense to the

---

[1] This point might possibly be contested. It might be held that the fact that we shake hands rather than embrace is a reflection of the coldness and reserve of the English temperament, and that if we started to embrace instead, this might help to make us more out-going. But this is no objection to my argument; for once we start to bring in considerations of this kind, we are no longer considering simply the conventional aspect of shaking hands.

fact of sacrificing one's life for the sake of an ideal. Now clearly, ethical relativism leaves all this intact—indeed, it emphasizes that the 'force of moral demands' is to be looked for in this direction, and not by resort to meta-moral expedients. We would indicate the force of any moral concept in the same way, by showing its relation to other concepts, the importance of its role within a system of norms and values, its necessary prominence within a whole way of life. And we could say that somebody who failed to see the force of a particular moral notion had failed to understand the meaning of that concept within our language and our culture. But now, how can we attach any sense to the idea that *all* our moral concepts might lose their force? Against what could this 'loss of importance' be measured? Are we to suppose some scale outside and apart from our systems of moral concepts, to which they can be referred? The only possible hypothesis is that ethical relativism might lead us to think that the very idea of 'moral demands' is in some way incoherent, and that what we had supposed to be 'moral demands' were really something else; but the only plausible candidate for the 'something else' is 'conventions'—the candidate which we have just rejected.

We have been arguing that by situating the standards of ethical judgement in the *concepts* rather than in the *beliefs* of a society we can deal more effectively with Moore's and similar objections. However, our formulation may be thought to create its own difficulties. It seems to lead to the paradoxical result that, in a sense, ethical relativism can never be properly stated, at any rate not in concrete instances. Suppose we say, for example, of a particular culture: 'Trust is not regarded as a virtue in this culture.' Now clearly, the concept that we are talking about here is *not* what *we* mean by 'trust'. It is not related to other concepts and to particular modes of behaviour in the way that defines our concept of trust. What concept is it, then? We can answer this question only by showing how the concept is defined by the practices to which it is related. But then we again face the problem that we can describe these practices only in terms of our own concepts, and so we are again unable to express the specific rationality of that culture. Therefore, we seem bound to arrive at the conclusion that any such concept can be defined and understood only from within that culture. Insofar as we describe and account for the practices and concepts of an alien culture in terms of our own concepts, we see in them what is really a reflection of our own culture. This is the paradox at the heart of social anthropology. Therefore, in a sense, the thesis of cultural relativism (where this means that the practices of a culture can be understood and explained only in terms of the concepts of that society, and vice versa) cannot be verified empirically. For where we *can* describe observed culture differences—where we can say, for example, that truth-telling is remarkably rare in a particular society—this implies that the society has the *same* concept as our concept of truth-telling, i.e. that this is *not* a case of cultural relativity in the aforementioned sense. Cultural relativism, in that sense, is an *a priori* thesis about the way in which we have to (logically have to) understand cultural differences. These observed differences lead us to the thesis only insofar as they may eventually lead us to see what is *wrong* with saying, for example, 'Trust is not regarded as a virtue in that culture'.

In the remainder of this chapter I want to look at some considerations which modify this seemingly sceptical conclusion. Although the important fact remains that the relativity of different ethical norms to different cultures is to be stated not in terms of differing beliefs but in terms of the differing meanings of normative concepts, this does not make other cultures totally opaque. We shall see grounds for supposing that inter-translatability between different normative languages is always possible, so that we can come to see the normative concepts of another culture as possible extensions of our own concepts.

4. THE HUMAN CONDITION

If we consider how a utilitarian philosopher might argue against any form of ethical relativism, the following presents itself as a possible objection: that certain biological and psychological facts about the human species make it inevitable that all men will share certain universal wants and desires, and that, therefore, the ethical concepts of every culture, despite their superficial differences, will ultimately be reducible to these same fundamental wants. Reference might be made, for example, to some of the considerations with which Mrs. Foot is concerned in her paper on *Moral Beliefs*. She suggests there that ethical conceptions are necessarily connected with notions such as those of human good and harm, and that not just anything counts as human good or harm. It follows from the facts of human existence, for example, that a man who suffers an injury is always harmed thereby. Consider the following passage:

... we should ... query the suggestion that someone might happen not to want anything for which he would need the use of hands or eyes. Hands and eyes, like ears and legs, play a part in so many operations that a man could only be said not to need them if he had no wants at all. That such people exist, in asylums, is not to the present purpose at all; the proper use of his limbs is something a man has reason to want if he wants anything. I do not know just what someone who denies this proposition could have in mind. Perhaps he is thinking of changing the facts of human existence, so that merely wishing, or the sound of the voice, will bring the world to heel?

(Moral Beliefs, p. 94)

On the basis of considerations of this kind, it might be argued that any culture must necessarily possess the concepts of human good and harm and injury, and that its ethical values are bound to be based on such facts as that to say that something constitutes an injury is necessarily to provide a reason for avoiding it.

Now I think it is true that these 'facts of human existence'—such as the fact that a man cannot effectively act in the world or alter his environment unless he has the use of his bodily organs—are bound to be reflected in any conceivable system of values and norms. But what is equally important is that they are not bound to be reflected in any one particular way.[1] This is apparent even within our own culture. 'The proper use of his limbs is something a man has reason to want if he wants anything'—but he may *not* want anything. That is to say, an ethic of resignation is not only conceivable, but represents a major ethical tradition. It is obviously most in place against a religious background, although not necessarily confined to such a framework in a narrow sense. We could compare also the Buddhist notion that 'the secret of happiness is to stop desiring'. And—lest it should seem that such an ethic is merely an eccentric and almost unrealizable extreme— the notion of resignation does not necessarily rule out all human action, but may simply mean that the point of such action is not primarily (in Mrs. Foot's revealing phrase) to 'bring the world to heel'. Now to someone who adheres to an ethic of this kind, the notion of injury is likely to have a very different significance from that which it has for Mrs. Foot; we might even say that they have *different concepts* of 'injury' and of 'harm'. And similarly, although it would seem that the evaluative concepts of any culture must relate in some way to these 'facts of human existence', this will by no means guarantee that all human cultures must necessarily have the same concepts of 'harm' and 'injury', or derive the same norms of behaviour from them. Therefore, we can by no means argue that attempts to justify human actions must appeal to the same ultimate reasons in any culture. Undeniably, the 'facts of human existence' are bound to constitute in some sense the 'foundations' of any system of ethical concepts; but the mistake is to suppose that they are foundations in a *reductionist* sense. The true relation between such facts and ethical concepts might perhaps be indicated by saying that they constitute the 'raw material' of ethics,

---

[1] Here I have drawn heavily upon a paper by D. Z. Phillips and H. O. Mounce: 'On Morality's Having a Point' (*Philosophy*, 1965).

which, though common to every system of ethical concepts, may be given a different significance by different systems.[1]

The recognition of such facts, then, does not require us to abandon the notion of ethical relativism. But it does mean that we can always find some point of contact between the evaluative concepts of another culture and those of our own. It may still be that the 'raw material' is assimilated into the two cultures in very different ways, so that the one set of concepts is vastly different from the other. But at any rate we can at least get to grips with the other culture, if only to the extent of being able to *locate* the points at which the respective concepts diverge. The non-comprehension is not total.

5. 'ANY CONCEIVABLE HUMAN SOCIETY'

Other arguments, rather different from the sort which can be derived from Mrs. Foot, have been put forward to show that there are certain ethical concepts which must (logically must) be possessed by any conceivable culture. These arguments are based not on the biological facts of the human condition, but on consideration of what is involved in the very idea of a human society. For example, Peter Winch has argued that any conceivable human society will necessarily regard truth-telling as a virtue (*Nature and Convention*), and the same argument appears in Alasdair MacIntyre's *Short History of Ethics* (pp. 77 and 95–6). For if it were not the case that most of the statements made by most of the people in a society were true, the use of language by them would be impossible; and the use of language is a logically necessary characteristic of anything that we should agree to call a human community (as distinct, say, from a number of human beings living in close physical proximity to one another). Both writers suggest that similar arguments could be employed in connection with other virtues, such as justice. This suggestion could perhaps be developed by arguing that a concept of justice is built into the very idea of 'agreement' or 'common action'. Similarly an argument could perhaps be formulated to the effect that any society is bound to possess the concepts of rights and duties, freedom and obligation; for it is difficult to see how a human collectivity in which any person could do exactly what he liked and could always, at will, prevent any other person from doing what he wanted, could be called a human society.

[1] Cf. Winch's discussion, in *Understanding a Primitive Society*, of the 'limiting notions' which determine 'ethical space', and Sartre's discussion, in *Existentialism and Humanism* (pp. 46–7), of 'the human condition', by which he means 'all the limitations which *a priori* define man's fundamental situation in the universe', and of which he says that 'every human purpose presents itself as an attempt either to surpass these limitations, or to widen them, or else to deny or to accommodate oneself to them'.

K

How does this affect the argument about ethical relativism? In one respect it represents a much stronger limitation on the possibilities of cultural variety than do the biological facts of the human condition. In the latter case it is simply certain facts that are bound to be reflected in any conceivable system of ethical concepts. But in the case of 'truth-telling', we are concerned with a particular *value* that is bound to be recognized in any conceivable society. On the other hand, both Winch and MacInture emphasize two important reservations. In the first place, it is not necessarily the case that truthfulness must have the *same* moral significance in any human society. Different cultures may have different concepts of truth-telling, different codes of honesty. I am not sure how far Winch or MacIntyre would want this to be taken, but I think it can be taken quite a long way. Winch has some bother with the problem of showing that truth-telling must necessarily be regarded as a *moral* virtue at all, and indeed I do not think that he really succeeds in showing this. He does succeed in demolishing the hypothesis of a society in which people tell the truth only to the extent that this is necessary to get others to do what they want. But this argument is not enough; giving truth-telling that kind of significance is not the only alternative to giving it a moral significance. The sense in which there *must* be a norm of truth-telling in any conceivable society can be seen from the fact that we cannot teach a child to speak a language without reproving him when he makes false statements. Therefore, in a sense, in teaching him the language we are teaching him the norm of truth-telling. But it is quite another thing to teach him that honesty is a moral virtue. Strictly speaking, in the former case we have not even really taught the child the concepts of 'telling the truth' and 'lying'; we have merely taught him the difference between making true statements and making false statements, and in so doing we have taught him the need to make true statements rather than false ones. But consider the many different ways in which we may react to the making of false statements. Not all false statements, or even all deliberately false statements, are lies. Here I have in mind not just the cases where the making of false statements may be justifiable (e.g. a 'white lie' to save someone embarrassment) or morally neutral (e.g. as philosophical examples), but even more importantly, the different kinds of reproof that may be appropriate. Consider the following very different cases:

(a) X asks Y for some money, on the pretence that he is collecting for a charity, but spends the money on himself. This is perhaps the kind of case we most often have in mind when we speak of a 'lie', namely one where we can specify what is wrong with it by characterizing it as an instance of 'deceit'. And if we wanted to spell out what is meant by 'deceit' here, we could relate it to such concepts as those of 'using other people as means to one's own ends' or of 'exploiting other people'.

(b) An academic writer includes in a book a statement which he knows to be inaccurate or misleading, because to correct it or examine it more closely might upset his argument. I am not sure whether one would speak of this as a 'lie' or as a case of 'deceit'; perhaps one might, but for my own part I think I should hesitate to do so, mainly because the kinds of human relationships involved here are not the direct inter-personal ones of case (a). Moreover, there is not so much of a sense of the reader 'depending on' or 'trusting in' the writer's words. It is no accident that we have a special concept of 'intellectual dishonesty'. To elucidate it, we should have to examine what is involved in such notions as that of a 'community of scholars'.

(c) A politician, like Dostoevsky's Grand Inquisitor, misinforms the people because he thinks it better to tell them what they prefer to hear, rather than make life difficult for them and perhaps present them with the agony of an unbearable choice. We might still speak of deceit here, but in this case we could hardly explicate the concept by saying that the politician is 'exploiting' the people or 'using' them, for his action is entirely altruistic. In trying to clarify what is wrong with such an action, however, we might speak of the politics of paternalism, of a particularly subtle kind of unfreedom, of the total impoverishment of the spiritual life of such a society, and so on.

(d) We could contrast all these cases with one where, say, a man is filling in his income tax forms and, for no reason at all (perhaps on impulse), deliberately states his income to be more than it really is, and so has to pay more tax. Clearly there is nothing morally wrong in this. What is wrong with it is not that it is immoral, but that it is stupid.

The general point which I want to draw from all these examples is that in order to show what kind of a wrong is constituted in each case by the failure to tell the truth, we relate the notion of a 'lie' or 'dis-honesty' to other moral concepts ('deceit', 'intellectual integrity', etc.). We see it in the context of particular kinds of human relationships—both the positive ones which are offended against and the negative ones which are brought into existence ('community of scholars', 'paternal-ism', 'using people' etc.). This does not mean that lying is wrong not in itself but only insofar as it falls under some other heading; for by relating it to other concepts, we show what lying *is*. But what does follow is that not only the kind of moral significance that truth-telling has, but the very possibility of its having any moral significance at all, depends upon the existence in the respective culture of certain moral concepts, certain kinds of relationships, certain ways of life.

The second reservation made by Winch and by MacIntyre is that, from the fact that any society must logically recognize a norm of truth-telling, it does not follow that any individual who tells a lie is necessarily being illgoical or irrational. Here again, I do not know how far they would want to take this; but it does seem to me that there are various different possibilities here. In the first place it is obvious that a man who on a particular occasion thinks it right to tell a lie is not always being irrational. I have in mind those cases where someone might think that the wrongness of telling a lie is overridden by other moral considerations (e.g. lying to save another's life); I think that these are also the kinds of cases that Winch has in mind.[1] Someone else might indeed object that it *is* always wrong to tell a lie, and this in turn would be intelligible; but I do not think anyone could claim that the man who feels justified in lying on such an occasion is being irrational.

But to take this a step further, I think that any given individual could also quite rationally decide not to regard truth-telling as a virtue. In other words, he would not just decide that particular circumstances might justify him in telling a lie, but would decide, as a matter of general policy, not to attach any importance to truth-telling at all. And I do not simply mean that people may actually do this, but that they may have perfectly intelligible reasons for doing so. The sort of justification he would give might perhaps be of the kind that I attributed to the egoist (see above, p. 197). So although truth-telling is bound to be recognized as a virtue in any human society, it does not follow that it is bound to be recognized as a virtue by everyone.

The final step which I want to take is to say that it is quite conceivable that *everyone* in a given society might, for reasons of this kind, cease to regard truth-telling as a virtue. What does follow from Winch's and MacIntyre's arguments is that, if such people were really consistent and thorough-going, their society would rapidly disintegrate and eventually cease to exist. Not only would they no longer be able to act in common, but they could not even teach their children to use language at all, and, therefore, such a society could not survive for more than a generation at the most. This is true not just on causal grounds but on logical ones; we have seen that the original argument about truth-telling is based on the existence of a logical relation between the notion of truth-telling and the notion of a human society. Thus it is no more impossible for everyone in a given society to cease to regard truth-telling as a virtue than it is impossible for all the members of a given society to decide that they no longer wish to preserve their society. Of course, my whole thesis is designed to show that if human beings did not constitute a society they could have no evaluative concepts and would be incapable of either rational evaluation or rational action. But there is no logical objection to the hypothesis that human beings *might* become incapable of all this.

---

[1] Cf. p. 250: 'I have said that there could not be a human society in which truthfulness were not in general regarded as a virtue. This does not mean that no one can ever be justified in lying. But it does imply that a lie always needs special justification if it is not to be condemned.'

From this whole discussion of the notion of truth-telling, then, I conclude that in any human society there will necessarily be a norm of truth-telling, but that nothing follows from this either about *what* concept of truthfulness any society will possess or about what actions will actually be performed or be regarded as justified in any given society. So, once again, the basic notion of cultural relativism remains intact, but has to be qualified. Since any normative language is bound to contain *some* concept of truth-telling (and similarly with other normative concepts essential to the very idea of a human society), any two normative languages are bound to be to that extent inter-translatable even though they are not precisely parallel.

6. SYSTEMS AND CULTURES

At this point we can usefully return to a problem which we left unresolved at the end of chapter 4—the problem of determining what is meant by an 'ethical system'. In the last two sections of this chapter we have encountered certain considerations which must be at the heart of any set of ethical concepts. We have emphasized that these considerations are fundamental in the sense that any set of ethical concepts must take account of them and must make it possible to attach some kind of ethical significance to them; but that they are not bound to be given any one particular kind of ethical significance. They do not constitute a limited number of 'ultimate values' to which all other values are in some way reducible. Given the existence of these considerations, however, any human culture will inevitably possess:

(i) Concepts which serve to identify certain basic human needs. These needs, in whatever light they are looked at, are bound to be recognized at least in the form of hypothetical imperatives: the necessity to find food and drink and shelter, to work and therefore to avoid injury and enjoy health, in order to live.

(ii) Concepts which are needed in order to determine how much importance is to be attached to these needs in relation to other human satisfactions, and to the different satisfactions in relation to one another. Primarily these concepts would have to offer a view of man. Examples in our own culture would be the kinds of concept employed by Hobbes when he depicts men in a state of nature competing for self-preservation, by Mill when (*malgré lui*) he exalts the dissatisfied philosopher above the contented pig, by Nietzsche when he contrasts 'slave ethics' with 'noble morality', or by Sorel when he contrasts man as consumer with man as producer.

(iii) Concepts which are needed in order to determine how much importance is to be attached to human needs and satisfactions in general, in relation to the non-human world. As we have previously indicated, central among these are concepts which serve to distinguish between the humanistic attitude and the religious attitude. And since we are in effect concerned here with the value assignable to human life, relevant also will be concepts which offer particular ways of seeing the fact of death—perhaps as the ultimate undesirable, or as the handing on of the torch, as man's final rest, or as the beginning of true existence.

(iv) Concepts which offer ways of seeing one's relationships to other human beings—in our own culture, these include concepts such as 'honesty', 'justice', 'duty', 'respect', but also concepts such as 'independence', 'nobility', 'self-affirmation', as well as those which refer to more specific relationships (family relationships, sexual relationships, institutional roles, etc.).

The notion of an ethical 'system' was introduced in chapter 3 with the idea that one criterion of a 'normative concept' might be its being situated within such a system. We can now re-phrase this suggestion by saying that any normative concept must connect in some way with the fundamental concepts which we have just considered. An ethical system will thus be a set of concepts embodying some one particular attitude to the above considerations—human needs and satisfactions, man's relation to the non-human world, and his relation to other men. This definition would seem to apply satisfactorily to the examples which we looked at in chapter 4.

The notion of a 'culture' employed in this chapter is thus wider than that of an ethical 'system'. We have implied that within a culture one may find a number of differing ethical systems. The following schematic picture therefore suggests itself. Any human culture is bound to possess normative concepts belonging to the above four categories, as well as many other normative concepts which nevertheless will depend on these basic concepts for their sense. The concepts will differ from one culture to another, but since the categories will remain the same, it will always be possible to arrive at some degree of understanding of the concepts and norms of an alien culture. Within any one culture the normative concepts will not dictate a single ethical point of view. There will be divisions, the most fundamental of which will entitle us to speak of the existence of different ethical systems within the culture. But here too the universality of the categories will enable us to situate these systems in relation to one another; if this were not so, we could not see them as *conflicting* systems.

But this picture remains over-simplistic, and demands a further qualification. The boundaries between cultures are by no means as clear-cut as I may have seemed to suggest. Even where we can distinguish two separate cultures, it does not follow that they are entirely insulated from one another. The possible degrees of contact may range from virtual indistinguishability to complete isolation. As examples of these two extremes we might take the cultural differences between northern and southern England, and the isolation of European cultures from those of the American continent prior to the fifteenth century. Clearly in the former case it would be absurd to suggest that there is one set of ethical values for the north of England and another for the south, but this would be quite plausible in the second case. In general we may say that when there is some degree of contact between two cultures (by which I mean not just conflict, but some kind of positive contact— commercial transactions, political treaties, etc.), to that extent there are bound to be shared standards of rationality. Consider another example. There is clearly a distinction to be made between the French culture and the English culture, and this distinction extends to the recognition of divergent ethical and evaluative norms. There are evaluative concepts which can be expressed in the French language but cannot be exactly translated into English, and vice versa (Hare mentions an example of this).[1] But there is obviously no vast divergence between the rationalities encapsulated in the two languages. There is, for example, no difficulty in seeing English ethical philosophers and French ethical philosophers as talking about the same things. And here it is significant that we can also talk about 'the European culture' as a single entity; for to the extent that there is a high level of intercourse (including intellectual inter-course) between the two cultures, they can also be seen as two parts of a single culture. Therefore the notion of ethical relativism is not to be interpreted as an over-simplified claim that there are a clear and specific number of totally discrete cultures, all perfectly distinguishable, and an equal number of sets of normative concepts standing in a simple one-to-one relationship to them. Nevertheless there *are* cases where there is no contact or intercourse between different cultures, and where we clearly have no option but to see them as completely *separate* cultures. It is notable that the possibility of social anthropology as an academic discipline was created by the discovery of cultures with which there had previously been no contact and which had little or no intercourse with

---

[1] *Language of Morals*, p. 121: 'The close connexion of standards of values with language is illustrated by the plight of the truly bilingual. A writer equally at home in English and French relates that once, when walking in the park on a rainy day, he met a lady dressed in a way which the English would call sensible, but the French "ridicule"; his mental reaction to this had to be expressed bilingually, because the standards he was applying were of diverse origin; he found himself saying to himself (slipping from English into French) "Pretty adequate armour. How uncomfortable though. Why go for a walk if you feel like this? Elle est parfaitement ridicule." This cleavage of standards is said sometimes to produce neuroses in bilinguals, as might be expected in view of the close bearing of standards of values upon action.' I should add that Hare does not, of course, interpret the 'close connexion of standards of values with language' in the way I do.

one another; they could therefore be seen as fairly self-contained, with clear boundaries between them, so that it was possible to state the thesis of cultural relativism clearly in a way that one could not do if one considered only, for example, the relations between different European cultures.

6. Tradition and Change

1. DURKHEIM ON VALUE-CHANGE

In our discussion of Durkheim we noted that he recognizes the possibility of objecting to his theory of morality on the grounds that it does not leave room for rational dissent from, or rational attempts to change, the prevailing norms of one's society. He formulates the potential objection as follows:

> To see morality in this manner is to preclude all possibility of judging it. If morality is the product of the collective, it necessarily imposes itself on the individual, who is in no position to question it whatever form it may take, and must accept it passively. We are thus condemned to follow opinion without ever having the right to rebel against its dictates.
>
> *(Sociology and Philosophy*, pp. 59–60)

Although I attempted in the last chapter to draw some important distinctions between Durkheim's position and the one I wish to defend, it will be apparent that the objection is one which might be levelled at my own arguments as well as at Durkheim's.

Now I have already indicated one sense in which a person can dissent from the prevailing morality of his society. I tried to make it clear in chapters 3 and 5 that the 'norms' which I have been talking about are not to be identified with 'what most men do'. In talking about 'norms', what we are really talking about are the *concepts* existing in a particular society. Admittedly, in order to determine what concepts are possessed within a society we do ultimately have to look at its patterns of behaviour; and although, of course, we have to look at its language too, we cannot tell what the words in the language mean unless we look at how men *act* in connection with them. But this logical relation between concepts and ways of acting is not a simple relation of identity. For example, if we are to say that the concept of justice is possessed by a society, it does not necessarily have to be the case that most men in that society act justly. (In particular, we have seen how the notion of a *system* sometimes makes it possible to say that most people in a society act in a manner contrary to a certain norm of that society.) Therefore, there is one clear sense in which a man could dissent from or attempt to change some aspect of current behaviour within his society; for he could say that this particular way of behaving was contrary to the society's own norms.

But if this were the only way in which it was possible to criticize prevailing morality, it would be a very limited way. What is much more important is whether we can give a sense to the notion of changing existing values by creating *new* norms, *new* concepts. The same question is posed by Durkheim's own reply to the envisaged objection. He indicates two ways in which it is possible to rebel against existing moral opinion. In the first place

> It is possible that, as a result of some passing upheaval, some funda-mental moral principle is hidden for a time from the public conscience which, not feeling it, denies that it is there (theoretically and explicitly, or practically and in action; it does not matter). The science of morals can appeal from this temporarily troubled moral condition to that which pre-existed . . .
>
> (*Sociology and Philosophy*, p. 60)

This corresponds to the possibility which we have mentioned—that someone might criticize current ways of behaving by appealing to already-existing norms. Durkheim's second possibility is that 'apart from the present order of morality maintained by the forces of tradition' there might appear 'new tendencies'. These 'new ideas' would be 'related to recent changes in the conditions of collective existence, and made necessary by these changes'; in other words, they would be reflections of changes in the social structure. In envisaging this, Durk-heim goes some way towards making room for the possibility of creating radically new normative concepts; but at the same time he still sets limits to this possibility. I have already (in chapter 5) criticized Durk-heim's view of the relation between ethics and social structure, on the grounds that it gives a logically privileged status to one particular class of norms. The same point is apparent here. Durkheim implies that certain norms, namely those which go to make up the 'social structure', are themselves immune from criticism, and that criticism of any other norms can only be on the grounds that they are out of step with autonomous changes in the 'structural' norms. Now in a way I am sympathetic to Durkheim's account; I shall try to show that radical value-change does, in fact, very often happen when changes in some aspect of social life alter the significance of other norms and values. But what I want to resist is the suggestion that such changes *must*—logically must—be initiated by autonomous (unwilled and unwillable) changes in the social structure. I want to resist any attempt to set limits to the degree of radicalism that is possible in the criticism of one's society's values. I intend to do this by looking at concrete historical examples of value-change and showing that, however radical they may be, their revolutionary nature is in no way incompatible with the fact that they can also always be seen as an extension of existing norms. The normative character of ethical rationality and the pursuit of ethical radicalism are not even potentially in conflict, and to suppose otherwise is to misunderstand the nature of radical change.

2. THE UTILITARIAN ACCOUNT OF VALUE-CHANGE

I also want to go even further and argue that the historical examples which I shall be looking at make much better sense from the point of view of my own position than within a utilitarian perspective. Utilitarianism is in its very nature committed to a misunderstanding of the nature of radical change. What sort of account can a utilitarian in fact give of value-change? He can recognize the following cases in which a change in values might occur and might deserve to be regarded as justified:

(a) Men might acquire new ultimate wants. If it is to be supposed that these new wants might just emerge from nowhere, without any explanation being possible, then the suggestion is totally mysterious and intrinsically implausible. If, on the other hand, the appearance of new wants can be explained as a consequence of changes in the physical or social environment, the utilitarian will find himself having to give a determinist account of ethics which is equatable with the most rigid social conformism. Suppose, for example, that technological developments eventually result in a race of media-drugged morons who are blissfully content. *Ex hypothesi*, these new ultimate wants are not amenable to rational criticism. Therefore, the change in values is not a result of rational thought and decision but is simply causally determined. Hence the historical connection of utilitarian modes of thought with the tyranny of technology.

(b) Men might calculate that new means of satisfying their wants have become preferable. This might happen either because the old means have ceased to be effective or because new and more efficient techniques have been discovered. For example, a utilitarian might argue that, with the ever-accelerating advance of industrialization and automation, and of economic centralization, production will be more efficient if industries are owned by the state instead of by private individuals. (The example is not an arbitrary one; it is a historical fact that Fabianism has its roots in utilitarianism.) If the stress is to be put on this rather than on (a) as the normal origin of changes in values, utilitarianism will have to be linked to the concept of a supra-historical 'human nature' and 'natural wants' (cf. Nowell-Smith: *Ethics*, p. 182). It will have to be supposed that men have always had more or less the same wants, and that history is the record of their attempts to find ever more efficient means of satisfying these wants. Hence the historical connection of utilitarianism with the politics of pragmatism and the rhetoric of progress.

But, of course, both these kinds of value-change would appear in history (at least in their pure form) only in a society whose members were themselves utilitarians. Since utilitarianism may or may not be the predominating ethic of a society, a utilitarian would also have to recognize, in addition to (a) and (b), the following kinds of value-change occurring in history:

(c) a change from a non-utilitarian ethic to utilitarianism—this would be a change from irrationality to rationality;

(d) a change from utilitarianism to a non-utilitarian ethic—this would be a change from rationality to irrationality;

(e) a change from one non-utilitarian ethic to another—this would be a change from one form of irrationality to another.

A utilitarian history of ethics would presumably recognize an initial period of enlightenment represented by the Sophists, Aristotle and the Epicureans, the long dark ages of irrationality represented by Scholasticism and its legacies, and the gradual re-emergence of enlightenment exemplified by writers such as Hobbes, Hume, Bentham and Mill. The connection of this distortingly simplified historical view with a broadly utilitarian conception of ethics is apparent in recent English academic philosophy.

3. FROM TRADITIONALISM TO THE SPIRIT OF CAPITALISM

The first historical example of a change in values which I want to consider is that discussed by Weber in his essay *The Protestant Ethic and the Spirit of Capitalism*, not only because it is one of the most important instances of radical value-change in European history but also because the notion of rationality has an absolutely central place in Weber's examination of it. This is especially apparent in his *Introduction* to the whole series of studies on the sociology of religion (reprinted as the *Introduction* of Parsons' translation). Weber begins by pointing out that a distinctive element in all branches of Western culture has been a certain kind of rationalization of activity, apparent in the application of systematic method, the employment of mathematical calculation and the emergence of trained specialists. The capitalist economy is one exemplification of this specific rationality. But why has the modern rational capitalistic organization of labour emerged only in the West?

This can be partly explained by the existence of rational structures of law and administration—i.e. a calculable and predictable legal system, and systematic administration based on formal rules—for without these there could be no certainty in economic calculations and no guaranteed expectation of returns. But to say this is really only to restate the problem, for these institutions are simply further manifestations of the specific rationalism of Western culture, which has still to be explained. Here Weber makes the first point that is of particular importance for our present interests: there is no one single form of rationality. Different kinds of rationality are to be found corresponding to different fields of activity and different points of view.

> There is, for example, rationalization of mystical contemplation, that is of an attitude which, viewed from other departments of life, is specifically irrational, just as there are rationalizations of economic life, of technique, of scientific research, of military training, of law and administration. Furthermore, each one of these fields may be rationalized in terms of very different ultimate values and ends, and what is rational from one point of view may well be irrational from another. Hence rationalizations of the most varied character have existed in various departments of life and in all areas of culture.
>
> (*The Protestant Ethic and the Spirit of Capitalism*, p. 26)

The most important application of this principle is that utilitarian rationality is only one form of rationality. We have already noted that from the utilitarian viewpoint other ethics are seen as irrational, and, as we shall see later, this means that from such a viewpoint it is impossible to understand particular historical instances of ethical change.

In the same paragraph Weber makes a second equally important point. Although any explanation of the distinctive nature of Western rationalism must recognize the fundamental importance of the economic factor,

> the opposite correlation must not be left out of consideration. . . . The development of economic rationalism . . . is at the same time determined by the ability and disposition of men to adopt certain types of practical rational conduct. When these types have been obstructed by spiritual obstacles, the development of rational economic conduct has also met serious inner resistance. The magical and religious forces, and the ethical ideas of duty based on them, have in the past always been among the most important formative influences on conduct.
>
> (Ibid., pp. 26-7)

These sentences are important because they show clearly what Weber was trying to do in this essay. He was not looking for 'the cause of capitalism'; indeed, only in a very limited sense could his discussion be called a causal account at all. He was not attempting a total and generalized explanation of how modern Western capitalism came into existence. He was concerned with the specific problem: how could the adoption, in practical conduct, of the new mode of rationality inherent in capitalism be sanctioned by pre-existing ethical conceptions. In other words, what Weber is looking for is what I have claimed *must* be found in any instance of rational value-change.

Weber considers that any discussion of the distinctive rationality of Western civilization must recognize the importance of what he refers to as 'the spirit of capitalism'. He illustrates it by quotations from Benjamin Franklin:

> Remember that *time* is money. He that can earn ten shillings a day by his labour, and goes abroad, or sits idle, one half of that day, though he spends but sixpence during his diversion or idleness, ought not to reckon *that* the only expense; he has really spent, or rather thrown away, five shillings besides.
>
> Remember, that *credit* is money. If a man lets his money lie in my hands after it is due, he gives me the interest, or so much as I can make of it during that time. . . .
>
> Remember, that money is of the prolific, generating nature. Money can beget money, and its offspring can beget more, and so on. . . . He that murders a crown, destroys all that it might have produced, even scores of pounds.
>
> (Ibid., pp. 48–9)

Weber comments that it would be a mistake to interpret this advice in a utilitarian perspective. What is distinctive about it is that the making of money is recommended not as a means to material prosperity but as an *ethical duty*.

> The *summum bonum* of this ethic, the earning of more and more money, combined with the strict avoidance of all spontaneous enjoyment of life, is above all completely devoid of any eudaemonistic, not to say hedonistic, admixture. It is thought of so purely as an end in itself, that from the point of view of the happiness of, or utility to, the single individual, it appears entirely transcendental and absolutely irrational.
>
> (Ibid., p. 53)

Notice how Weber implicitly assumes what I have argued for in earlier chapters, that one cannot fit absolutely any behaviour into a utilitarian scheme simply on the hypothesis of unusual wants. In this particular case, we cannot reveal Franklin's ethic as rational merely by saying 'Presumably people like Franklin just *like* making money for its own sake'. For in itself and regarded as an ultimate want, this is an irrational want, and it can be shown to be rational only by being given some further justification. But as we have just seen, in this case no further justification of a utilitarian kind is appropriate, since the making of money is not regarded by Franklin as a means to the satisfaction of any other wants. Therefore, all that a utilitarian can say of Franklin's ethic is that it is completely irrational. Here, however, Weber applies the first of the two important points which we have just noted. What is irrational from one point of view may be rational when seen from the point of view of very different ideals. Specifically, the earning of money as an end in itself, so irrational from a utilitarian point of view, becomes rational when it is seen as

> the result and the expression of virtue and proficiency in a calling; and this virtue and proficiency are . . . the real Alpha and Omega of Franklin's ethic. . . . This idea . . . of one's duty in a calling is what is most characteristic of the social ethic of capitalistic culture, and is in a sense the fundamental basis of it. It is an obligation which the individual is supposed to feel and does feel towards the content of his professional activity, no matter in what it consists, in particular no matter whether it appears on the surface as a utilization of his personal powers, or only of his material possessions (as capital).
>
> (Ibid., p. 54)

Weber now applies the second of the two aforementioned principles: the introduction of this ethic of duty in a calling as a new mode of practical rationality must have been capable of being justified in terms of already-existing ethical conceptions.

> In order that a manner of life so well adapted to the peculiarities of capitalism could be selected at all, i.e. should come to dominate others, it had to originate somewhere, and not in isolated individuals alone, but as a way of life common to whole groups of men. This origin is what really needs explanation.
>
> (Ibid., p. 55)

Weber goes on to state the problem in more specific terms. The pre-capitalist economic ethic was that of traditionalism. Weber uses this term to designate the attitude which derives from the mediaeval Christian church and can be summed up in the words of the Lord's Prayer: 'Give us this day our daily bread.' Economic activity is sanctioned to the extent that it is necessary for the meeting of basic human needs, since this is a necessity imposed by natural law. But there is no scope for man to exhibit positive virtue in economic activity. And economic activity beyond what is necessary for meeting daily needs (i.e. for maintaining a sort of economic equilibrium) is regarded as avarice. Weber therefore has to explain how the change could come about from this economic traditionalism to the notion that one has an ethical duty to make as much money as one can. In effect, he has to find a 'bridge' ethic—an ethic which developed out of the ethical conceptions justifying traditionalism, and which could in turn lead to the notion of 'duty in a calling'. It is necessary to be quite clear here about the nature of the problem. Of course, it was quite possible for individuals to disregard the traditionalistic ethical condemnation of money-making beyond one's needs. The late mediaeval period saw the rise of a class of prosperous merchants and bankers and financiers, well before the emergence of the 'spirit of capitalism'. But what has to be shown is how this kind of activity could come to be seen as an *ethical duty*, and how it could become a whole way of life for whole groups of people.

Before proposing an answer, Weber considers the suggestion that the development of the spirit of capitalism could be understood as part of a general process of rationalization of all fields of life. This is a way of looking at value-change which we have previously seen to be one of the ways characteristic of utilitarianism; it corresponds roughly to my categories (b) and (c) on pp. 145–6. But Weber is obviously bound to reject this suggestion. Of the objections which he offers, the two most important are simply re-assertions of familiar themes: (i) If by rationalism is meant rationalization from a utilitarian point of view, then 'we have already convinced ourselves that this is by no means the soil in which that relationship of a man to his calling as a task, which is necessary to capitalism, has pre-eminently grown' (Ibid., p. 77). (ii) We must repeat once more that

> . . . one may—this simple proposition, which is often forgotten should be placed at the beginning of every study which essays to deal with rationalism—rationalize life from fundamentally different basic points of view and in very different directions. Rationalism is an historical concept which covers a whole world of different things. It will be our task to find out whose intellectual child the particular concrete form of rational thought was, from which the idea of a calling and the devotion to labour in the calling has grown, which is, as we have seen, so irrational from the stand-point of purely eudae-monistic self-interest, but which has been and still is one of the most characteristic elements of our capitalistic culture.
>
> (Ibid., pp. 77–8)

The core of Weber's essay is his thesis that the ethic of 'duty in a calling' has its origin in the ideas of Protestant Christianity and especially of Calvinism. Weber detects the origin of the conception of a 'calling', in its new sense, in Luther's translation of the Bible. The conception acquires its importance from Luther's rejection of the idea of a spiritual hierarchy within the Church. Man has a direct and immediate relationship with God, being justified in God's sight not by works but by faith alone. Therefore, in particular, there is no special virtue in the monastic life; indeed, since such a life involves a renunciation of one's responsibilities in this world, it is a positive evil. Every man can live a life acceptable to God, whatever his position in life—that is to say, in whatever calling God has placed him. Every calling has the same value in God's eyes. However, Luther's concept of the calling remained essentially traditionalistic. At first he interpreted the concept as an aspect of the traditional Christian attitude of indifference to the things of this world: since man's sole concern is to prepare himself for the world to come, he has no business to bother himself with the distinctions of this world, and, therefore, one calling is as good as another. Later, as Luther himself became more involved in secular affairs, he added a more positive emphasis—the idea of a calling as a special task in this world, assigned to the individual by God. But after Luther had moved into opposition to the sects and the peasant rebellions, this aspect came to be outweighed by the idea that the existing social order is something ordained by God and not to be disturbed. Therefore the final emphasis was less on the idea of a calling as a special task assigned to the individual by God, and more on the idea of it as something to be accepted—the limits imposed on the individual's activity in this world, rather than an opportunity for positive virtue.

The concept of a calling received its positive emphasis from Calvinism. This fact might at first seem paradoxical. Calvin, even more strongly than Luther, denied the efficacy of any worldly activity to win salvation for a man. Not even faith could do so, let alone works. This followed directly from the central doctrine of Calvinism, that of predestination. Salvation was reserved solely for those who had been chosen as God's elect since the beginning of the world, in accordance with his own inscrutable will. To suppose that any man can win salvation for himself by his own merits would be to set limits to God's freedom and power. How then could the Calvinist emphasis on worldly activity arise? Because for the individual Calvinist, unable to depend for salvation on any priest or church or sacraments, living in intense spiritual isolation, the question which assumes overwhelming significance is: 'Am I one of the elect?' Calvin himself said that the question ought not to be asked; it was an attempt to prise open God's secrets. But the psychological pressures made it impossible for the individual to

L

suspend his questioning. Subsequent Calvinist leaders therefore prescribed a way of answering it. One should immerse oneself in intense worldly activity, for this alone can give one the certainty of election. A man's state of grace is manifested in the fact that God works through him; he is the tool of the divine will. Therefore all his actions will be actions serving to increase the glory of God, since that is the sole end for which this world has been created. Only one of the elect is able to augment the glory of God by real, and not merely apparent, good works. The characteristic features of this activity will be the following:

(a) It will be activity within the world. Calvinism, like Lutheranism, rejected the idea that the monastic life was superior and more pleasing to God. God has created this world, and human society within it, to glorify his name, and, therefore, human labour within it serves that end.

(b) It will be systematic activity. For the Catholic, good works can be regarded as a succession of individual acts, which may atone for individual sins or add to his chances of salvation. But the Calvinist posits an absolute distinction between the elect and the damned. Therefore the whole life of one of the elect must be on a totally different level. Even a single lapse is not something that can subsequently be atoned for but a sign that the man is not one of the elect. The activity of the elect must thus be rationalized through and through, subjected to a consistent method.

(c) It will be ascetic activity. The Calvinist rejects all sensuous artistic beauty because of its connotations of idolatry and its connection via Catholicism with the illusion that it may be a means to salvation. Moreover, asceticism is, as it was for the monastic orders, a technique for submitting one's life to the systematic rationalization which we have just mentioned. It is a way of achieving mastery over all irrational impulses and of bringing all one's actions under constant self-control.

(d) It will be activity in a calling. For only within a fixed and clearly defined calling can a man's work acquire the requisite systematic and methodical character. If it is not work in a calling, it is bound to be casual and irregular.

We can now see that the ethic of 'duty in a calling' did not simply arise out of nowhere. It was the ethic which followed naturally from the whole Calvinist scheme of ideas. On the one hand the notion of 'proof of salvation' provided the Calvinist with a tremendously powerful incentive towards restless systematic activity in a secular calling. On the other hand, the ascetic aspect of Calvinism meant that this ceaseless activity was never conceived of as having for its purpose the satisfaction of material wants. Hence there arises precisely that combination of strenuous acquisitive activity with a complete absence of enjoyment of the gains thereof, which is so irrational from a utilitarian point of view. And because this kind of activity was capable of being given a religious justification, it could be adopted on rational ethical grounds despite the traditionalistic condemnation of it.

This is not, of course, a complete exposition of Weber's essay. I have emphasized only those aspects of it which illustrate my own argument. It seems to me that they do illustrate it, because what emerges from Weber's account is that although the change from a traditionalistic economic ethic to an ethic of money-making without limit was an absolutely revolutionary change in values, nevertheless the new ethic could be seen as a development of existing ethical ideas. But I want to make it quite clear in what respect I am using this is an example. I certainly do not intend it to be regarded as an empirical proof of the thesis that revolutionary value-changes always and necessarily proceed by way of an extension of existing values. Obviously one cannot base such an empirical argument on only one case, and it could readily be objected that in other cases such a continuity would not be found. But the three points which I do want to make are:

(1) The fact that the new ethic can be justified in terms of previously existing ethical conceptions does not prevent it from being as radical a change in values as could be imagined. And therefore my claim that *all* instances of value-change, if they are to count as rational, must equally be in some sense an extension of existing values is not open to the objection that this would rule out the possibility of radical change.

(2) Weber implicitly assumes precisely what I am arguing, that any new ethic does have an 'origin' in the sense of being a development of pre-existing idea. And if we think in terms of concrete examples such as this one, we must surely agree that Weber's assumption is the natural and logical assumption which anyone would make. Historians always do look for the 'origins' of ideas in this sense. And this isn't an empirical assertion about historians, it is an assertion about the logic of the concept of 'explanation' as applied to human beliefs and ideas.

(3) One cannot hope to understand cases of radical value-change so long as one equates all rationality with utilitarian rationality. Weber's account exemplifies the need to recognize alternative rationalities. The contrast he draws between the rationality of utilitarianism and the rationality of Calvinism is in fact a particular instance of the fundamental ethical division which we discussed in chapter 4 between a humanistic ethic which stresses the need for man to utilize his environment and a religious ethic which stresses the need for man to respect his environment. We suggested there (p. 103) that it is especially against the background of a religious attitude that one can intelligibly propose an ethic to the effect that 'it is not for man to determine what the world should be like; rather, a man's task is to do the work that falls to his lot, and above all to do it well'. We argued that such an ethic is just as rational as a utilitarian ethic, but that they nevertheless constitute

radically different rationalities. From this point of view, then, we can legitimately describe a change from one ethic to another as a *radical* change, while still seeing it as rational. It is in fact the utilitarian who, because he sees practical rationality as a gradational concept admitting only of differences in degree which can be ranged in order on a single scale and measured by the consistency with which ends and means are accommodated to one another, is incapable of truly appreciating the nature of radical value-change.

4. From the Catholic Ethic to the Protestant Ethic

To complete my argument I need to be able to show that the Protestant ethic itself, although constituting a radical break with Catholicism, can be seen as a development of concepts within Catholicism. Weber, of course, does not show this—it is not the problem he is concerned with. But the point is readily apparent, and the arguments which would spell it out in detail are implicit in Weber's elucidation of Lutheranism and Calvinism as coherent religious systems. Thus, for example, in giving an account of what Lutheranism is and how Luther arrived at it, we should first have to note that the issues which he raises are, and by their very nature can only be, raised within a particular systematic ideology, viz. the ideology of Catholic Christianity. For example:

(a) Luther raises the question: 'How far are God's actions and purposes capable of being understood by men?' This is, of course, a question which can be asked within other religious traditions besides that of Christianity. But the meaning which this question has for Luther is determined by the fact that he asks it from within the Christian tradition. If, for example, the God about which he asked it had been the God of the philosophers—the God of Plato, or of Aristotle, or (anachronistically) of the Deists—both the way of answering it and the answer itself would have been very different. But the God about whom Luther is asking is the God of the Old and the New Testaments, and of the mediaeval Catholic church, a God whom Luther regards as having revealed himself to men in the past in certain particular ways, and whose relation to men is defined by this tradition. Consequently, factors within this tradition lead Luther to the theological conclusion that the nature of man and the nature of God are totally different, separated by an unbridgeable gulf, and thence to the ethical conclusion that men can never hope to comprehend God's plans and purposes or to attain to the kind of righteousness which he would demand.

(b) Luther raises the question: 'What can a man do to live in a manner pleasing to God, and obtain salvation from him?' Again, this is a question which can be asked in any religious tradition. But the meaning which it has for Luther is constituted by the fact that he poses it in particular terms which are traditional and inherited—concepts such as 'faith', 'works', 'grace', 'redemption', etc.

(c) Luther raises the question 'What value is to be ascribed to worldly activity?' This leads to a further question 'What is the relation between the material world and the spiritual world?' and this in turn involves the question 'What is the relation between the soul and the body?' Clearly these are questions which can be asked (in the way in which Luther asks them) only in a particular kind of metaphysic, one which is in some sense dualist. And the very meaning of the notions 'soul' and 'spiritual world' is determined by the particular religious tradition in which Luther is operating; they would have a very different meaning within the world-view of, for example, Homeric Greece.

It might be objected that this inherited vocabulary within which Luther is operating—'God', 'faith', 'works', 'grace', 'redemption', 'soul', 'spiritual'/'material', etc.—is not a specifically ethical vocabulary, and that the example, therefore, cannot be used to illustrate the creation of a radically new ethic out of inherited ethical concepts. It is surely clear, however, that a word like 'grace' is connected, not contingently but by virtue of its very meaning, with certain ways of behaving and certain ways of understanding and evaluating human behaviour. Perhaps it is not 'simply' an ethical word; for it is inseparable not only from particular ways of behaving but also from particular 'factual' judgements about the world. But it is part of my argument that words which are supposedly 'purely ethical' (like the paradigmatic 'good' and 'right' of numerous philosophical texts) are not the typical cases of ethical words. The fact is that insofar as Luther raises his questions within the metaphysical system of Christianity he is *ipso facto* raising them within an existing *ethical* system.

This system not only determines the kinds of question that he asks but also the kinds of answer that he arrives at. It is by looking at the Christian tradition, seen as the interventions of God in history, that one can conclude as Luther does that the Christian God is not a mere anthropomorphic super-hero like the Gods of the Greek pantheon, but is totally separate and distinct from our human nature. It is by looking at the Old and New Testaments as the record of God's revelations of himself to men that one can conclude that God can be known not by logic and rational thought but only to the extent that he chooses to reveal himself. And it is for this reason that, according to Luther, men can never hope to please God simply by doing good works, since their sense of righteousness can never correspond to God's sense of righteousness. But this does not mean that a man can never live in a manner that is justifiable before God; for the central Christian doctrines of the Incarnation and the Atonement imply that men can be reconciled to

God through faith in him. Hence there arises the characteristic Lutheran interpretation of the antithesis 'faith/works'. Luther also concludes from the traditional emphases within the Christian faith that there is an absolute severance between the material world and the spiritual world, and between the soul and the body. This is a further indication that activity which belongs to the material world has no spiritual value in itself. The secular order and the life of the body are imposed on men by God as a punishment, an expression of his power. Therefore no positive virtue can reside in the fulfilment of worldly duties except insofar as this constitutes obedience to divine commands; it is an illusion to suppose that human activity can 'improve' the secular world.

In saying that the system within which Luther is operating 'determines' the way in which he resolves the issues he has raised, I do not mean that his conclusions are the only possible ones within that system. The Catholic version of Christianity, for example, can equally well be erected upon the fundamental concepts of the Christian tradition without radical inconsistency or irrationality. What I mean is that it is within the Christian system that Luther's conclusions can be seen as rational and justifiable answers to the problems he has raised. The system suggests these as possible answers, although it may suggest others as well.

The two points which I have made so far—that both Luther's questions and also his conclusions are what they are because they arise from within a particular ideology—perhaps amount to no more than the recognition that he was a reformer, not a founder of a new religion. And this, of course, is obvious. But there is a third point to be made, which at the same time gives greater significance to the other two. It is precisely the fact that Luther is working from within an existing ideology that gives his ideas their radical nature. The points which he questions are not isolated and detached, but intricately related to a whole interlocking system of beliefs. Therefore, the initial questioning necessarily leads to a re-interpretation of the total system. We can see this logical inter-relationship working itself out as a chronological development in Luther's own life. At first he regards himself as concerned with a purely theological point—the relative efficacy of faith and works. But this very soon leads him to condemn the practice of selling indulgences; for the individual Christian is justified before God solely and directly by the power of his faith, and therefore the short cut offered by the Church in return for these very limited financial 'good works' is neither necessary nor sufficient. This particular challenge by Luther rapidly escalates into a questioning of the very purpose of the Church as an institution. For what is true of indulgences is true of all the other practices by which the Church purports to obtain salvation for the individual Christian. It is true, for example, of all the sacraments—

confession, baptism, the eucharist, etc. Certain of these may have a symbolic value, but no more than any other 'works' are they efficacious in themselves as means to salvation. Luther is also inevitably led into conflict with the notion of ecclesiastical authority. For if every individual Christian stands in a direct relationship to God through faith, then this relationship does not require to be mediated via an ecclesiastical hierarchy. Neither a priest nor a monk nor even the Pope himself is nearer to God than any faithful Christian. Nor is there any justification for the exercise of power by the Church within the secular world. As we have seen, Luther posits an absolute severance of the spiritual world from the material world. Therefore the Church belongs solely to the former; it is simply the community of all believers. The secular world has no spiritual value, and is therefore in itself no concern of the Church. From a spiritual point of view all that is required is complete acceptance of and obedience to the secular order of authority which God has instituted as an expression of his power. Hence Lutheranism expresses itself politically as the decline of 'Christendom' as a political entity and the rise of nationalism. The specifically ethical aspects of all this are, first, the notion of the primacy of the individual conscience in spiritual matters; second, the idea that, since there is to be no spiritual hierarchy, the Christian life has to be lived in the world, not in a monastery—this, together with the belief that the material world nevertheless has no value in itself, is the origin of that 'worldly asceticism' which Weber talks of; third, the idea that obedience to secular authority must be absolute, not conditional upon the conformity of that authority to any standards of moral or political right, and that any attempt at the amelioration or reform of the secular order is fundamentally misplaced. It must be emphasized that all these points are not to be seen as the *results* of Lutheranism, as a contingent sequence of historical conse-quences. Rather, they are the *meaning* of Lutheranism, the meaning which it necessarily receives from the context of ethical and religious ideas into which it is born. And it is just because it has a meaning within this context that we can speak of it as being a *radical* change— one which goes to the root of existing ethical conceptions and therefore entails a systematic re-interpretation of them.

The interpretation of Lutheranism which I have offered might be objected to on the grounds that what Luther did was not so much to base radically new ideas on traditional concepts, as simply to re-assert the traditional ideas and condemn lapses from them. Certainly Luther tended to see himself as effecting a return to the pure forms of primitive Christianity, rather than as an innovator. Nevertheless I believe that simply to interpret Lutheranism in this way would be to miss its significance. The world in which the doctrines of Lutheranism were elaborated was a world in which the Christian Church was a major political power. Therefore any Christian teachings about the Church were bound to have a different meaning in that world from their meaning in the world of primitive Christianity. More specifically, when the Church was simply a small face-to-face community of practising Christians there was no opposition between the idea that salvation was to be obtained through the Church and the idea that every faithful Christian had a direct relationship with God. But the Roman branch of the Church developed until it became what was in effect a secular power. This development does not necessarily have to be seen as a decline from the pristine purity of the Church (though it was that too); it can equally be seen as the triumph of spiritual values and institutions over secular values and institutions, and, therefore, as natural and justifiable within the Christian scheme of beliefs. In the process, however, the Catholic Church became an institutionalized hierarchical system of authority. Consequently when Luther wished to reassert the principle of justification by faith, he could do so only by introducing the dichotomy 'individual/Church'. In effect, therefore, the traditional concept, re-asserted in changed circumstances, acquired a new meaning and became a new idea. Similarly with the question whether the Church should exercise power over the secular princes. This question means one thing if one is asking whether a Christian prince should give priority in all things to his commitment to the Christian community. But it means another thing if one is asking whether the Church, having become in effect a quasi-secular power, should take precedence among the secular powers. Luther gives the answer 'No' because the question itself has changed its meaning. The case of Lutheranism is accordingly an excellent example of how, using pre-existing ethical concepts, one may nevertheless build from them a radically new ethic.

A clear statement of the interpretation of Lutheranism which I have been defending, coupled with an equally clear assertion of precisely that philosophical position which I have been attacking, can be found in Roy Pascal's *The Social Basis of the German Reformation* (a book from which I have obtained much of my information about Luther). After arguing that Lutheranism provided a metaphysical and ethical system which suited the needs of the settled, authoritarian German middle class, Pascal adds:

It must not be thought, of course, that this whole system was the abstract product of the middle class, simply and solely the rationalization of the economic needs of the contemporaries of Luther. The metaphysical system, especially particular concepts, of such a class might be imagined in a different form than Lutheranism. They evolved, however, historically from a former state of society, together with the middle class itself. They are modifications of ideas and values which permeated the whole of society, and at no point in history is a complete revision of concepts possible unless a complete revolution in authority is aimed at. Luther's class enjoyed some part of authority before the Reformation, however, and consequently did not wish for a complete revolution. Indeed, it needed to sustain some authority in order to maintain its privileges against the claims of other classes. Thus Luther worked inside the traditional framework of ideas, and even preserved the traditional concept of dogma.

(Op. cit., pp. 241-2)

That the ideas of Lutheranism were modifications of pre-existing ideas and values is what I have been arguing. But Pascal seems to suppose that this was only contingently the case, and is to be contrasted with a possible alternative situation in which there is 'a complete revision of concepts' because a 'complete revolution in authority is aimed at'. However, I think we have to ask what this 'complete revision' could conceivably amount to. One can imagine a revision of concepts differing from the Lutheran revision in degree—involving a more radical departure from previous modes of life but nevertheless taking its starting-points from certain existing ethical concepts. Indeed, one does not have to imagine it, for the anabaptists and levellers led by Münzer and Pfeiffer, Luther's contemporaries, precisely fit that description. In a sense, they were not 'working inside the traditional framework of ideas' as Luther was. Certainly they aimed at 'a complete revolution in authority'. But, equally certainly, they based their doctrines on certain fundamental Christian concepts; indeed, the doctrines were basically a more thorough-going and consistent development of Luther's own principles. Their radicalism thus differed from that of Luther only in degree. They did not aim at a complete revision of concepts in the sense of attempting to impose an entirely new set of concepts having absolutely nothing in common with existing concepts. And what I am claiming is that nothing could conceivably count as doing this. For if we try to suppose such a situation we immediately come up against those difficulties which are inherent in the idea of a private language. To put it simply, how could such concepts be given a meaning?

What goes for Lutheranism goes equally for Calvinism. Like Luther, Calvin begins with certain assertions about the nature of God as defined by the Christian tradition. To Luther's assertion of the inscrutability of divine purposes he adds a particular stress on the concept of divine omnipotence. This is then connected to the concept of 'salvation' in a radically new way. Calvin thus arrives at the notion of 'predestination', which is central to his whole system. When applied systematically this notion necessitates a re-interpretation of virtually all Christian doctrines including the fundamental ethical concepts of Christianity. But, of course, to give this account of Calvinism is at the same time to stress the significance of the fact that Calvin *is* employing the traditional ethical concepts of Christianity. As with Luther, what makes Calvinistic ethics a radical new departure is not *how many* previous concepts are rejected, but *how central* a place is occupied within the received system by the ideas which Calvin questions. And of course beliefs about the nature of God occupy *the* central place within a religious system; therefore new ideas at this point necessarily have ramifications throughout the system.

Examples could be multiplied. But if I have succeeded in making clear the sort of thing I have in mind when I say that a radically new ethic always also involves an extension of existing ethical concepts, then the multiplication of examples is unnecessary. For, of course, it is obvious that any new ethic always has to be presented and argued for, and what is important is not this *fact* but its *significance*. Once the latter has been made apparent for a few cases, it is equally apparent for all. If I turn now to one further example, this is because it seems to me to raise certain important new points. I want to look at the most important contemporary example of a revolutionary change in values, namely the rejection of liberal morality in the name of socialist morality.

5. FROM LIBERAL MORALITY TO SOCIALIST MORALITY

To show that the socialist ethic took up and extended pre-socialist ethical concepts, we could use the same kinds of argument as we have used in previous examples. We could consider the character of working-class socialism as a social movement; at this level, we could point to the ideals of the Dissenting churches—anti-authoritarianism, local democratic self-government, the egalitarian interpretation of Christian ethics —as one of the most important origins of the egalitarian and democratic ideals of the English working-class movement; or we could point to the way in which the concept of 'the rights of man', derived from bourgeois political theorists such as Locke, was developed by Paine so as to become one of the crucial formative influences on the embryonic working-class ideology in the 1790s.[1] We could also consider the relation between socialist and pre-socialist ideas at a more theoretical level. We could note how concepts in liberal moral and political theory such as 'justice' and 'liberty' are taken up into socialist theory, where they are re-interpreted; the liberal concepts of 'justice' and 'liberty' are criticized as being inadequate, and this criticism leads to a formulation of alternative, socialist concepts of 'justice' and 'liberty'.[2] In particular,

[1] See Chapters 2 and 4 respectively of E. P. Thompson: *The Making of the English Working Class*.

[2] W. B. Gallie, in his essay on 'Liberal Morality and Socialist Morality', contrasts the two in something like this manner.

we could note how Marx arrived at his formulation of socialist theory via the Hegelian concepts of freedom and harmony.[1] The concept of freedom is absolutely central to Marxism. Certainly Marx does not accept the concept uncritically, but his redefinition consists in giving the concept an extended content by emphasizing the emergence in society of new kinds of limitations on freedom; therefore, conversely, one could not hope to understand Marx's critique of existing society without presupposing the concept. In the economic works of the mature Marx there is less attention to this sort of traditional moral discussion; but unless it is to some extent presupposed, we can give no sense to the role of the concept of 'exploitation', for example, in Marx's economic theory. It might be objected that Marx is using the term not with the intention of passing any moral judgement, but simply as a neutral scientific description. But Marx could not have made the move from descriptive economics to political prescription, in the way that he does, other than by employing concepts with the sort of moral force that the concept of 'exploitation' has.

This interpretation of Marx, however, has often been challenged. It has been suggested that the presentation of socialist theory as an ethical critique of existing society was merely a youthful aberration on Marx's part. This suggestion seems to gain support from numerous passages in Marx's works, from the *German Ideology* onwards, where he pours scorn on those who engage in moral condemnation as a substitute for revolutionary action. These passages might be taken to imply that Marx rejects the very possibility of a meaningful condemnation of capitalist society in terms of ethical concepts which are shared with the bourgeoisie and which can at the same time constitute the ground of working-class opposition to bourgeois hegemony. Such an interpretation can be readily incorporated into an economic-determinist version of Marxism with a corresponding treatment of the notion of 'superstructures'. On this view, all intellectual theories, including all ethical theories, are in some sense illusory; they have no independent reality, and are mere 'reflections' of the relations between social classes. In Engels' writings, for example, conflicting moralities are seen as distorted expressions of the material interests and needs of conflicting classes.

My particular reason for mentioning this version of Marxism is that it might seem to have a certain affinity with my own position. I have laid stress on what I have referred to as the *social* nature of ethics, and have argued that rational ethical judgements are necessarily grounded in the norms of some human collectivity, some social group. From this it might be inferred that classes, e.g. the bourgeoisie and the proletariat in capitalist society, constitute such social groups. In that case each

[1] See Eugene Kamenka: *The Ethical Foundations of Marxism.*

class would constitute a 'form of life' with its own standards of rationality, including its own ethical standards. These standards would make it possible to arrive at ethical judgements which could be accepted as rational within that social class, but there could be no objective and rational argument concerning the conflicting claims of the alternative moralities. Therefore, between the bourgeoisie and the proletariat of capitalist society there could be only disagreement and conflict. And this picture bears an obvious resemblance to the aforementioned interpretation of Marxism, though without the notions of 'material interests' and economic reductionism.

Something like this position seems to be maintained by Alasdair MacIntyre in his *Short History of Ethics*—but I stress the word 'seems', because I am by no means certain that this would be a correct interpretation of what he says. In passages such as the following, I find suggestions of at least two possible views:

> Suppose a society . . . in which the form of life presupposes agreement on ends. Here there are agreed criteria for the use of 'good'. . . . In this society there is a recognized list of virtues, an established set of moral rules. . . . Is moral criticism in such a society impossible? By no means; but it must proceed by an extension of, and not by a total break with, the established moral vocabulary. . . .
>
> . . . In our society the acids of individualism have for four centuries eaten into our moral structures, for both good and ill. But not only this: we live with the inheritance of not only one, but of a number of well-integrated moralities. . . . Within each of these moralities there is a proposed end or ends, a set of rules, a list of virtues. But the ends, the rules, the virtues, differ. . . . It follows that we are liable to find two kinds of people in our society: those who speak from within one of these surviving moralities, and those who stand outside all of them. Between the adherents of rival moralities and between the adherents of one morality and the adherents of none there exists no court of appeal, no impersonal neutral standard. . . .
>
> . . . Marx resembles Hegel and the English idealists in seeing a communal framework as presupposed by morality; unlike them, he sees that it no longer exists; and he proceeds to characterize the whole situation as one in which moralizing can no longer play a genuine role in settling social differences. It can only be an attempt to invoke an authority which no longer exists and to mask the sanctions of social coercion.

All this, of course, does not entail that the traditional moral vocabulary cannot still be used. It does entail that we cannot expect to find in our society a single set of moral concepts, a shared interpretation of the vocabulary. Conceptual conflict is endemic in our situation,

because of the depth of our moral conflicts. Each of us, therefore, has
to choose both with whom we wish to be morally bound and by what
ends, rules and virtues we wish to be guided. These two choices are
inextricably linked. In choosing to regard this end or that virtue
highly, I make certain moral relationships with some other people,
and other moral relationships with others impossible. Speaking from
within my own moral vocabulary, I shall find myself bound by the
criteria embodied in it. These criteria will be shared with those who
speak the same moral language. And I must adopt some moral
vocabulary if I am to have any social relationships. For without rules,
without the cultivation of virtues, I cannot share ends with anyone
else. I am doomed to social solipsism. Yet I must choose for myself
with whom I am to be morally bound. I must choose between
alternative forms of social and moral practice. Not that I stand morally naked until I have chosen. For our social past determines that
each of us has some vocabulary with which to frame and to make
his choice.

(Op. cit., pp. 265-8)

Here we find precisely that emphasis which I have maintained on the
grounding of ethical judgements in the standards of a society. We find
also the conclusion which I have been attempting to derive from it, that
'moral criticism . . . must proceed by an extension of, and not by a total
break with, the established moral vocabulary'. From this it would
follow that we are able to make a rational comparison between rival
moralities, e.g. between bourgeois morality and socialist morality; for
between these moralities there is a certain continuity of ethical concepts.
And in the last paragraph MacIntyre offers hints in this direction, as in
the denial that 'I stand morally naked until I have chosen'. But we also
find suggestions of an alternative view: that one's commitment to one
of two rival moralities is ultimately a matter of allegiances. On this view,
if I align myself with one social group I shall thereby situate myself
within one morality, and if I align myself with some other social group
I shall thereby situate myself within an alternative morality; but the two
moralities, and the two groups, do not share any continuity of ethical
concepts by reference to which I can choose with which of them to
align myself. MacIntyre's inclination towards such a view comes out
more strongly in his discussion of Marx:

. . . Within bourgeois society there are two social groups at least,
constituted by the dominant and the dominated class. Each of these
has its own fundamental goals and form of life. It follows that moral
precepts may find a role within the social life of each class. But there
are no independent transcendent norms which are above those issues

which divide the classes. Certainly, many of the same precepts will occur in the moralities of each class, simply in virtue of each class being a human group. But these will not serve to determine the relations between classes.

According to MacIntyre, these considerations explain Marx's attitude to the passing of moral judgements:

> Marx .., believed that in matters of conflict between social classes the appeal to moral judgements was not only pointless but positively misleading. So he tried to excise from documents of the First International appeals for justice for the working class. For to whom are these appeals being made? Presumably to those responsible for exploitation; but they are acting in accord with the norms of their class, and although individual philanthropic moralists may be found among the bourgeoisie, philanthropy cannot alter class structure.

What one *can* do, nevertheless, is to

> ... appeal not to some independent classless tribunal but to the terms in which one's opponents have themselves chosen to be judged. So in the *Manifesto* Marx throws back the charges levelled against communism by bourgeois critics, arguing that they stand condemned not on his premises but on their own.

However,

> ... the use of moral vocabulary always presupposes a shared form of social order. Appeal to moral principles against some existing state of affairs is always an appeal within the limits of that form of society; to appeal against that form of society we must find a vocabulary which does not presuppose its existence. Such a vocabulary one finds in the form of expression of wants and needs which are unsatisfiable within the existing society, wants and needs which demand a new social order. So Marx appeals to the wants and needs of the working class against the social order of bourgeois society.
>
> (Ibid., pp. 212–14)

Here MacIntyre seems to imply that although the bourgeois social order may be condemned from the standpoint of bourgeois ethical concepts, this is not the same as the condemnation of it from the standpoint of socialist morality. There are, in other words, two irreconcilable ethical vocabularies, each being an element in the form of life of a separate social group. Whereas I have suggested that socialist ethics inherits from bourgeois ethics such concepts as 'liberty', 'justice', and 'exploitation', MacIntyre would perhaps want to say that this is no more than the inheritance of certain words. He would suggest, perhaps, that the word 'liberty' means something different in the context of socialist morality from what it means in the context of liberal morality; of course there are connections and of course it is not purely arbitrary that the same word is used in both cases, but nevertheless what we have here are ultimately two different concepts. And there cannot be reasons or arguments for adopting one concept rather than the other. Which concept one uses will depend on which perspective one already occupies, and this is not something amenable to rational choice but is rather a question of where one finds oneself. If I am a bourgeois, I will see 'liberty' in one way; if I am a worker, or if I align myself with the workers, I will see it in another.[1]

For the sake of a convenient label I shall refer to this as 'MacIntyre's position', even though there is equally good evidence in his book for ascribing a different position to him. It is clearly important to discuss the relation between this position and my own, since this raises again (as in the previous chapter) the whole question of what sort of social unit I have in mind when I speak of 'the social nature of ethics'. And if the relevant kind of social unit *can* be a particular class within a society, so that my emphasis on the social basis of ethics does lead to something like MacIntyre's position, then the charge of social conformism might be reformulated by saying that my account allows for the possibility of a radical change in the ethic of a society only when this takes the form of a new social class achieving predominance and imposing its own ethic, and that therefore I cannot allow for a change in values which is both *radical* and also *rational*.

However, I do not think that my own argument does lead to such a position. In order to mark off the difference between that position and my own, I want to look at MacIntyre's claim that the different social classes in modern society no longer share a common ethical vocabulary. To what extent is this true? Well, we might say, at any rate they all share the English language. As a matter of fact I think that this is very relevant to the present argument. But of course this relevance has to be demonstrated. As a first step towards showing it, I want to look more closely at the positive content which MacIntyre gives to his thesis. It remains rather sketchy in the *Short History of Ethics*, but is given much greater substance in MacIntyre's lectures entitled *Secularization and Moral Change*. In the first of these three lectures MacIntyre attributes the loss of a common ethical vocabulary and of shared and established norms primarily to the urbanization of the Industrial Revolution, which meant

---

[1] The ascription of these views to MacIntyre is supported by what he says about Montesquieu in the middle paragraph on p. 180 (op. cit.).

the destruction of the older forms of community and the emergence of new kinds of class division involving relations of class conflict. This 'changing structure of society makes it only too obvious to all parties that the alleged authoritative norms to which appeal is made are in fact man-made, and that they are not the norms of the *whole* community to which in their own way men of *every* rank are *equally* subject' (op. cit., p. 14). More specifically, for the new urban working-class it is all too obvious that the traditional norms of Christianity are being used 'too often, and too publicly, (as) a device to secure the class interest of the ruling classes'—to sanction a spurious 'public security', to render working-class children 'honest, obedient, courteous, industrious, submissive and orderly', or to impose factory discipline (Ibid., p. 19). The consequence of this class conflict was that separate classes built up their own moralities, although these class moralities ultimately proved inadequate to articulate the aspirations and values of the respective classes. In the second lecture MacIntyre outlines the content of three main class moralities:

(1) The upper-middle-class morality typified in the public-school prefect.

Its principal virtues are loyalty to the group and the cultivation of a corresponding feeling that there are really no limits to what you may do to outsiders.

A further characteristic attitude is

the suggestion that your own group is the bearer of the essential past, and within this morality . . . there is a very strong sense of continuity with a past that is largely the product of genealogical imagination. . . . This false picture of the group as inheriting its position is used to justify its antipathy to careerism, an antipathy which is accompanied by a feeling that members of this particular group have a *right* to a certain sort of job. It is wrong to be too ambitious and it is wrong to plan and contrive too much, because this would suggest that you are uncertain of your claim on society. You must be honest because it is beneath your dignity not to be, and your honesty, your right to a certain type of position, and your loyalty to the group are together put to the service of a paternalism towards those over whom it is your vocation to rule.

(Ibid., pp. 38–9)

(2) The morality of the middle-class businessman, rooted in survivals of the puritan ethic.

Thrift is a key virtue, hard work is seen as a virtue in itself and not merely as a means to an end, and self-help and self-advancement have a maximal value.

(Ibid., p. 41)

(3) The morality of the Trade Union movement.

A worker can better himself only by bettering his class. Trade Union morality rests on the view that a man's links are chiefly with those with whom he works. Its tenets are that a worker is essentially equal with those with whom he works, that he is also essentially equal with those who claim superiority to him, and that in knowing that he is equal to them he has his chief weapon against them. . . . At the same time there is a disbelief in paternalist help. . . . Instead there is a deep belief in mutual assistance, and . . . in the virtues of solidarity and fraternity.

(Ibid., p. 42)

At this point it may be appropriate to recall some sentences previously quoted from MacIntyre:

. . . to appeal against (the existing) form of society we must find a vocabulary which does not presuppose its existence. Such a vocabulary one finds in the form of expression of wants and needs which are unsatisfiable within the existing society, wants and needs which demand a new social order. So Marx appeals to the wants and needs of the working class against the social order of bourgeois society.

I suspect, therefore, that MacIntyre may regard these aspirations of the working class—equality, solidarity, fraternity—as the ground of socialist morality and of the socialist critique of existing society. Let us therefore look more closely at this concept of 'solidarity', for example. We should first remember the obvious fact that this concept did not suddenly emerge out of nowhere—did not, as it were, spring fully armed from the heads of the workers. It was a value which the embryonic working class arrived at in struggling to make sense of their personal experience. And this struggle was precisely the struggle to make sense of a radically new situation by means of an inherited vocabulary. Therefore the new concept gets its meaning from this traditional vocabulary adapted to the new situation. In a sense, admittedly, it was forced on the emergent working class by external circumstances. It can be argued that it was simply a plain fact that the worker could better himself only by bettering his class; in their struggle for a better life, the only weapon which the working class possessed was their numerical

M

superiority, and this could constitute an effective weapon only if there was class unity. However, the very fact that the working class confronted and evaluated its experience in terms of these options—individual self-advancement or mutual assistance—is not something that can be taken for granted but rather is to be explained as due to the ethical concepts inherited from pre-industrial, pre-working-class experience. Here again, for example, we can refer, as we have done previously, to the ethical concepts derived from Christianity, and especially from the Dissenting churches, and their influence on working-class values and methods of organization. Of course, the ethic of 'loving one's neighbour', or the notion that all men are equal in the sight of God, are not the same as the concept of working-class solidarity; but it is by virtue of the fact that our common language contains concepts of the former kind that a space is available in it, as it were, for the latter concept.

Moreover, the concept of 'solidarity' was not just that of a technique for survival but also, as I have already indicated, one which was able to give a sense, a meaning, to working-class experience. To explicate it by saying that a worker can better himself only by bettering his class is to represent only the utilitarian aspect of it. But the concept was also one which was capable of making working-class experience more than just a struggle for survival, of giving the harsh realities of the struggle an ethical value. It was a concept which ennobled what it referred to. And this was made possible by the meaning which the concept necessarily acquired from its history and its place in our language.

In what sense, then, is this evidence of a common vocabulary? Insofar as the concept of solidarity is a working-class concept, and not one employed by members of the bourgeoisie, the two classes do not share a common vocabulary. But insofar as the concept of solidarity gets its meaning from a common language, a language shared by both the dominant and the dominated class, there is a *potential* common vocabulary, a stock of ethical concepts available to all users of the language, whether or not they actually employ them. The point is that the concept of 'solidarity' is one which *can* be as meaningful to the public-school paternalist or the middle-class businessman as it is to the working-class Trade Unionist. And conversely the values of independence and hard work are values whose meaningfulness *can* be apprehended by the Trade Unionist, even though they might make little sense or seem inappropriate if he were to attempt to apply them to his own personal experience. Now to the extent that there are ways of making the various ethical concepts meaningful to members of all classes, there are available to all users of the language the means of making a rational assessment of the working-class ethic, or a rational choice between the bourgeois ethic and the working-class ethic. There is a continuity between the two ethics analogous to the continuities we have observed in previous examples; the radical revision is at the same time an extension and development of inherited ethical concepts. To point up the analogy we might ask whether Lutheranism and Catholicism share a common vocabulary. Here, as in the case of bourgeois morality and working-class morality, we have to answer that in a sense they do not. The concept of 'the priesthood of all believers', the Lutheran concept of a calling, and so on, are not concepts which are shared with Catholicism. And yet we can understand the relation between Lutheranism and Catholicism only if we see that relation as constituted by disputes which can themselves be formulated and resolved (one way or the other) only by means of a common vocabulary and a common stock of concepts.

My argument can be brought out in another way by looking at MacIntyre's own presentation of the working-class ethic. He begins with the following quotation from a writer on industrial relations:

> A very persistent attitude of the British working class is the belief that any member who tries to better himself is a class traitor who is disloyal to the workers, and two important results of this are the difficulties experienced by the ambitious worker who wants to become a manager or attain an even higher position in industry, and the intelligent boy or girl of working class origin who wants to go to a University to study for a professional career. The former is likely to experience the contempt of his mates, and even have other difficulties put in his way, the latter apart from the deep seated notion that anyone who is studying is in some way queer is likely to meet the other attitude that anyone who is not earning as much money as possible is soft.
>
> (Quoted ibid., pp. 41–2)

MacIntyre comments that 'this is a characteristic view of the working class as seen from the standpoint of and through the distorting and myopic lenses of the middle class.' He then goes on to re-state the Trade Union ethic in much more favourable terms, so that it can be seen as a meaningful and consistent way of life. And he does this by using a different vocabulary—the vocabulary of equality and fraternity and solidarity and mutual assistance—and by showing how 'the deep belief in mutual assistance . . . takes over some of the functions of the pre-industrial extended family and of the pre-industrial community', and so on. Now the point which I want to stress is that in this way MacIntyre makes the working-class morality intelligible to members of the middle class who are unacquainted with the working-class way of life. Therefore, 'the distorting and myopic lenses of the middle class' are not a barrier which makes it in any sense logically impossible for the middle class to understand the working-class ethic. At most they are a psycho-logical barrier. For it is by using the resources of a common ethical language that MacIntyre makes the working-class ethic intelligible. Moreover, in making it intelligible he is *ipso facto* providing possible reasons for adhering to it—not reasons which consist in deriving it from something else which is external to the ethic, but reasons which consist simply in showing what the ethic is. And the fact that the ethic is made intelligible by relating it to other concepts in the language—e.g. the concept of the family, which pre-dates it—shows again how this possibility of making it intelligible and offering reasons in support of it is connected with the continuity between it and pre-working-class ideas.

At this point it might be objected that when the concept of 'solidarity' is made intelligible in this way, this enables one to understand it only in an 'external' manner. One can appreciate the practical force of this concept, it might be said, only when one understands it from experience, i.e. by sharing the experience of the working class. And since, in that case, the concept could operate as a reason for acting in certain ways only for those who belonged to the relevant social group, this could be used as an argument in support of MacIntyre's position. I think it is true that there is this distinction between 'understanding from experi-ence' and 'understanding from outside'. It is true not just of this example but of many others. For example, it might be said that one has not understood what love is until one has actually experienced it. Now the first, and perhaps obvious, point to be made here is that this 'understanding from experience' is not to be thought of as a *greater degree* of understanding—i.e. of the same kind of understanding. It is a different kind of understanding altogether—and the only way of bring-ing out what kind of understanding it is, is by saying that it just *is* understanding from direct experience. When a person, after learning all there is to learn about love 'from outside', subsequently comes to understand what love is from direct experience, this does not enable him to say or to specify anything further about what love is like; for, *ex hypothesi*, he was already able to say all that can be said about love. He does not learn anything further about the relation between love and other kinds of activity or other kinds of experience. Similarly, someone who understands all that there is to be said about the concept of solidarity, and for whom this concept has been made perfectly in-telligible on a verbal level, but has never shared in actual working-class experience, does not need this experience in order to see the concept of solidarity as a justification for certain kinds of action. He can still recognize the force of the concept, and can act on it, or can criticize middle-class ways of life from the standpoint of this concept. It may be that, as a matter of fact, in his own deliberations about how to act or to assess actions this concept does not carry as much weight in opposition to alternative ideas as it would do if he had had direct experience of working-class life. But that is rather different.

My claim that the rival ethics of different social classes are nevertheless situated within a common language and a common ethical vocabulary can be approached from another angle. Classes are not static social blocs with rigid boundaries. For all the reality—the oppressive reality —of class divisions, individuals in our society do participate in a common social life. Certainly I would want to argue that the poverty and barrenness and dehumanization of this common social life are direct consequences of an economic division of labour creating distinct social classes. But this very fact can be significantly stated only if there is some minimal participation in a common social life. In the complete absence of the latter, one cannot use the vocabulary of 'class division' at all. MacIntyre, indeed, recognizes this participation in a common social life as a historical fact of our society. He notes that the separation into independent class moralities was broken down to some extent by the necessity for class interaction and cooperation. I should regard this not as a contingent fact, but as an *a priori* truth about the concepts of 'class' and 'society'. MacIntyre recognizes that, insofar as this interaction and cooperation was necessary, it was inevitable that there should to some extent be a common ethical vocabulary, even though the basic division into class moralities persisted. But he tends to minimize this fact by asserting that the common stock of ethical concepts was limited to what he calls the 'secondary virtues'. Such virtues as 'a pragmatic approach to problems, cooperativeness, fair play, tolerance, a gift for compromise, and fairness' are, he says, the ones which inevitably come to the forefront with the development of class cooperation. But he argues that an ethical vocabulary containing only concepts of this sort is incomplete, since 'their existence in a moral scheme of things as virtues is secondary to, is if you like parasitic upon, the notion of another primary set of virtues which are directly related to the goals which men pursue as the ends of their life' (Ibid., p. 24). MacIntyre's assumption here that any ethic, if it is to be complete and intelligible, must be teleological, i.e. must stress 'goals' to be achieved, is one which I have previously rejected. Hence even if it is the case that the shared ethical concepts of a society are limited to virtues of this kind, this does not necessarily entail that the society does not possess an adequate common ethical vocabulary. But, of course, it is true that men do pursue goals, and although it does not follow that an intelligible and comprehensive ethic must be one which stresses goals as the fundamental values, it does follow that any ethic must provide a basis for some kind of attitude towards the pursuit of goals. But the moral scheme of which the so-called 'secondary virtues' are a part *is* such an ethic. As MacIntyre recognizes, it is in effect the ethic of liberalism. On pp. 44–5 MacIntyre speaks of the inevitable growth of liberal ideas as a further factor contributing to the breakdown of the divisions between class moralities. The essence of the liberal ethic is that the goals which an individual chooses to pursue, the purposes which give a meaning and a direction to his personal life, are a matter of subjective predilection. Therefore, where a society is divided among divergent social classes and sharply divergent ways of life, but where there is nevertheless a need for co-operation and intercourse between these classes and movements at the level of economic necessity, liberalism is supremely fitted as an overall ethic within which these different elements can interact. It recognizes the existence of a plurality of radically different ways of life by emphasizing the freedom of the individual to choose his personal values; social activity is then seen primarily as what is necessary to guarantee this individual freedom—hence the importance of MacIntyre's 'secondary virtues'. And this is why, to the extent that there is a common ethical vocabulary in our society, an important element in it consists of many of the concepts that belong within the liberal ethic.

However, what I want to stress ultimately is not the existence of a 'common vocabulary' but that of a 'common language'. That is to say, although it is undeniable that different social groups do employ different evaluative concepts, the concepts are situated in, and draw their meaning from, a common language, and consequently the concepts associated with a particular social group are accessible to someone from outside that group. The vocabulary of liberalism does to some extent constitute a common ethical vocabulary, but what is more important is that the ability of different classes to see it as a meaningful vocabulary is an indication of the existence of a common normative language in this more fundamental sense. To recognize the existence of this common normative language is to see the concepts of the working-class ethic as a development and extension of pre-working-class normative concepts, and hence to see the change from the one ethic to the other as a rational change. Similarly—and in apparent contradiction to MacIntyre I believe that this is something *different*, though obviously closely connected—we can see the concepts of the socialist ethic as extensions of liberal norma-tive concepts, and can therefore see this development too as a rational one. Finally, corresponding to this historical fact is the fact that a rational case can therefore be made for the socialist ethic which does not presuppose a prior acceptance of the ethic and which at the same time does not appeal to supposed 'independent transcendent norms' or 'impersonal neutral standards'. And this conclusion, if it is valid, seems to me to be of some importance.

Bibliography

The following is a list of the works referred to in the text. In those cases where a work is available in more than one form or in more than one edition, I have listed only the particular source which I have used.

G. E. M. Anscombe: *Intention* (Basil Blackwell, 1957).

G. E. M. Anscombe: 'Modern Moral Philosophy' (in *Philosophy*, 1958).

A. J. Ayer: 'On the Analysis of Moral Judgements' and 'The Principle of Utility' (both in *Philosophical Essays*, Macmillan, 1954).

Jonathan Bennett: 'Whatever the Consequences' (in *Analysis*, 1965–6).

Jeremy Bentham: *Deontology* (ed. Bowring, London, 1934).

G. A. Cohen: 'Beliefs and Roles' (in *Proceedings of the Aristotelian Society*, 1966–7).

Joseph Conrad: *Lord Jim* (Penguin Books, 1949).

Emile Durkheim: 'The Determination of Moral Facts' (in *Sociology and Philosophy*, translated by D. F. Pocock, Cohen and West, 1953).

Emile Durkheim: *Moral Education* (translated by E. K. Wilson and H. Schnurer, Free Press of Glencoe, 1961).

Philippa Foot: 'Moral Beliefs' (in *Theories of Ethics*, O.U.P., 1967).

W. B. Gallie: 'Liberal Morality and Socialist Morality' (in *Philosophy, Politics and Society*, First Series, edited by Peter Laslett, Basil Blackwell, 1963).

David P. Gauthier: *Practical Reasoning* (O.U.P., 1963).

Russell Grice: *The Grounds of Moral Judgements* (C.U.P., 1967).

A. Phillips Griffiths and R. S. Peters: 'The Autonomy of Prudence' (in *Mind*, 1962).

R. M. Hare: *The Language of Morals* (O.U.P., 1952).

R. M. Hare: *Descriptivism* (reprinted from the *Proceedings of the British Academy*, Vol. XLIX, O.U.P., 1963).

R. M. Hare: *Freedom and Reason* (O.U.P., 1963).

R. F. Holland: 'The Autonomy of Ethics' (in *P.A.S.S.V.*, 1958).

David Hume: *A Treatise of Human Nature, Book III: Of Morals* and *An Enquiry Concerning the Principles of Morals*. (Both in *Hume's Moral and Political Philosophy*, edited by Henry D. Aiken, Hafner Library of Classics, 1948).

E. Kamenka: *The Ethical Foundations of Marxism* (Routledge & Kegan Paul, 1962).

Arthur Koestler: *Darkness at Noon* (Penguin Books, 1947).

D. H. Lawrence: *The Rainbow* (Penguin Books, 1949).

David Lyons: *Forms and Limits of Utilitarianism* (O.U.P., 1965).

Alasdair MacIntyre: 'Hume on "Is" and "Ought"' (in *Philosophical Review*, 1959).

Alasdair MacIntyre: *A Short History of Ethics* (Macmillan, 1966).

Alasdair MacIntyre: *Secularization and Moral Change* (O.U.P., 1967).

Karl Marx: *Economic and Philosophical Manuscripts* (in Erich Fromm: *Marx's Concept of Man*, Frederick Ungar Publishing Co., 1961).

B. F. McGuiness: 'I Know What I Want' (in *P.A.S.*, 1956–7).

J. S. Mill: *Utilitarianism* (edited by Mary Warnock in The Fontana Philosophy Series, Collins, 1962).

G. E. Moore: *Principia Ethica* (C.U.P., 1903).

G. E. Moore: 'The Nature of Moral Philosophy' (in *Philosophical Studies*, Routledge & Kegan Paul, 1922).

Jan Narveson: *Morality and Utility* (Johns Hopkins Press, 1967).

P. H. Nowell-Smith: *Ethics* (Penguin Books, 1954).

Roy Pascal: *The Social Basis of the German Reformation* (Watts, 1933).

D. Z. Phillips and H. O. Mounce: 'On Morality's Having a Point' (in *Philosophy*, 1965).

George Pitcher (ed.): *Wittgenstein: The Philosophical Investigations* (Macmillan, 1968).

Anthony Quinton: 'The Foundations of Knowledge' (in *British Analytical Philosophy*, ed. Williams and Montefiore, Routledge & Kegan Paul, 1966).

Jean-Paul Sartre: *Existentialism and Humanism* (translated by Philip Mairet, Methuen, 1948).

Henry Sidgwick: *The Methods of Ethics* (Macmillan, 1907).

Georges Sorel: *Reflections on Violence* (translated by T. E. Hulme and J. Roth, Collier Books, 1961).

J. L. Stocks: *Morality and Purpose* (Routledge & Kegan Paul, 1969).

E. P. Thompson: *The Making of the English Working Class* (Penguin Books, 1968).

K. A. Walton: 'Rational Action' (in *Mind*, 1967).

Mary Warnock: *Ethics Since 1900* (O.U.P., 1960).

Max Weber: *The Protestant Ethic and The Spirit of Capitalism* (translated by Talcott Parsons, George Allen and Unwin, 1930).

Peter Winch: *The Idea of a Social Science* (Routledge & Kegan Paul, 1958).

Peter Winch: 'Nature and Convention' (*P.A.S.*, 1959–60).

Peter Winch: 'Understanding a Primitive Society' (in *American Phil. Quart.*, 1964).

Peter Winch: 'The Universalizability of Moral Judgements' (in *The Monist*, 1965).

Peter Winch: *Moral Integrity* (Basil Blackwell, 1968).

Ludwig Wittgenstein: *Philosophical Investigations* (Basil Blackwell, 1953).

Ludwig Wittgenstein: *Remarks on the Foundations of Mathematics* (Basil Blackwell, 1956).

Index